American Book Company
The Standards Experts

MASTERING THE COMMON CORE
GRADE 8
ENGLISH LANGUAGE ARTS

Author: Zuzana Urbanek

Project Coordinator: Zuzana Urbanek

Reviewer: Ginger Howe

Executive Editor: Dr. Frank Pintozzi

American Book Company
PO Box 2638
Woodstock, GA 30188-1383
Toll Free: 1 (888) 264-5877   Phone: (770) 928-2834
Fax: (770) 928-7483   Toll Free Fax: 1 (866) 827-3240
www.americanbookcompany.com

ACKNOWLEDGEMENTS

The authors would like to gratefully acknowledge the technical contributions of Marsha Torrens and Becky Wright and the proofreading expertise of Susan Barrows.

We also want to thank Mary Stoddard for her expertise in developing many of the graphics for this book.

© 2012 American Book Company
PO Box 2638
Woodstock, GA 30188-1318

ALL RIGHTS RESERVED

The text of this publication, or any part thereof, may not be reproduced or transmitted in any form or by any means, electronic or mechanical, including photocopying, recording, storage in an information retrieval system, or otherwise, without the prior written permission of the publisher.

Printed in the United States of America

01/12

| Preface | vii |

Chapter 1 How to Write Constructed Responses — 1

Writing Constructed Responses 2
   Read the Question Carefully 2
   Write Clearly 2
   Use Neat Handwriting 3

Chapter 2 Literary Elements — 9

Genres of Literature 9
Literary Elements 11
   Plot 12
      Summarizing the Plot 13
   Theme 14
      Theme and Central Idea 15
   Characterization 20
   Point of View 22
   Setting 27
   Mood and Tone 27
Chapter 2 Summary 30

Chapter 3 Literary Devices — 31

Literary Devices 31
Figurative Language 31
   Nuances of Meaning 32
Sound Devices 41
Chapter 3 Summary 44

Chapter 4 Analyzing Literature — 45

Inference Skills 45
Comparing and Contrasting Literature 53
   How Structure Affects Meaning and Style 53
   Analyzing How Modern Literature Draws on Tradition 59
   Analyzing Adaptations of Texts 65
Chapter 4 Summary 66

Literature Review   **67**

Chapter 5 Understanding Informational Texts   79

Central Idea and Details 79
    Summarizing 80
Author's Purpose and Style 83
    Author's Purpose 84
    Author's Style 86
Chapter 5 Summary 90

Chapter 6 Analyzing Informational Texts   91

Facts and Interpretations 92
    Inferences and Conclusions 92
Connections and Distinctions 95
    Organization 95
        Comparison and Contrast 95
        Chronological or Sequential Order 95
        Cause and Effect 96
        Problem and Solution 96
Argumentation 99
    Responding to Conflicting Evidence 100
Media 103
Chapter 6 Summary 106

Informational Text Review   **107**

Chapter 7 Vocabulary   117

Building Vocabulary 118
    Context Clues 118
        Words with Multiple Meanings in Context 119
    Greek and Latin Roots and Affixes 121
    Dictionary Skills 123
Analyzing Word Meaning 127
    Denotations and Connotations 128
    Literal and Figurative Meanings 128
Chapter 7 Summary 133
Chapter 7 Review 134

Chapter 8 Research   137

Research Sources 137
    Primary and Secondary Sources 138
    Electronic Sources 138
    Organizational Features 139
Evaluating Sources 141
    Developing Research Questions 141
    Choosing the Best Sources 142
Using Sources 143

    Citing Sources 143
    Ways to Incorporate Sources 144
Chapter 8 Summary 147
Chapter 8 Review 148

Chapter 9 The Writing Process — 155

STEP 1: Planning 155
    Purpose for Writing 156
    Audience 156
    Developing Ideas 157
STEP 2: Drafting 160
    Organization and Coherence 160
    Clarity and Style 162
STEP 3: Revising 164
    Guidance and Support 164
    Making Improvements 165
STEP 4: Proofreading and Editing 167
STEP 5: Publishing 168
Chapter 9 Summary 169
Chapter 9 Review 170

Chapter 10 Types of Writing — 173

Persuasive Writing 174
    Making a Claim 174
    Providing Evidence 175
    Responding to Counterclaims 176
    Analyzing Conflicting Viewpoints 177
    Providing a Strong Conclusion 179
Informative Writing 184
Narrative Writing 188
Chapter 10 Summary 193
Chapter 10 Review 194

Chapter 11 Conventions — 197

Verbs: Voices and Moods 198
    Active and Passive Voice 198
    Verb Moods 199
    Using Voices and Moods 200
Verbals 203
    Gerunds 203
    Infinitives 203
    Participles 203
Punctuation 206
    Comma 206
    Dash 207
    Ellipsis 208
Spelling 209
Chapter 11 Summary 211
Chapter 11 Review 212

Chapter 12 Speaking and Listening — 215

Analyzing Presentations 216
Making a Presentation 220
    Structure of a Speech 220
    Delivering a Speech 221
Group Communication 224
Chapter 12 Summary 227
Chapter 12 Review 228

Index — 231

Preface

Mastering the Common Core in Grade 8 English Language Arts will help students who are learning or reviewing the Common Core State Standards. The materials in this book are based on the Common Core standards and the model content frameworks as published by the Partnership for Assessment of Readiness for College and Careers (PARCC) consortium.

This book contains four sections:

1) General information about the book

2) A literature unit (chapters 2–4) with a Literature Review practice chapter

3) An informational texts unit (chapters 5–6) with an Informational Texts Review practice chapter

4) Six additional chapters that review the concepts and skills and provide further practice

Standards are posted at the beginning of each chapter and at the beginning of each practice.

Teachers: See the "Answer Key and Teacher Resources for *Mastering the Common Core in Grade 8 English Language Arts*" to read tips for using this book and access additional material for classroom and one-on-one use.

We welcome comments and suggestions about the book. Please contact the authors at

American Book Company
PO Box 2638
Woodstock, GA 30188-1383

Toll Free: 1 (888) 264-5877
Phone: (770) 928-2834
Fax: (770) 928-7483
Website: www.americanbookcompany.com

About the Author and Project Coordinator:

Zuzana Urbanek serves as ELA Curriculum Coordinator for American Book Company. She is a professional writer and editor with over twenty-five years of experience in education, business, and publishing. She has taught a variety of English courses at the college level and also has taught English as a foreign language abroad. Her master's degree is from Arizona State University.

About the Reviewer:

Ginger Howe has over twenty years of experience teaching middle school language arts and high school English. She has a bachelor's degree in Language Arts Education and a master's degree in Human Relations from the University of Oklahoma. She currently serves as the Secondary Language Arts and Reading Coordinator for Moore Public Schools in Oklahoma.

About the Executive Editor:

Dr. Frank J. Pintozzi is a former Professor of Education at Kennesaw State University. For over twenty-eight years, he has taught English and reading at the high school and college levels as well as in teacher preparation courses in language arts and social studies. In addition to writing and editing state standard-specific texts for high school exit and end-of-course exams, he has edited and written several college textbooks.

Preface

Common Core Standards by Chapter	
Standard	Chapters
RL 1	2, 4, Literature Review
RL 2, 3	2, Literature Review
RL 4	3, Literature Review
RL 5	4, Literature Review
RL 6	2, 3 Literature Review
RL 7	4, Literature Review
RL 8	Not applicable to literater
RL 9	4, Literature Review
RL 10	2–4, Literature Review
RI 1	5, 6, Informational Texts Review
RI 2	5, Informational Texts Review
RI 3	6, Informational Texts Review
RI 4, 5	5, Informational Texts Review
RI 6	5, 6, Informational Texts Review
W 1, 2	2, 4, Literature Review, 6, Informational Texts Review, 10
W 3	Literature Review, Informational Texts Review, 10
W 4	Literature Review, Informational Texts Review, 9
W 5, 6	Informational Texts Review, 9
W 7–9	Literature Review, Informational Texts Review, 8
W 10	Literature Review, Informational Texts Review, 9, 10
SL 1	4, Literature Review, Informational Texts Review, 12
SL 2	4, Literature Review, 6, Informational Texts Review, 12
SL 3	4, Literature Review, 6, Informational Texts Review, 12
SL 4	Informational Texts Review, 12
SL 5, 6	Informational Texts Review, 12
L 1–3	Literature Review, Informational Texts Review, 11
L 4	Literature Review, Informational Texts Review, 7
L 5, 6	3, Literature Review, Informational Texts Review, 7

Chapter 1
How to Write Constructed Responses

Welcome to *Mastering the Common Core in Grade 8 English Language Arts*! This book will help you review skills that will help you get ready for Common Core testing.

As you read this book, you will see practices with questions for you to answer. This is good practice for any future tests you take. Many of the questions are multiple choice; that means you need to choose an answer from the choices given.

Some questions, however, ask you to write your own answer in a blank. Other questions ask you to write a longer text on your own paper. You will be asked to read and write about different passages, both fiction and nonfiction texts. Items emphasize the important understandings you are expected to gain from reading, and you will base your written responses on the reading passage.

The instructions for what to write will let you know what is expected of you. Be sure to read the constructed-response prompt carefully.

A **constructed response** is a paragraph or a short essay about a topic.

A **prompt** is an introduction with a question you need to answer or an idea you need to address.

Trained readers score responses to questions based on scoring rubrics, which are scales that describe different levels of performance. The trained readers follow scoring procedures that have been developed to ensure a high degree of objectivity and reliability. This chapter will help you get ready to answer those questions that ask you to write out your answers.

Before we review writing a constructed response, let's take a look at the general scoring rubrics for a constructed response.

Chapter 1

Rubric for 4-Point Scoring of Writing	
4 pts	The response indicates that the student has a thorough understanding of the reading concept asked for in the task. The student has provided a response that is accurate, complete, and fulfills all the requirements of the task. Necessary support and/or examples are included, and the information is clearly text-based.
3 pts	The response indicates that the student has an adequate understanding of the reading concept asked for in the task. The student has provided a response that is accurate and fulfills all the requirements of the task, but the required support and/or details are not complete or clearly text-based.
2 pts	The response indicates that the student has a partial understanding of the reading concept asked for in the task. The student has provided a response that includes information that is essentially correct and text-based, but the information is too general or too simplistic. Some of the support and/or examples and requirements of the task may be incomplete or omitted.
1 pt	The response indicates that the student has very limited understanding of the reading concept asked for in the task. The response is incomplete, may exhibit many flaws, and may not address all the requirements of the task.
0 pts	The response is inaccurate, confused, and/or irrelevant, or the student has failed to respond to the task.

You want to get the highest score you can when you write. Here are some ways to make sure you write the best responses.

WRITING CONSTRUCTED RESPONSES

Here are some steps to keep in mind when you write short answers. These steps will help you write the best answers you can.

READ THE QUESTION CAREFULLY

First of all, read the prompt carefully. Make sure you understand what it is asking you to write about, and make sure your response is only about that topic. If you need help, ask your teacher.

WRITE CLEARLY

Answer each question clearly and completely. For example, if a question asks about why or how something happened, be sure to talk about the sequence of events as well as causes and effects. If it asks you to compare and contrast two people or events, be sure to talk about how they are alike or different.

Being clear also means that your writing must be grammatically correct. Use complete sentences, and be sure to check your spelling. Also look for and fix any other mistakes such as punctuation errors, missing words, and misplaced modifiers. If you find an error, erase it completely, or cross it out. Write what you actually mean directly above it or next to it.

How to Write Constructed Responses

USE NEAT HANDWRITING

Make sure that people reading your answer can tell what it says. Write in a neat way that others can read.

Now read the following selection. Then study how a student replied to an extended-response question. Be sure your response has a beginning, a middle, and an end and that it provides an answer to the writing task with support based on the text. The sample response that follows this passage is a model response, and the test graders would likely assign the highest point value (4) to this response. This is followed by another response that would earn two (2) score points.

Life Is but a Dream

Steve got up one Saturday morning, barely awake. He stumbled into the kitchen and grabbed some orange juice. His roommate, Jeff, came in a little later.

"Man, that was a strange dream I had last night," Jeff yawned sleepily.

"What did you dream, Jeff?" Steve asked.

"Well, I dreamed that you and I were at a gas station. We found some fire hoses and were dousing each other with water. Then, you jumped into your pickup truck and wrecked it in the woods."

"That's pretty weird," Steve muttered. "Because I had a similar dream last night. Only, in mine, I was driving my truck, and it slipped and spun out of control on a patch of ice. It was probably that junk food we ate last night."

Just then, the phone rang. Jeff picked it up. "Hello," he said.

"Hi, is this Steve?" the woman asked.

"Just a second," Jeff said and handed the phone to Steve.

"Hello," Steve answered.

"Hi, my name is Allison. I work with your girlfriend, Jenny. She just twisted her ankle and wants to know if you can pick her up."

"OK. Tell her I'll be right there," Steve said. "I'm on my way now." After he hung up, Steve told Jeff what had happened. Then he jumped in his truck.

"Rats," Steve griped aloud, "I'm almost out of gas." He pulled into a gas station near his apartment and fueled up. After paying the attendant, Steve drove onto the road. It was a four-lane road with no divider lane. It was raining, so he had to drive carefully. Driving in the left lane. Suddenly, as the car in front of him stopped to make a left turn, Steve had to slam on his brakes. Steve's truck began to skid forward.

Chapter 1

> Quickly, Steve turned the wheel to the right. But because he was hydroplaning, the truck went to the left instead of to the right, directly into oncoming traffic. Steve braced himself as he hit a smaller truck in a head-on collision. Then it was over. Steve opened his eyes in shock at the scene before him. His truck was bashed in past the radiator.
>
> Luckily, Steve was wearing his seat belt and was unhurt. The front end of the car Steve had hit was smashed up, and the engine was on fire. Steve helped the driver out of his burning vehicle. The driver in this car was also unhurt because his airbag had opened. The police came, and the fire trucks were called in to put out the fire. Totally freaked out, Steve called Jeff on his cell phone.
>
> "Jeff," he said shakily, "I think that maybe you were supposed to pick up my girlfriend, Jenny, today …"

The constructed-response question on the Common Core test might read as follows:

> **Writing Task**
>
> Describe the two dreams in this selection. Explain how each dreaming character reacts to the dream. Use details and examples from the passage to support your ideas.

What would your response be? Practice writing a response that answers this prompt. Then look at the sample responses, and study the scoring comments that follow each one.

Model Student Response: 4-Point Score

> Jeff and Steve are two characters in "Life Is but a Dream." Both have dreams concerning an accident involving Steve's truck.
>
> In Jeff's dream, there is comic relief of playing with fire hoses before Steve jumps in his truck and wrecks it. He does not take the dream seriously or see danger ahead for Steve's life.
>
> In Steve's dream, he is driving his truck when he loses control on a patch of ice. Steve does not take the dream seriously either, and he immediately attributes it to the junk food they ate the night before.
>
> Neither character is alarmed by the dream. There is no foreboding sense of danger. But then Steve wrecks his truck is real life. He is aware that maybe he was not supposed to pick up his girlfriend, and just maybe his dream had substance after all. The story seems to say that we should not dismiss things just because they may be unplesant.

How to Write Constructed Responses

Score: 4 Points

The response states that the dreaming characters have one thing in common: they do their best to block out painful ideas and go after more pleasant ones. The response gives a reason for dismissing the dream: eating too much junk food. The unpleasantness of the dream or even wondering if there might be some meaning or warning in the dream is not something that either one is willing to face at the time. In dismissing the dream, they both can go on with their lives as if nothing has happened. Only after Steve's wreck can they assign any substance or validity to the dreams. We are more likely to dismiss our dreams if they don't make us feel good.

Annotation (comments from scorers)

The response correctly addresses all aspects of the item; the student correctly explains each character's dream and how he reacts to the dream. The student uses sufficient details and information from the selection to support the response. The response has no serious errors.

Model Student Response: 2-Point Score

> Jeff and Steve are kinda dum that they don't relize dreams mean somthing. Neither guy listens to their dream. So Steve gets into a acident and finaly knows he should pay attenshun. Dreams are important we have to listen to what they tell us.

Score: 2 Points

The response shows partial understanding of the reading and the task. The writing veers off task and does not answer the question. Instead of answering how the characters react, it discusses the importance of dreams and their connection to life events. In addition, there are numerous errors that might affect understanding of the response.

Annotation (comments from scorers)

The response correctly identifies that the characters in the story did not take either dream seriously. However, it does not provide details and examples about how each character reacted to his dream. It focuses on the writer's opinion about paying attention to dreams. Serious mistakes throughout the response include spelling and usage errors (*kinda dum*, *relize*, *something*, *a acident*, *finaly*, *attenshun*) and a run-on sentence (last sentence).

Now read the next passage. Then study how two students replied to a constructed-response question.

Chapter 1

I Dreamt …

by Suleiman Rustam

I dreamt last night that we had parted.
We strolled no longer through the lane.
No nightingale its trilling started
In gardens sear—all life was pain
My misery like a cloud above me
Deprived my soul of laughter's lilt
I asked, "Why does my love not love me?
In what, O love, consists my guilt?"
My tortured thoughts were turbid, sickly.

To questions there was no reply.
How could her fancy change so quickly?
How could such love abate and die?
I woke to memories reassuring,
For yesterday, to my great pride,
I heard sweet words of love, ensuring
That you will never leave my side.
To die a little, parting seems,
So let us only part in dreams.

The constructed-response question on the Common Core test might read as follows:

> **Writing Task**
>
> Evaluate the troubled nature of the poem's narrator, and explain four results or consequences of his dream.

What would your response be? Practice writing a response that answers this prompt. Then look at the sample responses, and study the scoring comments that follow each one.

Model Student Response: 3-Point Score

> In "I Dreamt …" the poet has a dream that actually is a nightmare. In it, his greatest fear becomes a reality. The speaker has lost the loved one who made life worth living. He is very upset.
>
> But, when the poet wakes up, he hears in his heart the words of his sweetheart from the day before. This assures him of her undying love. He knows they will never part. Finally, the poet is relieved. He knows it was just a dream and not reality.

How to Write Constructed Responses

Score: 3 Points

The response states that the poet has a nightmare, and he is troubled. It shows adequate understanding of the passage and the writing task. The response includes some support from the poem but it is vague and not specifically text-based. It is difficult to tell whether four distinct results or consequences are mentioned.

Annotation (comments from scorers)

The student identifies and explains the dream and states that the poet is tortured in his thoughts over what he has done to lose this love in his life. The student's response is brief and less thorough than a 4-point response in stating how troubled the poet is in his dream. The student does address and explain results or consequences of his dream, but four distinct results are unclear.

Model Student Response: 1-Point Score.

> the narator has a dream and they break up. but it turn out to be just a dream. Everything is OK

Score: 1 Points

This response states that the narrator has a dream, and the characters break up. Due to sentence construction, it is impossible to tell how this is meant (whether the characters break up in the dream or as a result). The response then states that it turns out to be just a dream and all is well. This is a maximum of two results or consequences mentioned as an answer to the prompt. The response is vague and limited.

Annotation (comments from scorers)

The response shows a lack of understanding or attention to the text and the writing task. It does not evaluate the troubled response of the narrator in the poem, nor does it include four results or consequence of the dream. The first sentence is unclear. Despite its extreme brevity, the response contains many mistakes such as capitalization errors (at start of first two sentences), a spelling error (*narator*), an agreement error (*it turn out*), and style issues (informality in *Everything is ok*).

Practice 1: Writing a Constructed Response

Both of the passages in this chapter are about dreams. Compare and contrast how the passages address the relationship of dreams and reality. Discuss how the works convey the effects of dreams on waking life. Are they similar or different in this aspect? Use information from the passages and your own ideas to support your answer.

Practice 2: Reviewing Responses of Others

Now that you have read the sample constructed responses, take a moment to notice which facts and details from the passages were used in some way when writing the responses. Use what you have learned to practice scoring the responses of others. Trade your papers (such as the constructed responses you wrote for practice 1 in this chapter) with another student. Practice scoring each others' responses. Then discuss why you scored the responses as you did.

Chapter 1

Chapter 2
Literary Elements

This chapter covers the following eighth grade strand and standards:

Reading: Literature

1. Cite the textual evidence that most strongly supports an analysis of what the text says explicitly as well as inferences drawn from the text.

2. Determine a theme or central idea of a text and analyze its development over the course of the text, including its relationship to the characters, setting, and plot; provide an objective summary of the text.

3. Analyze how particular lines of dialogue or incidents in a story or drama propel the action, reveal aspects of a character, or provoke a decision.

6. Analyze how differences in the points of view of the characters and the audience or reader (e.g., created through the use of dramatic irony) create such effects as suspense or humor.

10. By the end of the year, read and comprehend literature, including stories, dramas, and poems, at the high end of grades 6–8 text complexity band independently and proficiently.

Writing (in Writing Tasks throughout chapter)

1. Write arguments to support claims with clear reasons and relevant evidence.

2. Write informative/explanatory texts to examine a topic and convey ideas, concepts, and information through the selection, organization, and analysis of relevant content.

GENRES OF LITERATURE

Literature is any written work that is intended for others to read. It includes short and long works. As you know, the types of literature are called **genres**. There are four main genres, each of which has additional genres under it. Here are a few examples.

Literary Genres	
Genre	**Description**
Fiction	**Fiction is writing that tells a story drawn from the author's imagination, rather than from actual events.**
Mystery	A **mystery** is a story in which the characters face a problem that seems to be beyond explanation. Suspense or terror plays a big part in this subgenre. **Example:** Arthur Conan Doyle's *The Hound of the Baskervilles*

Chapter 2

Literary Genres (continued)	
Genre	Description
Science fiction	**Science fiction** stories typically are set in the future, or they may be set in outer space. Many science fiction stories include science and inventions that are not yet possible. Some contain warnings about what the future might be like if people continue to take certain actions. **Example:** Ray Bradbury's *Fahrenheit 451*
Fantasy	**Fantasy** stories usually take place in made-up worlds. They often include magic and supernatural elements. They are different from science fiction and horror in that they do not focus on imaginative science or on gruesome events. **Example:** J. R. R. Tolkien's *The Hobbit*
Nonfiction	**Nonfiction** is writing that is based on fact and tells about actual people, places, and events.
Autobiography	An **autobiography** is a book about the life of a real person, written by that person. **Example:** *Dangerous Days: The Autobiography of a Photojournalist* by J. William Turner
Biography	A **biography** is a book about the life of a real person, written by someone else. **Example:** *A Boy Called Slow: The True Story of Sitting Bull* by Joseph Bruchac.
Essay	An **essay** presents the ideas of the author with the purpose of making the reader consider the topic. Famous essayists throughout history have written about topics like philosophy, ethics, politics, and more. Essays are sometimes satirical, presenting a dark and mocking way to think about a serious subject. **Examples:** "A Modest Proposal" by Jonathan Swift; "The Ancestral Bond" by Ambrose Bierce
Drama	**Drama** is a type of story written to be acted out. It contains lines of dialogue for actors to recite, along with stage directions for the action.
Skit	A **skit** is a brief sketch performed by one or more actors. It is typically one to ten minutes long and is written to be comedic (funny). **Example:** skits on a TV variety show
One-act play	A **one-act play** is a short play consisting of just a single act, though it can have more than one scene. **Example:** *A Memory of Two Mondays* by Arthur Miller; *At Liberty* by Tennessee Williams

Literary Elements

Full-length play	A **full-length play** is usually divided into three acts (though some plays have as many as five). Each act typically is between thirty and ninety minutes long and may have several scenes (separate plot settings). The main categories of drama are comedy (protagonist succeeds) and tragedy (protagonist fails). Examples: *Our Town* by Thornton Wilder; *The Importance of Being Earnest* by Oscar Wilde; the plays of William Shakespeare
Poetry	**Poetry** is typically written in lines and stanzas. It usually does not follow the conventions of prose writing, but it might follow rules that define one of the many types of poems. Many poems convey deep emotion or depict a moment in time, while others tell stories. Most use sound devices more prominently than prose does.
Epic	An **epic** poem is a long, narrative (story) poem that tells about the extraordinary feats of a great legendary or national hero. **Examples:** *Beowulf* (about an Old English hero who fights mythical creatures); the *Odyssey* (about the voyages of the legendary Greek king, Odysseus)
Lyric	**Lyric** poems express emotion. Ancient lyric poems were set to music (typically using the lyre, a stringed instrument that inspired the name). Today, we still call poems that have been set to music *lyrics*. **Examples:** "A Lyric to Mirth" by Robert Herrick; "Butterfly Laughter" by Katherine Mansfield
Sonnet	A **sonnet** is a type of poem that usually has fourteen lines, each with ten syllables and an alternate-line rhyme scheme. Some sonnets follow slightly different rules, but all use contrasting ideas to communicate an emotion or state of being. **Examples:** "Ode to the West Wind" by Percy Bysshe Shelley; over 150 sonnets by William Shakespeare

No matter what form literature takes, it often provides insights into life. These insights can be observations, questions, or lessons. The more you can get out of what you read, the more it can help you understand life itself! This chapter and the next one review the elements (parts) and devices (techniques) that authors use to create literature such as stories, dramas, and poems.

LITERARY ELEMENTS

Literary elements are the building blocks of writing. Like the walls of a house, these elements provide the structures that authors use to create a work of literature. Writers introduce you to interesting characters. While getting to know these characters, you follow the plot (sequence of events) that shapes each story you read. Through your reading adventures, you come to understand certain themes (underlying messages) that are a part of the literature you explore. In this chapter, you will look at the elements that authors use in their writing.

Chapter 2

Elements like plot, theme, and characterization work together to create a meaningful story. For instance, an author might develop a story revolving around three contrasting sisters who are raised in a small southern town during the 1950s. They rally together during a crisis that threatens to tear their family apart. The author tightly intertwines the plot, characters, and setting to draw out meaning about southern culture and family bonds. As you read, keep in mind that all literary elements have impact on meaning.

PLOT

Plot refers to all the related events that move the story from its beginning to its end. A plot shapes a work of literature. In turn, everything that happens propels the plot. For example, pay attention to what characters say and do. How does the behavior of characters drive the plot? Also keep track of incidents that happen. What does each event have to do with how things turn out?

\	Plot and Its Features
Plot	The **plot** is the pattern of events in a story. The plot of *Harry Potter and the Sorcerer's Stone* follows young Harry, an orphan who discovers that he is a wizard, as he begins going to school to learn magic.
Introduction	The **introduction** (also called **exposition**) is the opening of a story where the author describes the setting, introduces the characters, and reveals the conflict. The narrator's point of view is usually revealed in the introduction. The persona or the personality of the narrator and the point of view will affect how the plot develops. For example, in Edgar Allan Poe's short story "The Tell-Tale Heart," the madman narrates the story. Imagine how differently the story would be written (and experienced by the reader) if one of the policemen narrated it.
Conflict	The **conflict** is the struggle between opposing forces in a story on which the narrative not only depends but uses to build and maintain reader interest. This struggle can be with nature, with one's self, with others, or with society. In Pearl S. Buck's *The Good Earth*, the main characters struggle against weather and Chinese cultural demands. Sometimes, conflicts are not resolved. This lack of resolution can affect a story in many ways, including an unhappy ending.
Climax	The **climax** is the turning point in a story. In Edgar Allan Poe's "The Fall of the House of Usher," the climax is when Roderick Usher reveals that his "dead" sister is actually alive.

 **Literary Elements**

Plot and Its Features (continued)	
Resolution	The **resolution** (also called **denouement**, pronounced day-noo-m*aw*n) is the final event of a plot. It can be the solution of a mystery, an explanation, or an outcome. The dramatic resolution of Shakespeare's *Hamlet* involves the death of most of the main characters.
Subplot	A **subplot** is an additional line of action in a story that in some way informs or supports the main plot. Short stories often do not have the space for subplots, but novels and long plays often have several going on at once. For example, in Shakespeare's *Much Ado about Nothing*, the main plot is about Claudio and Hero and the misunderstanding that nearly stops their wedding plans. A subplot to this is the romance of their friends, Benedick and Beatrice. Another subplot is the comic patrolling and reporting duties of the constable Dogberry. Subplots can influence and are affected by the main plot.

SUMMARIZING THE PLOT

A great way to figure out whether you understand a story is to summarize it. When you **summarize the plot**, think of only the most important facts. The "Five W's and H" will probably help you here. Ask yourself *who, what, when, where, why,* and *how* questions about the story or passage. These bare bones will give you a good foundation for an objective summary. Staying objective means you provide the main ideas and major details without offering your opinion or critique. There are other times when you will be asked to analyze and interpret a passage; we will discuss how to do that in chapter 4.

Here are the steps to writing an effective summary:

- Write down the subject and main idea of the passage. The first sentence of your summary should mention the title and author. Use a complete sentence.
- Next, list the major details. Again, use complete sentences. Be sure to use quotation marks to indicate exact words or phrases from the original source, but use quotations very sparingly, if you use them at all.
- As much as possible, a summary should be in your own words.

How long should your summary be? A general rule is to keep it to about one-fourth to one-third of the story's original length. So, if your original story is two pages long, a summary should be about half a page. Now read this passage and study the summary of it that a student wrote.

Chapter 2

Excerpt from "Tough Times on the Farm"

by Dennis Martin

I was raised in a small town on the shores of Lake Erie. The big water was only three blocks away from my house, and as a young boy I spent much of my time fishing from its shore with my two friends, Sparky and Dave. When I wasn't fishing, I was busy working. Life in the city brought many opportunities for a young boy to make money. First, there was my paper route. I would fold the papers in thirds, tuck in the ends real tight, load them in the basket on the front of my bike, and throw them on the porches of all my customers. Not only did I get paid every week, but during the holiday season, I would always receive nice tips from the homeowners. With the changing of the seasons came more means of making money for a boy of industrious inclinations. In the winter, I would shovel the snow off the walks for all the elderly people. In the spring and summer, I would cut their grass, and in the fall I would rake their leaves and clear their lawns of the ubiquitous buckeyes. Life was good, and I always had money to spend.

Student's Summary

> In "Tough Times on the Farm" by Dennis Martin, the narrator describes growing up in a town near Lake Erie. When he wasn't fishing with his friends, he was working at his paper route. In winter he would shovel snow, and in summer and fall he cut lawns and raked leaves. He always had money.

As you can see, this summary covers well the main points of the passage. It sticks to just what's in the passage, and it tells everything you need to know to understand the plot.

THEME

The **theme** is the central message or deeper meaning in a story, poem, play, or other work of literature. The theme usually develops slowly over the course of a text. It is shaped by the characters, the plot, and even the setting. In turn, the theme affects all of these other elements. Keep this in mind when you read, and look at how all of the elements interact. By identifying the theme, you can gain insights into literature and life. Themes are often universal messages, because people around the world share similar ideas about love, courage, honor, freedom, growing up, death, and so on.

 **Literary Elements**

Examples of Themes	
Theme	Work
Good always wins over evil.	*The Chronicles of Narnia*
Power corrupts.	*Animal Farm*
War forces men to change.	*The Things They Carried*
Nature works by its own set of laws.	*The Old Man and the Sea*
Individuals must think for themselves.	*Ender's Game*

Hints for Finding the Theme

- Look for clues in the title.
- Consider how the author develops characters, plot, and setting.
- Consider how the author uses symbols.
- Look at the wording the author uses.
- Write one sentence that sums up the author's message.

Different pieces of literature can have the same theme. In fact, some themes, especially those related to love, war, and courage, are so popular that people have been writing about them for hundreds of years.

THEME AND CENTRAL IDEA

Works of nonfiction may or may not have a theme, but they always have a **central idea**. This is the main point that each work communicates.

Read the two passages that follow to see how two different authors explore the same theme.

Example 1:

Type of Literature: Short story

Theme: Selfishness is a negative human trait.

> Many years ago, there was an Emperor, who was so excessively fond of new clothes, that he spent all his money on splendid outfits. He did not trouble himself in the least about his soldiers; nor did he care to go either to the theatre or the chase, except for the opportunities then afforded him for displaying his new clothes. He had a different suit for each hour of the day; and as of any other king or emperor, one is accustomed to say, "He is sitting in council," it was always said of him, "The Emperor is sitting in his wardrobe."
>
> – from "The Emperor's New Clothes" by Hans Christian Andersen

Chapter 2

Example 2:

Type of Literature: Novel

Theme: Selfishness is a negative human trait.

> The door of Scrooge's counting-house was open that he might keep his eye upon his clerk, who in a dismal little cell beyond, a sort of tank, was copying letters. Scrooge had a very small fire, but the clerk's fire was so very much smaller that it looked like one coal. But he couldn't replenish it, for Scrooge kept the coal-box in his own room; and so surely as the clerk came in with the shovel, the master predicted that it would be necessary for them to part. Wherefore the clerk put on his white comforter, and tried to warm himself at the candle; in which effort, not being a man of a strong imagination, he failed.
>
> – from *A Christmas Carol* by Charles Dickens

Notice that neither author came right out and said that his character was selfish. Instead, each author revealed this by describing his character's actions and attitudes. In "The Emperor's New Clothes," we can tell from what the emperor chooses to spend his money on (or not spend his money on) that his own personal comfort is the most important thing to him. In *A Christmas Carol*, we can tell who Scrooge values more by who gets the bigger fire.

Themes and central ideas may relate regardless of subject areas. For instance, a poet may write a poem exploring the emotional devastation of war while a historian may write a research paper exploring the economic devastation of war. How a theme or a central idea is treated depends on the subject and the person handling it. Let's look at how two different writers work with a similar **theme** and **central idea** in similar subjects.

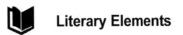 **Literary Elements**

Example 3:

Type of writing: Fiction

Subject: Literature

Theme: Money and power cannot help someone escape a dreaded disease.

> The "Red Death" had long devastated the country. No pestilence had ever been so fatal, or so hideous. Blood was its Avatar and its seal—the redness and the horror of blood. There were sharp pains, and sudden dizziness, and then profuse bleeding at the pores, with dissolution. The scarlet stains upon the body and especially upon the face of the victim, were the pest ban which shut him out from the aid and from the sympathy of his fellow-men. And the whole seizure, progress, and termination of the disease, were the incidents of half an hour.
>
> – from "The Masque of the Red Death," by Edgar Allan Poe
>
> *In the rest of the story, rich Prince Prospero isolates himself and his court in his palace. He hopes to escape the fate of the rest of the land. But someone dressed as the "Red Death" comes to the party. The Prince is shocked and makes him remove his mask. It turns out to be Death. Through symbolism, the story shows that one cannot use money or power to escape disease.*

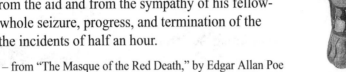

Example 4:

Type of writing: Nonfiction

Subject: Science

Central idea: Tuberculosis is a serious disease.

> Tuberculosis is an infection of the lungs. It can be transmitted from one person to another when an infected person sneezes, coughs, or even speaks. People with tuberculosis often have a bloody cough, fever, and listlessness. Tuberculosis can be prevented by vaccines and treated with antibiotics.

Note that Poe's examination of disease in "The Masque of the Red Death" includes emotional words like *hideous* and *sympathy*. Poe shows the fear and horror that goes along with the infectious disease. By contrast, the scientist's description of a similar disease, tuberculosis, is more clinical. It describes the facts that relate to the disease: what it is, how it is transmitted, what the symptoms are, and how it is treated. It does not show emotion, because that is not the purpose of a scientific report. While literature tends to use description and imagination, science relies on fact. Therefore, a similar theme and central idea are treated differently in these types of writing.

Chapter 2

Understanding the theme and/or the central idea of a passage is vital. It helps you to see the full meaning of the work. It also allows you to analyze it, which we will discuss in chapter 4.

Practice 1: Plot and Theme

RL 1, 2, 3, 10

DIRECTIONS Read the passage, and answer the questions that follow.

Banding Together

1   When Sylvia and I decided to start a jazz ensemble in our eighth grade band so we could perform during the Spring Festival, we did not realize what we were getting ourselves into. It seemed like a great idea at first. Sylvia played flute, I played trombone. Within two days, we had recruited Dave to play trumpet and Janet to play saxophone. All we really needed now was a drummer, and we found one in Tobias, a dedicated student who played the sticks on any surface he could reach.

2   Next, we talked to the band director, Mr. Greeley, about finding a place to practice. He said, "Our school is proud of its strong musical heritage. You had better be ready to pay the price if you expect me to let you perform in front of the student body and the parents. Look at yourselves! Janet, you have a terrible squeak. Dave, half the time I see you, you are struggling with allergy attacks. Tobias, you break sticks as if they are going out of style." He then turned to me. "And you always have your head tilted to the left when you play the trombone. I have to look at you sideways. I hope this ensemble knows what it's getting into. Not one of you is even first or second chair." Then he added, shaking his finger at all of us, "But—if you are determined, you can practice after school in the custodial closet. There is no room in the band room since the chorus uses the space then. If you need music, come see me. You have six weeks until the festival."

3   This talk was a real downer for all of us. Then Sylvia said, "We'll show Mr. Greeley what we can really do. But it's not going to be easy."

4   "Yeah, let's do it!" I said, "We can practice for two hours after school three days a week. Whatever it takes." We all agreed to this schedule, and we soon got started.

5   At first, things worked out great. In the practices, Janet helped Tobias by reinforcing his sticks with duct tape, Sylvia coached me toward better posture, and Tobias brought his air purifier from home to keep Dave's allergies from acting up.

6   For the first three weeks, we really started getting together as a group. Practicing and playing with mops falling on our heads and janitors chuckling as they reached around us to grab their cleaning supplies all became staples of our practice sessions.

 **Literary Elements**

7   In the hallways at school, we were constantly ridiculed behind our backs. "Those losers? Play jazz? Whatever!" "Have you heard them? Please don't let them out of the janitors' closet!" "Do yourselves a favor—play for the hearing impaired!"

8   During full band practice at the three-week mark, Mr. Greeley called us aside. "All right. I want to hear this. Play it for me tomorrow before school, and you had better be primed. See you at 7:30."

9   We were equally excited and scared. "What if we mess up?" Tobias fretted. "Impossible," I said. "We've been practicing for three weeks!"

10 I couldn't have been more wrong. Dragging ourselves in at 7:15, we set up and prepared to play our favorite piece from Stevie Ray Vaughan, "Testify." Mr. Greeley walked in and calmly sat down, but we were all tense and jumpy. We completely choked. Tobias snapped his reinforced stick; Janet squeaked away from the first note; I was listing precariously to the left again; and poor Dave appeared to be playing through his asthma inhaler rather than his trumpet.

11 But we finished the song because we were determined, and Mr. Greeley noticed the effort. He approached us and said, "You all played horribly, just horribly, but I admire your determination and courage. From now on, I will direct you, but we will have to practice every day until festival and stick with it until we get it right. Now let's see about moving some more cleaning stuff so we'll have room to practice."

12 "All right!" we all shouted in harmony. And so we soldiered forward.

13 Practices were intense. Mr. Greeley pushed us to a level of excellence we'd never imagined. Each of us had conquered our own personal fears. In doing so, we went from mediocre players to the top of our class.

14 On the day of the performance, we were not even nervous. After playing in front of Mr. Greeley, and after practicing every day, we knew we had given this effort our very best. We played beautifully, and the audience rewarded us with a standing ovation. We were victorious because we had fought against the unflattering names that we had given ourselves, that other students had also called us, and that our band director even initially labeled us with. We believed that we could achieve excellence, and, in the end, that was all that mattered.

1 Paragraph 11 belongs to what part of the plot?

  A Exposition

  B Climax

  C Denouement

  D Theme

Chapter 2

2. In the second paragraph, Mr. Greeley gives a list of things that the band members have to deal with. Why is this important to the plot?

   A It demonstrates the difference of opinion between Mr. Greeley and the kids.

   B It shows readers that Mr. Greeley really does not like this group of kids.

   C It provides insight into why the characters have conflict between each other.

   D It gives readers an idea about the challenges the band members will face.

3. The band wants to play well, but they run into roadblocks. What is the turning point in the story that shows they might achieve their goal? Why does it happen?

   _____

   _____

Read the second sentence of Paragraph 10.

Dragging ourselves in at 7:15, we set up and prepared to play our favorite piece from Stevie Ray Vaughan, "Testify."

4. This sentence is included to show what?

   A A glimpse of how the story will turn out in the end

   B The dilemma that the main characters must deal with

   C Clues about the time period and setting of the story

   D The relationships between the kids in the band

> **Writing Task**
>
> Write a paragraph explaining the theme of this story. Use evidence from the passage to support your idea. Use your own paper to write a thoughtful and well-developed paragraph. Make sure your writing is well organized, your ideas are clear, and any errors you find are corrected.

CHARACTERIZATION

Characterization is the manner through which an author reveals the characters in a narrative. Getting to know characters is like getting to know new friends—or even new enemies! A writer can reveal characters in a variety of ways, including direct descriptions of how they look and what they think. But characterization also includes nonphysical traits you can observe about a character, such as how he speaks, other characters' opinions of him, his actions, and how he reacts to others.

Various characters also play different roles. This includes the protagonist, antagonist, and possibly a narrator within the story. In many stories, the protagonist (main character) tells his or her own story, but not always. Look at the following charts for more facts about characters and how we learn about them.

 **Literary Elements**

Character and Its Features	
Antagonist	This is an opponent or rival of the protagonist. The antagonists in Ernest Hemingway's *Old Man and the Sea* are the sharks.
Character	Characters are people (or animals, or other beings) that appear in a literary work. Celie and Nettie are the main characters in Alice Walker's *The Color Purple.*
Influences	An influence is an outside pressure or force that can change the thoughts and actions of a character. For instance, if a character knows that a certain way of dressing is the way to make friends, it may change what the character wears. How a character reacts to influences says a lot about the character.
Motivations	There are reasons behind the actions of characters. These reasons are often needs or desires. For example, a character who is enslaved will want to gain freedom. A character who has freedom will want to keep it. In John Steinbeck's *The Pearl*, Kino and his family want to escape poverty.
Narrator	The narrator tells the story. In Maya Angelou's *I Know Why the Caged Bird Sings*, the narrator is a young girl who is also the main character. Sometimes the narrator is a character, and sometimes it is an unknown speaker.
Protagonist	This is the main character. Romeo and Juliet are protagonists in Shakespeare's famous play named for them.
Relationships	This includes a character's background and contact with other people. In Hemingway's *The Sun Also Rises*, Jake's tortured relationship with Lady Brett Ashley controls much of his attention.
Revealing Character Traits	
An author has several ways to reveal characters to the reader.	
Actions	Sometimes the actions of a character speak louder than words to show the character's true self. The main characters in O. Henry's "The Gift of the Magi" show their love through the sacrifices they make.
Description	An author tells how characters look, dress, and what their ages are, just as you might describe a friend of yours to someone.
Dialogue	Conversation between two people in a story is called dialogue. Huck and Jim engage in many dialogues as they travel along the Mississippi River in Mark Twain's *Adventures of Huckleberry Finn.*
Narration	If the narrator is one of the characters, he or she reveals a great deal though narration. The speaker will tell how other characters feel or think about another character or will describe how they act.

Chapter 2

You already know that events in the plot propel the action of a story. What characters do and say also move the story along. At the same time, their dialogue and behavior reveal a great deal about characters. As an example, look at the next passage.

Excerpt from "The Tell-Tale Heart"

by Edgar Allan Poe

I loved the old man. He had never wronged me. He had never given me insult. For his gold I had no desire. I think it was his eye! Yes, it was this! He had the eye of a vulture—a pale blue eye, with a film over it. Whenever it fell upon me, my blood ran cold; and so very gradually I made up my mind to take the life of the old man and thus rid myself of the eye forever. You fancy me mad. But you should have seen me. You should have seen how wisely I proceeded—with what caution I went to work!

Who is the narrator of this passage? You can tell that it is someone in the story. He or she speaks in the first person and talks about relating with another character, the old man. You don't know the narrator's name, but as he or she calls the other character old, the narrator is likely younger.

POINT OF VIEW

Every story has a **narrator**. This is the speaker who tells the story to the reader. Look at this chart of narrative styles.

Features of Point of View	
First Person	The narrator tells the story from the *I* point of view. In "The Tell-Tale Heart," Edgar Allan Poe tells the story from the main character's point of view.
Second Person	The speaker is talking to you and uses the pronoun *you*. Second-person point of view is rarely used in fiction, but is fairly common in poetry, short essays, and songs. For example, the songs "You Are My Sunshine" and "You've Got a Friend," and Jamaica Kincaid's story "Girl" use the second person point of view.
Third Person	An outside observer tells a story describing characters as "he," "she," or "they," as in Mildred D. Taylor's *Roll of Thunder, Hear My Cry*.
• omniscient	The narrator is capable of knowing, telling, and seeing all that happens to the main characters. In Louisa May Alcott's *Little Women*, an all-knowing narrator tells the story and describes the inner thoughts of all the characters.
• limited	The speaker tells the story knowing only what is seen, heard, and felt by the thoughts and viewpoint of one character, usually the main character, but sometimes an outsider. In *The Red Badge of Courage*, author Stephen Crane tells a realistic story about the Civil War through the eyes of Henry, a young soldier in the Union Army.

Literary Elements

As you can see, a story written in **first-person point of view** tells a story from a character's perspective. This might be a main character or a minor one who observes and reports.

The excerpt from "The Tell-Tale Heart" that you read in the last section is told by a character in the story. By using the first-person point of view, the author provides special insight into the narrator. For example, if the passage from "The Tell-Tale Heart" used third-person point of view, you would most likely not have insight into the speaker's motives. You might not know exactly why the narrator felt it necessary to harm the old man. Obviously, things would also be very different if the old man were the narrator. If that were the case, he might wonder what is bothering his friend lately. He might be a bit frightened by the younger person looking strangely at his eye.

I, Me

Likewise, your own point of view as a reader plays a role. Reading "The Tell-Tale Heart," for instance, you might feel that the narrator is imagining things. There might be a difference between what a character knows or sees and what you can figure out. An author can use this **difference in points of view** to create effects like suspense or humor.

A story in **third-person point of view** is told by an unnamed storyteller who stands back from the story as it is told, describing characters as *he*, *she*, or *they*. Washington Irving's *Rip Van Winkle* is an example of third-person point of view. For example, the narrator begins describing the main character in this way: "Rip Van Winkle, however, was one of those happy mortals, of foolish, well-oiled dispositions, who take the world easy, eat white bread or brown, whichever can be got with least thought or trouble, and would rather starve on a penny than work for a pound."

Them, They

Point of view is crucial to the story. You know that an author writes for a specific purpose, but he or she also chooses the point of view to get the most effect out of the story. Point of view affects the story's interpretation.

Practice 2: Characters and Point of View

RL 1, 2, 3, 6, 10

> **DIRECTIONS** Read the passages, and answer the questions that follow each one.

From "The Bohemian Girl"

by Willa Cather

The transcontinental express swung along the windings of the Sand River Valley, and in the rear seat of the observation car a young man sat greatly at his ease, not in the least discomfited by the fierce sunlight which beat in upon his brown face and neck and strong back. There was a look of relaxation and of great passivity about his broad shoulders, which seemed almost too heavy until he stood up and squared them. He wore a pale

Chapter 2

> flannel shirt and a blue silk necktie with loose ends. His trousers were wide and belted at the waist, and his short sack coat hung open. His heavy shoes had seen good service. His reddish-brown hair, like his clothes, had a foreign cut. He had deep-set, dark blue eyes under heavy reddish eyebrows. His face was kept clean only by close shaving, and even the sharpest razor left a glint of yellow in the smooth brown of his skin. His teeth and the palms of his hands were very white. His head, which looked hard and stubborn, lay indolently in the green cushion of the wicker chair, and as he looked out at the ripe summer country a teasing, not unkindly smile played over his lips. Once, as he basked thus comfortably, a quick light flashed in his eyes, curiously dilating the pupils, and his mouth became a hard, straight line, gradually relaxing into its former smile of rather kindly mockery. He told himself, apparently, that there was no point in getting excited; and he seemed a master hand at taking his ease when he could. Neither the sharp whistle of the locomotive nor the brakeman's call disturbed him. It was not until after the train had stopped that he rose, put on a Panama hat, took from the rack a small valise and a flute case, and stepped deliberately to the station platform. The baggage was already unloaded, and the stranger presented a check for a battered sole-leather steamer trunk.

1. Which of the following sentences best describes the young man?

    A He is poorly dressed and feeling uncomfortable.

    B He is hardworking and curious.

    C He is dressed strangely and very excited.

    D He is strong, relaxed, and a stranger in this place.

2. What does the following sentence say about the character?

    His head, which looked hard and stubborn, lay indolently in the green cushion of the wicker chair, and as he looked out at the ripe summer country a teasing, not unkindly smile played over his lips.

    A He is tired from his long trip and wishes it were over.

    B He is a stubborn man but is feeling pleased.

    C He enjoys teasing people.

    D His head is very large and strange-looking.

3. What point of view does the author use?

    _____

    _____

 **Literary Elements**

Excerpt from "The Red-Headed League"

by Sir Arthur Conan Doyle

This excerpt is from a story about the famous fictional detective Sherlock Holmes. The narrator is Holmes's friend and colleague, Dr. Watson. Watson has come to see Holmes and finds him talking with Jabez Wilson, a man with fiery red hair who needs the detective's assistance.

I did not gain very much, however, by my inspection. Our visitor bore every mark of being an average commonplace British tradesman, obese, pompous, and slow. He wore rather baggy gray shepherd's check trousers, a not over-clean black frockcoat, unbuttoned in the front, and a drab waistcoat with a heavy brassy Albert chain, and a square pierced bit of metal dangling down as an ornament. A frayed top-hat and a faded brown overcoat with a wrinkled velvet collar lay upon a chair beside him. Altogether, look as I would, there was nothing remarkable about the man save his blazing red head, and the expression of extreme chagrin and discontent upon his features.

Sherlock Holmes's quick eye took in my occupation, and he shook his head with a smile as he noticed my questioning glances. "Beyond the obvious facts that he has at some time done manual labor, that he takes snuff, that he is a Freemason, that he has been in China and that he has done a considerable amount of writing lately, I can deduce nothing else."

Mr. Jabez Wilson started up in his chair, with his forefinger upon the paper, but his eyes upon my companion.

"How, in the name of good-fortune, did you know all that, Mr. Holmes?" he asked. "How did you know, for example, that I did manual labor. It's as true as gospel, for I began as a ship's carpenter."

"Your hands, my dear sir. Your right hand is quite a size larger than your left. You have worked with it, and the muscles are more developed."

"Well, the snuff, then, and the Freemasonry?"

"I won't insult your intelligence by telling you how I read that, especially as, rather against the strict rules of your order, you use an arc-and-compass breastpin."

"Ah, of course, I forgot that. But the writing?"

"What else can be indicated by that right cuff so very shiny for five inches, and the left one with the smooth patch near the elbow where you rest it upon the desk?"

"Well, but China?"

Chapter 2

> "The fish that you have tattooed immediately above your right wrist could only have been done in China. I have made a small study of tattoo marks and have even contributed to the literature of the subject. That trick of staining the fishes' scales a delicate pink is quite peculiar to China. When, in addition, I see a Chinese coin hanging from your watch-chain, the matter becomes even more simple."
>
> Mr. Jabez Wilson laughed heavily. "Well, I never!" said he. "I thought at first that you had done something clever, but I see that there was nothing in it, after all."
>
> "I begin to think, Watson," said Holmes, "that I make a mistake in explaining .... My poor little reputation, such as it is, will suffer shipwreck if I am so candid."

4 What point of view does the author use?

   A First person

   B Second person

   C Third person limited

   D Third person omniscient

5 Based on the description in the first paragraph, what does Watson most likely think of Wilson?

   A He finds Wilson very clean and tidy in his appearance.

   B He thinks that Wilson is probably a shady criminal.

   C He believes Wilson may be quite intelligent and clever.

   D He sees Wilson as the typical British working-class person.

6 Which of the following can be said about Holmes?

   A He jumps to conclusions about people for no reason.

   B He often insults the intelligence of his clients.

   C He discovers much simply by looking at a person.

   D He feels that his observation skills are slipping.

7 Holmes drew the conclusion that the man had been to China by what means?

_____

_____

Literary Elements

8   Holmes' phrase "My poor little reputation, such as it is, will suffer shipwreck if I am so candid" means —

   A he is worried that his reputation will suffer if his predictions about his clients turn out to be wrong.

   B he thinks that Watson and Mr. Wilson don't understand his explanations.

   C he thinks that Watson is better at observing people than he is.

   D he is worried that his reputation will suffer if he gives away his secrets too freely.

Writing Task

In the second paragraph, Holmes rattles off details about the client he just met. Then he says, "I can deduce nothing else." What does this dialogue reveal about Holmes and his view of himself? Explain what you learn about Holmes in this speech and the story as a whole. Use your own paper to write a thoughtful and well-developed paragraph. Use evidence from the passage to support your ideas.

SETTING

Setting includes the place and time in a story. The setting of Edgar Allan Poe's "The Cask of Amontillado" is a murky wine cellar in the eighteenth century.

Features of Setting	
Place	This is the location where a story takes place. The Uncle Remus tales of Joel Chandler Harris take place in rural Georgia.
Time	This is when the story occurs. Stephen Crane's *The Red Badge of Courage* takes place during the Civil War.

MOOD AND TONE

Mood is the feeling a reader experiences while reading the text. To create a feeling, authors use images and details in the setting and plot.

Examples of Mood				
angry	creepy	excited	funny	mysterious
anxious	dismal	frenzied	joyful	sad

Chapter 2

Tone is an attitude that the author conveys. It is similar to tone of voice when we speak. Just as we show our feelings about what we are saying, the author shows feelings toward characters or parts of the story.

Examples of Tone				
affectionate	cold	humorous	pessimistic	satirical
cynical	formal	optimistic	rude	serious

As an example, Edgar Allan Poe's story, "The Cask of Amontillado," is told with a pitiless and vengeful **tone** by the main character. This adds to the **mood** of horror that the story arouses.

Practice 3: Setting, Mood, and Tone

RL 1, 2, 6

DIRECTIONS Read the passages, and answer the questions that follow each one.

Excerpt from *The Prince and the Pauper*

by Mark Twain

In the ancient city of London, on a certain autumn day in the second quarter of the sixteenth century, a boy was born to a poor family of the name of Canty, who did not want him. On the same day another English child was born to a rich family of the name of Tudor, who did want him. All England wanted him too. England had so longed for him, and hoped for him, and prayed to God for him, that, now that he was really come, the people went nearly mad for joy. Mere acquaintances hugged and kissed each other and cried. Everybody took a holiday, and high and low, rich and poor, feasted and danced and sang, and got very mellow; and they kept this up for days and nights together.

---

1. In what time and place is the story set?

   _____

   _____

2. The tone of the passage is somewhat cynical (mocking), pointing out the immense celebration of one birth while ignoring another. How do you think this might affect the mood of the rest of the book? Which mood will most likely be the strongest throughout the book?

   A Anxious   **B** Critical   **C** Joyous   **D** Hilarious

 **Literary Elements**

Excerpt from *Twenty Thousand Leagues Under the Sea*
by Jules Verne

When I got up, I saw that Captain Nemo and his first mate were on the platform. They were examining the ship's position, exchanging several words in their incomprehensible language.

Here was our situation. Two miles to starboard rose Gueboroar Island, whose coast extended from north to west like an immense arm. Toward the south and east, we could already make out the tops of several coral formations which the ebb tide was beginning to uncover. We had gone aground at high tide, which would make it difficult to refloat the *Nautilus*. Nevertheless the ship had suffered no damage, for her hull was solidly joined. But even though it could never sink or spring a leak, there was a serious danger of its remaining grounded forever on these reefs, and that would be the end of Captain Nemo's submarine.

I was thinking of all this when the captain came over looking as cool and calm as ever. He seemed neither disturbed or unhappy.

"An accident?" I asked.

"No, an incident," he replied.

"But an incident," I retorted, "that will force you once again to live on that land you have been fleeing!"

3   At the end of the passage, the mood is —

   A   tense.

   B   happy.

   C   relaxed.

   D   boring.

4   What is the setting of this scene?

   _____

   _____

Chapter 2

> ## CHAPTER 2 SUMMARY
>
> **Plot** is "what happens" in the story—all the related events that move the story from beginning to end. The plot shapes a work of literature.
>
> **Theme** is an author's underlying message in a piece of fiction.
>
> **Characterization** is the way that an author introduces a character, letting a reader get to know that person.
>
> A story written in **first-person point of view** tells a story from a narrator's perspective, using *I* and *me* in describing the plot.
>
> A story in **third-person point of view** is told by an unnamed personality who stands back from the story as it is told, describing characters as *he*, *she*, or *they*.
>
> **Setting** includes the place and time in a story.
>
> **Mood** is the feeling a reader experiences while reading the text.
>
> **Tone** is an attitude that the author conveys.

For more practice with this chapter's material, see the Literature Review on page 67.

Chapter 3
Literary Devices

This chapter covers the following eighth grade strand and standards:

> **Reading: Literature**
>
> 4. Determine the meaning of words and phrases as they are used in a text, including figurative and connotative meanings; analyze the impact of specific word choices on meaning and tone, including analogies or allusions to other texts.
>
> 6. Analyze how differences in the points of view of the characters and the audience or reader (e.g., created through the use of dramatic irony) create such effects as suspense or humor.
>
> 10. By the end of the year, read and comprehend literature, including stories, dramas, and poems, at the high end of grades 6–8 text complexity band independently and proficiently.
>
> **Language**
>
> 5. Demonstrate understanding of figurative language, word relationships, and nuances in word meanings.
>
>   a. Interpret figures of speech (e.g. verbal irony, puns) in context.
>
> 6. Acquire and use accurately grade-appropriate general academic and domain-specific words and phrases; gather vocabulary knowledge when considering a word or phrase important to comprehension or expression.

LITERARY DEVICES

In this section, you will read about the ways in which authors make writing interesting and memorable. This includes the use of figurative language and sound devices. These **literary devices** help to shape the literature that you read.

All writing has words, but the way that the words are used makes each story, novel, play, and poem unique. As you saw in chapter 2, all literature has certain devices that must be present. But authors can choose from among elements they can include.

FIGURATIVE LANGUAGE

Have you ever heard a statement similar to one of these?

- You could have knocked me over with a feather!
- My brother eats like a pig.
- She has a heart of gold.
- Charlie is a beast on the soccer field!

Chapter 3

These are all examples of **figurative language**. In literature, writers use figurative language to liven up their writing. They also use it to give precise expression to the ideas they wish to convey. Recognizing and understanding figurative language is an important part of reading literature.

Figurative language uses words or phrases that are not literally true. Often, one thing is described in terms of something else; to do this, the author uses imaginative comparisons. Figurative language is most often used to **convey meaning, mood, and images** in a passage.

NUANCES OF MEANING

To fully understand figurative language, you need to figure out the **nuances of word meaning** in context. Specific words and phrases have an impact on mood, tone, and meaning.

For example, the words *odor* and *aroma* can both mean "smell." However, if you told a chef that her dinner had an interesting aroma, the chef would probably thank you. But, if you told her that her dinner had an interesting odor, she would probably be offended. While both of these words denote, or mean, "smell," the connotation of aroma is positive while that of odor can be negative. (For more about denotation and connotation, see chapter 7.)

Example: Both the words *reliable* and *accountable* are denoted as *responsible*. However, without understanding their connotations, these words can be misused. Read the following sentences:

1. I can trust Janine to look after my pet iguana because she is such an *accountable* girl.

2. Jessie, who had accidentally overturned the pitcher, was held *reliable* for the damage.

In sentence 1, the word *accountable* seems awkward because of its connotation as *blameworthy* rather than *dependable*. In sentence 2, the word *reliable* seems awkward because of its connotation as *trustworthy* rather than *blameworthy*.

Now read the following selection from Geoffrey Chaucer's *Canterbury Tales*. Notice how the denotations and connotations of his words enrich the description of Chanticleer, the proud rooster:

> Chanticleer's comb was redder than coral, with a beautiful jagged edge just like the towers of a castle. His bill was as black and shining as jet; his legs and toes were blue as azure, with nails whiter than a lily flower; and his feathers were the color of shimmering gold.

Chaucer uses words like *coral, shining, towers,* and *shimmering gold* because of their strong connotations. Taken together, these lead to an emotional response: they bring up the image or feeling of majesty, beauty, and magnificence.

How words relate in context can greatly affect the meaning and mood in writing. Now, look at some of the types of figurative language you might find in literature.

Page 32

Literary Devices

Types of Figurative Language

Device	Definition	Example
Allusion	An **allusion** is a reference to a well-known place, literary or art work, famous person, or historical event. Today, these references are often related to pop culture. Allusions are dependent on the reader being familiar with the work or item mentioned.	If you tell your friends that your cousin reminds you of Bart Simpson, they would have a definite picture of that boy's personality!
Analogy	An **analogy** is a comparison of two unlike things that uses imagery to help understand a concept.	"Life is like a box of chocolates: you never know what you're going to get." – Forrest Gump
Hyperbole	**Hyperbole** is the use of overstatement or exaggeration. It is a special type of figurative language that allows writers to infuse shades of meaning into their descriptions of characters and plots. Many hyperboles can be funny.	"I have seen this river so wide it only had one bank." – Mark Twain
Imagery	**Imagery** is language that appeals to the senses. Most images are visual; they appeal to the sense of sight, creating pictures that readers can see in their minds. Other images appeal to the senses of touch, taste, hearing, or smell.	Joey awoke to the aroma of blueberry pancakes and bacon. He could hear the "sizzle pop" sound of the bacon frying in Grandma's iron skillet. Opening his eyes, he saw the floral pattern of the wallpaper that trimmed the tops of Grandma's guest-bedroom walls.

Chapter 3

_	Types of Figurative Language (continued)	
Irony	**Irony** is a contrast between expectation and reality. There are three common types of irony.	
	• **Verbal irony** involves a contrast between what is said or written and what is meant.	After a day of mischief, little Juan was tired. With a smile, his mother put him down for a nap, cooing sweetly, "Now, you can rest, *my little angel*."
	• **Situational irony** occurs when what happens is very different from what is expected to happen.	In Aesop's fable "The Tortoise and the Hare," a slow-moving tortoise *wins a race of speed* against a much-speedier hare.
	• **Dramatic irony** occurs when the audience or the reader knows something a character does not know.	In reading a tragic novel in which a character is gravely ill and going to die, the reader might learn of the character's fate *before* the character does.
Metaphor	A **metaphor** is an imaginative comparison between two unlike things in which one thing is said to be another thing. Metaphors, unlike similes, do not use words such as *like*, *as*, *than*, or *resembles*, to express comparisons.	The roar of the engines was thunder, and the sparks flying on the speedway were its partner, lightning.
Personification	**Personification** is a figure of speech in which a nonhuman thing or quality is given human characteristics. Often, the use of personified objects in literature conjures up vivid mental images that readers can picture.	The numbers danced off the page of my algebra test.

Literary Devices

	Types of Figurative Language (continued)	
Pun	A **pun** is a way of using words so that their meaning can be taken in different ways, which makes what is said humorous. A pun is often referred to as a *play on words*. **Example:** Notice the word play in the following excerpt from *Alice's Adventures in Wonderland*, by Lewis Carroll. "And how many hours a day did you do lessons?" said Alice, in a hurry to change the subject. "Ten hours the first day," said the Mock Turtle, "nine the next, and so on." "What a curious plan!" exclaimed Alice. "That's the reason they're called lessons," the Gryphon remarked: "because they lessen from day to day." The pun involves the similar sounds but vastly different meanings of the words *lessons* and *lessen*.	
Simile	A **simile** makes a comparison between two unlike things, using a word such as *like*, *as*, *than*, or *resembles*. Similes are commonly used to help writers express their ideas in a precise or imaginative manner.	He is crazy like a fox.
Symbolism	A **symbol** is a person, place, thing, or event that has its own meaning but also stands for something beyond itself. Symbols are used in everyday life. 	Examples of symbolism appear in "the Tell-Tale Heart" by Edgar Allen Poe. The narrator talks about an old man's "evil eye" which becomes a symbol for fear and paranoia. He kills the man and buries him under the house but says he still hears his heart beating. The sound symbolizes the narrator's guilt.

Chapter 3

Practice 1: Figurative Language
RL 4, 10, L 5.a

> **DIRECTIONS** Read and answer the questions.

1. Which of the following is an example of situational irony in the fairy tale "Cinderella"?

   A The mean stepsisters never work and are mad at Cinderella for ruining their dresses.

   B Cinderella is treated like a servant but is chosen by the prince over her pampered stepsisters.

   C The evil stepmother tries to get the prince to notice her daughters because she wants to be rich.

   D The king has a ball so the prince can choose a wife from many eligible young ladies.

2. If a friend told you her father reminds her of Ebenezer Scrooge, what would this allusion say about his personality?

   A He loves children.   C He is stingy with money.

   B He enjoys cooking.   D He gets haunted by ghosts.

3. In *Romeo and Juliet,* when Mercutio is about to die of a stab wound, he says, "Ask for me tomorrow and you shall find me a grave man." Explain what makes this a pun.

   _____

   _____

   _____

Literary Devices

> **DIRECTIONS** Read each passage, and then answer the questions that follow.

Colin had been nervous all day. He had been practicing his oral history report for three weeks, yet he felt unprepared. He shuddered to think how he would feel standing in front of his classmates trying to remember details about the Trail of Tears. Colin was so nervous about his speech that he had forgotten to write his name on his spelling quiz and made careless mistakes on his math test.

Now, as he sat at the lunch table, knowing the speech would be next period during social studies, Colin felt just like a newly hatched chick—he wanted to crawl right back into his shell. He slowly ate his lunch, lost in thought, going over the speech in his head. So consumed by worries about the coming speech, Colin forgot to grab a napkin and wipe his mouth after lunch. Unknowingly, he left the cafeteria and headed to social studies class with a milk moustache.

Finally, it was Colin's turn to speak. He got up and walked slowly to the front of the classroom, turning to face the other students. A soft ripple of giggles made their way to him, starting with a small point-and-sniggle from Amy Tinsley in the back. When Mrs. Boles looked up from her notes to see what the children found so amusing, she had to hold back her own giggle. "Colin, dear," she said in her gentle way, "you are wearing a milk moustache."

---

4 How does the use of irony affect this story?

  A The readers understand that Colin is nervous about his report.

  B The readers are first to know that Colin has a milk moustache.

  C The readers find out that Colin's teacher is named Mrs. Boles.

  D The readers know that the subject of Colin's report is the Trail of Tears.

5 By comparing Colin to a "newly hatched chick," what does the author tells us about Colin's speaking experience?

  A He has only made one speech, but he's happy to make another.

  B He has given speeches many times.

  C He loves to give speeches, especially on the Trail of Tears.

  D He has not made many speeches before.

Excerpt from "Life"

by Emily Dickinson

He ate and drank the precious words,
His spirit grew robust;
He knew no more that he was poor,
Nor that his frame was dust.
He danced along the dingy days,
And this bequest of wings
Was but a book. What liberty
A loosened spirit brings!

6 The main character "danced along the dingy days." What does the author mean by this?

    A He was employed in the cleaning business.

    B The book he was reading was about dancing.

    C Boring days went by quickly thanks to reading.

    D His life passed him by because he was preoccupied.

7 The poem says "this bequest [gift] of wings / Was but a book. What liberty / A loosened spirit brings!" What point is the author making about reading? Use the rest of the poem to support your idea.

_____

_____

_____

Sitting propped up by pillows in his bed, Kunal looked around his room. He saw his new computer system, complete with the latest technology and gadgets. It sat there on the desk that had been a surprise from his older brother who was away at college. On his right was the flat-screen television that his parents had bought for him. The corkboard beside the TV had little space left; it was crowded by funny pictures and get-well cards from friends and family. Kunal could not help but think of himself as incredibly lucky and loved, despite the heavy cast on his broken leg. He would have lots of time to use his computer and watch his TV now that he could no longer compete. He wouldn't be traveling to all the state and regional tournaments with the team. He had played basketball as long as he could remember, always perfecting his game. And now that he was so close, he might never get the scholarship he was hoping for. It would have made sense had he broken his leg playing. But he was in this cast because of taking a clumsy step off a curb!

8 Which type of imagery is used mostly in the following passage? Give at least two examples of which sense the author appeals to most.

_____
_____
_____
_____

9 What object could most be considered a symbol for Kunal not being able to play basketball?

  A The cast on his leg

  B The computer

  C His new television

  D His room

Chapter 3

> The next excerpt is from *My Bondage and My Freedom* by Frederick Douglass. He was a slave who gained his freedom and became a famous abolitionist (a person who believes there should be no slavery and often fights for this cause), speaker, author, and publisher.
>
> "Make a noise," "make a noise," and "bear a hand" are the words usually addressed to the slaves when there is silence among them. This may account for the almost constant singing heard in the Southern states. There was, generally, more or less singing among the teamsters, as it was one means of letting the overseer know where they were, and that they were moving on with the work. But, on allowance day, those who visited the great house farm were peculiarly excited and noisy. While on their way, they would make the dense old woods, for miles around, reverberate with their wild notes. These were not always merry because they were wild. On the contrary, they were mostly of a plaintive cast, and told a tale of grief and sorrow. In the most boisterous outbursts of rapturous sentiment, there was ever a tinge of deep melancholy. I have never heard any songs like those anywhere since I left slavery, except when in Ireland. There I heard the same *wailing notes*, and was much affected by them. It was during the famine of 1845-6.

10 The author compares the singing of the slaves with the singing of those affected by famine in Ireland. What does this help you to understand? Use evidence of imagery and analogy in the passage to support your ideas..

_____

_____

_____

_____

_____

Frederick Douglass

Literary Devices

SOUND DEVICES

Have you ever had to recite a poem? Some forms of literature, such as poetry, are written to be read aloud. In these cases, special **sound devices** help to shape the writing of these literary forms. Writers use the following sound devices to give creativity and style to their writing. As with other literary devices, sound devices are used to convey meaning, mood, and imagery.

Alliteration is the repetition of the same or very similar consonant sounds at the beginning of words. Alliteration helps emphasize words. It is used most often in poetry.

>**Example:** The whisper of the wind-blown willows (repeats the "w" sound).

Onomatopoeia refers to words that sound like what they are describing. Onomatopoeia helps to create the sound imagery of poetry.

>**Examples:** *meow, buzz, tick-tock, boom*

Rhyme is the repetition of accented vowel sounds and all sounds following them in words placed close together in a poem.

>**Example:** The cat in the hat sat on the mat. (*Cat*, *hat*, *sat*, and *mat* all rhyme.)

Two types of rhyme are internal rhyme and end rhyme.

Internal rhyme means that words within a line rhyme.

>**Example:** We fight with all our might to win by ten tonight!

Fight, *might*, and *tonight* all rhyme.

End rhyme occurs at the end of lines.

>**Example:**
>
>>Here a star, and there a star,
>>
>>Some lose their way.
>>
>>Here a mist, and there a mist,
>>
>>Afterwards – day!
>
>>– Emily Dickinson

In this poem, lines 2 and 4 use end rhyme.

Chapter 3

The pattern of end rhyme in a poem is called a **rhyme scheme**. Readers use separate letters of the alphabet to identify each new sound in a poem's rhyme scheme. For example, the following quatrain (a poem or stanza consisting of four lines) has an *abab* rhyme scheme:

> Thou art my life, my love, my heart *a*
> The very eyes of me *b*
> And hast command of every part *a*
> To live and die for thee. *b*
>
> – from "To Athena Who May Command Him Any Thing" by Robert Herrick

Just like in music, **rhythm** refers to the beat and pace of written words. This is achieved by stressing certain syllables. Especially in poetry (in which meter is used to measure syllables), rhythm becomes important in the overall structure of the writing. Depending on how sounds are arranged, rhythm can be fast or slow, choppy or smooth, pleasant or harsh. Rhythm in prose (stories and novels) comes from repetitions of sounds and pauses.

Notice the rhythm of the excerpt from *The Song of Hiawatha* by Henry Wadsworth Longfellow.

> By the shore of Gitchie Gumee,
> By the shining Big-Sea-Water,
> At the doorway of his wigwam,
> In the pleasant Summer morning,
> Hiawatha stood and waited.

The rhythm is repetitive, with the stress on the same syllables in each line. So, it sounds almost like a Native American chant.

Practice 2: Sound

RL 4, 10

DIRECTIONS Read the passage, and then answer the questions that follow.

Excerpt from "The Raven"

by Edgar Allan Poe

Once upon a midnight dreary, while I pondered, weak and weary,
Over many a quaint and curious volume of forgotten **lore**,
While I nodded, nearly napping, suddenly there came a tapping,
As of some one gently rapping, rapping at my chamber **door**.
"'Tis some visitor," I muttered, "tapping at my chamber **door**—
Only this, and nothing **more**."

Literary Devices

1. What literary sound device is used in the bolded words?
   A Alliteration
   B Onomatopoeia
   C End rhyme
   D Internal rhyme

2. In this poem, which literary sound device is used in the phrase "while I pondered, weak and weary"?

   _____

3. The rhythm of the poem is steady until the last line. Why does it most likely change then?
   A It trails off to show the reader that the narrator of the poem has left the room.
   B It ends abruptly to give an eerie, suspenseful feeling about what comes next.
   C It gets faster as the narrator becomes more frightened, and his heart beats faster.
   D It slows down to show that it is late at night, and the house is very quiet.

Excerpt from "Life"

by Emily Dickinson

Glee! The great storm is over!
Four have recovered the land;
Forty gone down together
Into the boiling sand.

---

4. Which of the following represents the rhyme scheme of this poem?
   A abcc
   B abcb
   C abaa
   D abbc

Chapter 3 Summary

Authors use **literary devices** to shape the literature they write.

Figurative language uses words or phrases that describe one thing in terms of something else and are not literally true.

Figurative language is most often used to **convey meaning, mood, and images** in a passage.

To fully understand it, you need to figure out the **nuances of word meaning** in context.

Common forms of figurative language include **allusion**, **hyperbole**, **imagery**, **irony**, **metaphor**, **personification**, **simile**, and **symbolism**.

Writers can also use **sound devices** to give creativity and style to their writing. These devices include **alliteration**, **onomatopoeia**, and **rhyme**.

A **rhyme scheme** is the pattern of end rhyme in a poem.

Rhythm is the beat and pace of written words.

For more practice with this chapter's material, see the Literature Review on page 67.

Chapter 4
Analyzing Literature

This chapter covers the following eighth grade strand and standards:

> **Reading: Literature**
>
> 1. Cite the textual evidence that most strongly supports an analysis of what the text says explicitly as well as inferences drawn from the text.
>
> 5. Compare and contrast the structure of two or more texts and analyze how the differing structure of each text contributes to its meaning and style.
>
> 7. Analyze the extent to which a filmed or live production of a story or drama stays faithful to or departs from the text or script, evaluating the choices made by the director or actors.
>
> 9. Analyze how a modern work of fiction draws on themes, patterns of events, or character types from myths, traditional stories, or religious works such as the Bible, including describing how the material is rendered new.
>
> 10. By the end of the year, read and comprehend literature, including stories, dramas, and poems, at the high end of grades 6–8 text complexity band independently and proficiently.
>
> **Speaking and Listening** 1–3 (in Activities throughout chapter)
>
> **Writing** 1–4, 10 (in Writing Tasks throughout chapter)

Analyzing literature takes careful reading. It also takes some thinking about what is under the surface.

INFERENCE SKILLS

In the chapter about literary devices, you read about how important it is to understand the expressions (words and phrases) that authors use. Sometimes what the author means will be clear. At other times, you might need to use **inferences skills** to figure out what's under the surface. In this section, you will review how to make inferences and draw conclusions and to support your analysis with evidence from the text. These skills are important for improving your understanding of what you read.

Chapter 4

Good readers are like detectives. They are able to evaluate **evidence** left by the author to **support an analysis** of the text. Keeping this evidence in mind, they can support what the text says and also their own ideas about it.

The ideas that you come up with on your own, based on evidence you find, are called **inferences**. An inference is an educated guess based on information given in a text, clues in the text, and previous experience and knowledge. You make inferences by "reading between the lines." Authors do not always directly state what they want you to understand. When you make an inference, you are noticing relevant details and clues in a text and then combining those clues with what you already know. This allows you to figure out events in a story.

For an example, read this passage from Richard Connell's "The Most Dangerous Game," and see if you can tell or infer what has happened to the character at the end.

> Rainsford sprang up and moved quickly to the rail, mystified. He strained his eyes in the direction from which the reports had come, but it was like trying to see through a blanket. He leaped upon the rail and balanced himself there, to get greater elevation; his pipe, striking a rope, was knocked from his mouth. He lunged for it; a short, hoarse cry came from his lips as he realized he had reached too far and had lost his balance. The cry was pinched off short as the blood-warm waters of the Caribbean Sea closed over his head.

Did you guess that this character has fallen into the sea? You can correctly infer that he has fallen overboard a ship because ropes and rails are common items on a ship and because the narrator describes the water closing over his head.

Now, read the following passage in which the topic is not stated but must be inferred. Notice how the details that provide the clues in the paragraph help you make an inference.

> Now that you've built up your arm and leg strength, you are ready to go. Before you begin, you need to remember that the sport requires more than a board and water. First, you need a great deal of balance. The waves are always changing and moving. The rider's feet must be positioned and repositioned on the board to avoid falling. Second, you need good vision. It is important to observe how your wave is changing and make adjustments. You also need to watch out for other people in the water. Third, you need patience. Much of the time, you will just be sitting on your board and floating in the water while waiting for the perfect wave. Even when that wave arrives, don't be surprised when you fall off. It takes some time to get the right combination of movements together to catch the perfect wave. When that wave comes, you'll be ready for an awesome experience!

Analyzing Literature

Did you infer that the topic of this passage is surfing? The following details provide clues.

Direct statements in the text:

- "First . . . a great deal of balance."
- "a board and water"

Clues that depend on connections and prior knowledge:

- "catch the perfect wave"; a phrase you have probably heard before
- water and waves mentioned; points to the ocean, not a lake or river
- "sitting on your board and floating in the water while waiting for the perfect wave"; describes what you might have seen surfers do

You could also draw other inferences about the selection. For example, you could infer that surfing is a challenging sport. The passage also suggests that surfing requires much practice.

Activity

RL 1

Reread the selection. Think of two other inferences you could make based on the passage. Write your inferences on the spaces provided. Then, discuss your inferences with a classmate or in a small group. What is the evidence for your inference? Is it something you found in the text or something you already knew? Are the statements you wrote down facts, or are they truly inferences that you needed to figure out?

Inference _____

Inference _____

Conclusions are general statements you can make and support with details from a text. Drawing a conclusion is one type of inference skill. If you read a story describing a sport where players use a bat to hit a ball and then run around bases, you can likely conclude that the sport is baseball.

To reach a valid (well-supported and logical) conclusion, you can use multiple sources of information. You combine the written texts with what you already know. Then you can come up with a statement about the topic. The conclusion would be based on all sources of information. It must also reasonably and logically follow the existing information. Drawing conclusions helps you find connections between ideas and events and allows you to better understand what you read and hear.

Read the following paragraph. Choose the most logical conclusion you can draw from this passage.

> Erin had been practicing for basketball tryouts. She had her older brother play with her every afternoon for weeks. She had dreams about playing basketball. On the morning of tryouts, her stomach began to ache.

Chapter 4

1. Erin will win a spot on the basketball team.
2. Erin is nervous about basketball tryouts.
3. Erin works hard for what she wants.

Which one did you choose? Here is an explanation of the answers:

Statement (**1**) is not a logical conclusion but is a prediction. Erin is not guaranteed to make the team. There could be heavy competition for only a few spots, or Erin might not be very good at the game.

Statement (**2**) is a logical conclusion. We can conclude Erin is nervous about tryouts since she has practiced for long hours and has a stomach ache in the morning.

Statement (**3**) is a not a logical conclusion. The passage only mentions basketball. There is no evidence that shows she works hard at everything she wants.

When you are asked to draw a conclusion about a passage, you need to read carefully, paying special attention to the facts and details. Whatever conclusion you come to has to be supported by information from the text.

Practice 1: Inference Skills

RL 1, 10, SL 1–3

DIRECTIONS Read the passages, and then answer the questions that follow.

Excerpt from *Adventures of Huckleberry Finn*

by Mark Twain

At first I hated the school, but by-and-by I got so I could stand it. Whenever I got uncommon tired I played hookey, and the hiding [whipping] I got next day done me good and cheered me up. So the longer I went to school the easier it got to be. I was getting sort of used to the widow's ways, too, and they warn't so raspy on me. Living in a house, and sleeping in a bed, pulled on me pretty tight, mostly, but before the cold weather I used to slide out and sleep in the woods, sometimes, and so that was a rest to me. I like the old ways best, but I was getting so I liked the new ones, too, a little bit. The widow said I was coming along slow but sure, and doing very satisfactory. She said she warn't ashamed of me.

Analyzing Literature

1. The passage suggests that the narrator is —
   A a good student.
   B not used to living indoors.
   C angry
   D trying to earn a living.

2. Which of the following events has most likely happened?
   A The narrator has run away from home.
   B The narrator lives in an orphanage.
   C The widow has made life easy for the narrator.
   D A fire has burned the narrator's house down.

3. What inference can you make about the widow? Support your answer with evidence from the passage.

   _____
   _____
   _____
   _____

4. Based on the passage, we can conclude that —
   A the narrator really enjoys sleeping in a bed.
   B no one likes the narrator very much.
   C the narrator is struggling with his new life.
   D the widow is a wealthy woman.

Picking a Pet

The decision to get a family pet is usually surrounded by happy emotions. You see an animal in a shop window or at a neighbor's where there has been a litter. You fall in love and bring the baby home. However, this kind of spur-of-the-moment decision may end up being a disaster. It is important to investigate different types of animals before making a decision. Many people would love a puppy or kitten that they can raise themselves. But there are also many abandoned or rescued animals that need good homes. It's always a good idea to arrange visits with the pet to see how you interact. All animals need attention, some more than others, so you should also consider how much time you have to spend with your pet.

Chapter 4

5. Based on the passage, which is a valid conclusion?

   A People who travel should not have pets.

   B You should not get a pet the first day you see it.

   C Only people with families should get pets.

   D It is better to get a pet from a shelter than pet store.

6. Explain the evidence for your conclusion.

_____

_____

_____

_____

Excerpt from "The Widow and the Parrot"

by Virginia Woolf

Mrs. Gage, as I have already said, was lame in her right leg. At the best of times she walked slowly, and now, what with her disappointment and the mud on the bank, her progress was very slow indeed. As she plodded along, the day grew darker and darker, until it was as much as she could do to keep on the raised path by the river side. You might have heard her grumbling as she walked, and complaining of her crafty brother Joseph, who had put her to all this trouble. "Express," she said, "to plague me. He was always a cruel little boy when we were children," she went on. "… I make no doubt that he's all aflame at this very moment in fire, but what's the comfort of that to me?" she asked, and indeed it was very little comfort, for she ran slap into a great cow which was coming along the bank, and rolled over and over in the mud.

---

7. Based on this paragraph, what can you infer about the relationship between Mrs. Gage and her brother? Be sure to support your answer with evidence.

_____

_____

_____

_____

 Analyzing Literature

Sonnet 43

by Elizabeth Barrett Browning

How do I love thee? Let me count the ways.
I love thee to the depth and breadth and height
My soul can reach, when feeling out of sight
For the ends of Being and Ideal Grace.
I love thee to the level of everyday's
Most quiet need, by sun and candle-light.
I love thee freely, as men strive for Right;
I love thee purely, as they turn from Praise.
I love thee with the passion put to use
In my old griefs, and with my childhood's faith.
I love thee with a love I seemed to lose
With my lost saints,—I love thee with the breath,
Smiles, tears, of all my life!—and, if God choose,
I shall but love thee better after death.

8 Based on the poem, what does the narrator believe about death? Support your answer with evidence.

_____
_____
_____
_____

Chapter 4

What Kills Birds?

There are many ways birds can die, but countless die each year from human-related causes. Hunters kill 121 million birds each year. An estimated 50 to 100 million birds are killed each year by cars and trucks on America's highways. Agricultural pesticides poison 67 million birds per year. Dr. Daniel Klem conducted a 20-year study that looked at bird collisions with windows. He found that 1 billion birds are killed each year by flying into glass windows.

9 Which of the following is a valid conclusion?

  A Bird populations are high and need to be controlled.

  B We can learn much by studying human impact on animal habitats.

  C It is often difficult to tell how deceased birds actually died.

  D Glass windows are the most dangerous human structure to birds.

10 Explain the evidence for your conclusion.

_____

_____

_____

_____

Activity

RL 1, 10, SL 1.a–d

Read two to three short stories from books, magazines, or the Internet. What inferences and conclusions can you make from the stories? Write down the facts or details that support your ideas.

Share your findings with other students. Remember to take turns listening and speaking. Consider the ideas of others and what they add to how you interpreted each article. Is there agreement about the inferences and conclusions? When you disagree, share the evidence for each point of view, and decide which idea is best supported.

 **Analyzing Literature**

COMPARING AND CONTRASTING LITERATURE

You know how to compare (analyze similarities) and contrast (analyze differences). There are several ways to **compare and contrast literature**. In this section, you will look at how the different structures of texts contribute to their meaning and style. You will examine how modern works draw on traditional stories. Finally, you will review ways to analyze how closely a play or film adaptation follows the text on which it is based.

HOW STRUCTURE AFFECTS MEANING AND STYLE

Works in each genre (type) of literature share certain **structure** and characteristics. If you need to, refer to the list of literary genres in chapter 2 to read about the qualities of each genre. For instance, myths explain how something in nature came to be; mysteries contain suspense and surprises; and poems convey emotion, use sound devices, and are written in stanzas. Understanding what genre a text fits into can help you understand more about its meaning.

Writers choose which genres to use based on what and how they want to communicate. This choice can have a great effect on a piece of writing. In some ways, the choice of **genre shapes meaning** in the writing. For instance, if an author wants to illustrate the emotions of war, he might write a poem. If he wants to discuss strategies of war, he might choose to write an essay.

In addition, each author uses language differently. A writer's unique way of conveying a point is called his **style**. You might recognize the style of certain famous writers the minute you begin reading something they wrote. Some write in long sentences filled with descriptive words. Others make brief but powerful statements. Here, for example, are two excerpts from texts about success, made by two different authors. Pay attention to the differences.

Example 1 is an excerpt from the "Number One Speech" speech by Vince Lombardi (1913–1970), famous coach of the Green Bay Packers in the 1960s.

> Winning is not a sometime thing; it's an all the time thing. You don't win once in a while; you don't do things right once in a while; you do them right all the time. Winning is a habit. Unfortunately, so is losing.
>
> There is no room for second place. There is only one place in my game, and that's first place. I have finished second twice in my time at Green Bay, and I don't ever want to finish second again. There is a second place bowl game, but it is a game for losers played by losers. It is and always has been an American zeal to be first in anything we do, and to win, and to win, and to win.
>
> […]

Chapter 4

> Running a football team is no different than running any other kind of organization—an army, a political party or a business. The principles are the same. The object is to win—to beat the other guy. Maybe that sounds hard or cruel. I don't think it is.
>
> [...]
>
> I don't say these things because I believe in the "brute" nature of man or that men must be brutalized to be combative. I believe in God, and I believe in human decency. But I firmly believe that any man's finest hour, his greatest fulfillment to all he holds dear, is that moment when he has to work his heart out in a good cause and he's exhausted on the field of battle—victorious."

Example 2 is the poem "Success" by Emma Lazarus (1849–1887), the poet whose words. "Give me your tired, poor / Your huddled masses yearning to breathe free" from the poem "The New Colossus" are inscribed in the base of the Statue of Liberty.

Oft have I brooded on defeat and pain,
The pathos of the stupid, stumbling throng.
These I ignore to-day and only long
To pour my soul forth in one trumpet strain,
One clear, grief-shattering, triumphant song,
For all the victories of man's high endeavor,
Palm-bearing, laurel deeds that live forever,
The splendor clothing him whose will is strong.
Hast thou beheld the deep, glad eyes of one
Who has persisted and achieved? Rejoice!
On naught diviner shines the all-seeing sun.
Salute him with free heart and choral voice,
'Midst flippant, feeble crowds of spectres wan,
The bold, significant, successful man.

What are the similarities? Both examples are about the idea of success through hard work. Both suggest that being the best is, well, the best! The two examples, however, address this subject is different ways.

The speech by Lombardi is inspired by winning on the field, specifically in football. It aims to motivate those who compete in sports, as in any walk of life. It challenges the audience to look at winning as the only option and entreats them to make it a habit. With its focus on winning being paramount, it does not offer much sympathy for those who struggle or just get by. The author's style is simple and straightforward. Points are clearly stated, with little meaning left for the reader to infer.

Analyzing Literature

Lazarus's poem, on the other hand, starts out by empathizing with (relating to) those who do not succeed but struggle in life. The narrator then chooses to look away from their daily grind for the moment and invites readers to celebrate great accomplishments. But how does the poetic structure and word choice affect the topic? In referring to average people as "the stupid, stumbling throng" and "flippant, feeble crowds of spectres wan," is the narrator really putting them down? Or is there a bit of irony here?

When you analyze literature, first think about the point a passage makes. What is the author communicating? Then listen to your gut. How does the work make you feel? Finally, look for evidence to support both the facts and the inferences you make. When you do this for each work, you can then compare and contrast two or more works convincingly.

Practice 2: Comparing and Contrasting Literature
RL 2, 10, SL 1–3

DIRECTIONS Read the passages, and then answer the questions that follow.

Excerpt from "The Gravel Road"

by Elizabeth Sutherland

Mountain mornings are chilly in western North Carolina, even in the early fall. Sometimes there's even a touch of frost. There was on this particular morning. I can still remember being a little cold and able to see my own breath as I headed down the old gravel road my brother, sister, and I had traversed so many times before. Like most Saturdays, the three of us rose early, grabbed our rusty metal buckets, and headed off to pick blackberries. Picking blackberries was how we earned money to buy school supplies. I'm not sure how far we actually walked most weeks to reach our prime blackberry-picking spot. I just remember that the walk always seemed too long and too short at the same time. It seemed long because we walked and walked, until the shabby, blue-collar trailer park where we lived was no longer visible and had given way to nothing but woods and the sound of gravel beneath our feet. The walk back seemed even longer. By the time we'd finished picking blackberries, we were tired, and the early morning chill had long since given way to the exhausting heat of the early afternoon sun.

And, yet, the walk never seemed long enough. The walk along that gravel road and the time spent in the blackberry field was, if nothing else, an escape. It was the closest to freedom my siblings and I knew. It was the one time each week we were together without the feeling that we might be beaten, verbally abused, or humiliated as the butt of some other kid's cruel comment or a teacher's insensitive remark. Along that quiet gravel road

Chapter 4

> and in that open field, it was just us. There we weren't abandoned, orphaned kids. We were just brother and sisters. We didn't have to worry about what the world thought of us—at least for a few hours. We could just be together. We could just be, period.
>
> But this day's trek down the gravel road was different. This time, I walked with nervous anticipation. I wasn't sure if I should be scared or excited … worried or hopeful. My brother and sister suspected nothing. To them, it was just another Saturday's hike to pick blackberries. As we walked along, the sound of rocks and dirt shuffling under our worn, dragging shoes, the sun gradually broke through the surrounding trees. My baby sister and older brother occasionally made small talk or stopped to pick up a random stick. I can't remember anything they said, I just remember that they seemed normal, the same way they always did. Perhaps they noticed I was quieter than usual—distracted. If they did, they didn't say anything. They didn't seem to notice anything was wrong or different. But even if they had, there's a good chance they still wouldn't have mentioned it. Our blackberry expeditions constituted the one time a week we chose to leave the despair of our daily existence behind, if only for a little while, in that dingy, foul-smelling trailer we called home. We dealt with enough sadness and anxiety every other moment of our lives; more than any kids our age ever should. The last thing any of us wanted to do was to disrupt our blackberry-picking expedition with any talk of concerns or dread. It's understandable if they chose to ignore any vibe of worry I might have been giving off that morning. Why risk weighing down our few moments of weekly freedom with talk and thoughts of the hell we lived in day to day?

1. Which is the best analysis of the author's use of the phrase "… the walk always seemed too long and too short at the same time"?

    A The phrase suggests that the walk was too far to travel without getting tired, but too short to reach the best blackberry-picking spots that they knew existed.

    B The phrase suggests that the walk was long from a physical standpoint, but that it was too short because the children would have to return to the trailer when it was over.

    C The phrase suggests that the walk was long from a physical standpoint but that it was not far enough for them to escape from the mountains of western North Carolina.

    D The phrase suggests that the walk along the gravel road to pick blackberries was very long, but the path the children took back to the trailer park was much shorter.

2. According to the narrator, what did the walk to pick blackberries represent for the children? Be sure to cite evidence for your idea.

    _____

    _____

Excerpt from *A Doll's House*

by Henrik Ibsen

This three-act play premiered in 1879. It focuses on the dilemma of Norwegian housewife Nora, who borrowed money in an illegal way when her husband Torvald was ill. She secretly paid it back for years out of her household allowance to save her husband's reputation. Before this scene, the lender of the money told Torvald what Nora had done. However, he then also said the debt was forgiven, and he would never tell anyone about it. Torvald was furious with Nora (though she had done it for him) and then forgave her and expected her to be grateful.

TORVALD. How unreasonable and how ungrateful you are, Nora! Have you not been happy here?

NORA. No, I have never been happy. I thought I was, but it has never really been so.

TORVALD. Not—not happy!

NORA. No, only merry. And you have always been so kind to me. But our home has been nothing but a playroom. I have been your doll-wife, just as at home I was papa's doll-child; and here the children have been my dolls. I thought it great fun when you played with me, just as they thought it great fun when I played with them. That is what our marriage has been, Torvald.

TORVALD. There is some truth in what you say—exaggerated and strained as your view of it is. But for the future it shall be different. Playtime shall be over, and lesson-time shall begin.

NORA. Whose lessons? Mine, or the children's?

TORVALD. Both yours and the children's, my darling Nora.

NORA. Alas, Torvald, you are not the man to educate me into being a proper wife for you.

TORVALD. And you can say that!

NORA. And I—how am I fitted to bring up the children?

TORVALD. Nora!

NORA. Didn't you say so yourself a little while ago—that you dare not trust me to bring them up?

TORVALD. In a moment of anger! Why do you pay any heed to that?

NORA. Indeed, you were perfectly right. I am not fit for the task. There is another task I must undertake first. I must try and educate myself—you are not the man to help me in that. I must do that for myself. And that is why I am going to leave you now.

TORVALD *[springing up]*. What do you say?

Chapter 4

NORA. I must stand quite alone, if I am to understand myself and everything about me. It is for that reason that I cannot remain with you any longer.

TORVALD. Nora, Nora!

NORA. I am going away from here now, at once. I am sure Christine will take me in for the night—

TORVALD. You are out of your mind! I won't allow it! I forbid you!

NORA. It is no use forbidding me anything any longer. I will take with me what belongs to myself. I will take nothing from you, either now or later.

TORVALD. What sort of madness is this!

NORA. Tomorrow I shall go home—I mean, to my old home. It will be easiest for me to find something to do there.

TORVALD. You blind, foolish woman!

NORA. I must try and get some sense, Torvald.

TORVALD. To desert your home, your husband and your children! And you don't consider what people will say!

NORA. I cannot consider that at all. I only know that it is necessary for me.

TORVALD. It's shocking. This is how you would neglect your most sacred duties.

NORA. What do you consider my most sacred duties?

TORVALD. Do I need to tell you that? Are they not your duties to your husband and your children?

NORA. I have other duties just as sacred.

TORVALD. That you have not. What duties could those be?

NORA. Duties to myself.

TORVALD. Before all else, you are a wife and a mother.

NORA. I don't believe that any longer. I believe that before all else I am a reasonable human being, just as you are—or, at all events, that I must try and become one. I know quite well, Torvald, that most people would think you right, and that views of that kind are to be found in books; but I can no longer content myself with what most people say, or with what is found in books. I must think over things for myself and get to understand them.

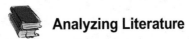
Analyzing Literature

3 From this conversation, which of the following is true about Torvald?

    A He is more concerned about appearances than about Nora's unhappiness.

    B He has known all along that he and Nora had a problem in their marriage.

    C He is most upset because Nora is leaving him to care for the children.

    D He loves Nora so deep that he will find it difficult to live without her.

4 How does the difference in structure affect what you know about the characters in each passage?

_____

_____

_____

_____

> **Writing Task**
>
> In both passages, you see characters who want to get out of a situation. Write an essay about what is similar about their problems, and what is different. Be sure to use evidence from the passages to support your ideas. Use your own paper to write a thoughtful and well developed essay. Make sure your writing is well organized, your ideas are clear, and any errors you find are corrected.

ANALYZING HOW MODERN LITERATURE DRAWS ON TRADITION

There is a saying that there are no new stories in the world. There certainly are many creative ways to tell a tale, but the more you read, the more you will see certain age-old storylines. As you read both classic and modern literature, you will see stories that remind you of others. **Many modern works of fiction draw on traditional stories, religious works, and mythology** for their plots, characters, or themes. Sometimes authors do this on purpose. They might retell a classic tale in a new way for modern audiences. Other times, authors may simply be influenced by works they have read. Bits and pieces might show up later in their own work.

Here is an example of a lasting tale and its transformation through different times in history.

Chapter 4

> In Roman myth, Pygmalion is a sculptor who is not very interested in having a relationship. However, he creates a statue of a woman so beautiful that he falls in love with it. He prays at the altar of Venus (goddess of love) to bring his creation to life. His prayer is answered, and he marries his living statue.
>
>
>
> In 1912, playwright George Bernard Shaw adapted this ancient story into a five-act play called *Pygmalion*. But the characters are Professor Henry Higgins, a phonetics teacher, and Eliza Doolittle, a flower-seller from the streets. Higgins, like the original Pygmalion, doesn't think much of women. But he makes a bet with a friend that he can take the low-born Eliza and pass her off as a duchess simply by transforming the way she peaks. He "brings her life" by teaching her to speak well, and then he realizes he has fallen in love with her. It added twists of setting as well as plot to the original tale. Most importantly, Shaw added a feminist twist. In the end, Eliza leaves the professor, who takes her for granted, and marries someone else.
>
> Shaw's story, in turn, was adapted into a stage musical (also later filmed) under the name *My Fair Lady*. The feature film stars Rex Harrison as Henry Higgins and Audrey Hepburn as Eliza Doolittle. Obviously it added musical numbers to communicate some of the plot, plus changed the ending to have Eliza stay with the professor, which most modern audiences thought was the happier ending.

Practice 3: Analyzing How Modern Literature Draws on Tradition

RL 9, W 1, 2

> **DIRECTIONS** Read the introduction, passages, and sample question below. Then answer the questions that follow.

The Lord of the Rings trilogy by J. R. R. Tolkien is well known by readers as three volumes of fantastical tales filled with heroism, wizardry, and extraordinary creatures. This trilogy is part of a larger series of books that Tolkien wrote dealing with the history and events of Middle-earth, a mythical setting he created. Tolkien draws on many sources for inspiration. Some readers have noticed that his magical stories contain biblical images, allegories, and themes—not unlike C. S. Lewis's The Chronicles of Narnia. In fact, Tolkien, a devout Catholic, was a friend of Lewis and influenced him to become a Christian. Read the following biblical passages and the brief synopsis of the three books that make up The Lord of the Rings. Then answer the question that follows.

 Analyzing Literature

Excerpts from the *Bible*

Jesus dies and is resurrected three days later

(1 Corinthians 15) ^{3} I passed on to you what I received, which is of the greatest importance: that Christ died for our sins, as written in the Scriptures; ^{4} that he was buried and that he was raised to life three days later, as written in the Scriptures; ^{5} that he appeared to Peter and then to all twelve apostles. ^{6} Then he appeared to more than five hundred of his followers at once, most of whom are still alive, although some have died.

The apostle Paul teaches the Law of Christ

(Galatians 6) ^{1} My friends, if someone is caught in any kind of wrongdoing, those of you who are spiritual should set him right; but you must do it in a gentle way. And keep an eye on yourselves, so that you will not be tempted, too. ^{2} Help carry one another's burdens, and in this way you will obey the law of Christ. ^{3} If you think you are something when you really are nothing, you are only deceiving yourself. ^{4} You should each judge your own conduct. If it is good, then you can be proud of what you yourself have done, without having to compare it with what someone else has done. ^{5} For each of you have to carry your own load.

Jesus as the bread of life

(John 6) ^{43} Jesus answered, Stop grumbling among yourselves. ^{44} People cannot come to me unless the Father who sent me draws them to me; and I will raise them to life on the last day. ^{45} The prophets wrote, Everyone will be taught by God. Anyone who hears the Father and learns from him comes to me. ^{46} This does not mean that anyone has seen the Father; he who is from God is the only one who has seen the Father. ^{47} I am telling you the truth: he who believes has eternal life. ^{48} I am the bread of life. ^{49} Your ancestors ate manna in the desert, but they died. ^{50} But the bread that comes down from heaven is of such a kind that whoever eats it will not die. ^{51} I am the living bread that came down from heaven. If you eat this bread, you will live forever. The bread that I will give you is my flesh, which I give so that the world may live.

God makes plans for us that might not be what we wanted

(Proverbs 16) ^{1} To man belong the plans of the heart, but from the Lord comes the reply of the tongue.

(Proverbs 19) ^{21} Many are the plans in a man's heart, but it is the Lord's purpose that prevails. (Job 15) ^{8} Did you overhear the plans God made? Does human wisdom belong to you alone?

(Isaiah 28) ^{29} All this wisdom comes from the Lord Almighty. The plans God makes are wise, and they always succeed.

Chapter 4

The significance of loyalty

(Judith 8) [27] God is not testing our loyalty as severely as he did theirs. God is not sending this punishment on us as revenge, but as a warning to us who worship him.

(Psalms 85) [11] Human loyalty will reach up from the earth, and God's righteousness will look down from heaven.

(Proverbs 3) [3] Never let go of loyalty and faithfulness. Tie them around your neck; write them on your heart.

(Sirach 45) [4] The Lord chose Moses out of the whole human race and consecrated him because of his loyalty and humility.

Summary of The Lord of the Rings trilogy by J. R. R. Tolkien

This sequel to *The Hobbit* begins with a flashback: Many years ago, in the mystical realm called Middle-earth, the Dark Lord Sauron forged a potent talisman called the One Ring to gain power over all the races of Men, Elves, and Dwarves. But Sauron was defeated in battle, and the ring was lost. It was eventually found by two hobbits. But one hobbit came under the ring's evil spell; he slew his cousin and took the ring for himself. He hid in the Misty Mountains, where the ring prolonged his life, turning him into a pathetic creature called Gollum. When Gollum lost the ring, the hobbit Bilbo Baggins found it.

Years later, Bilbo is leaving the Shire, home of the hobbits. He wills the One Ring (which he has been hiding) to his young cousin, Frodo Baggins. A visiting wizard, Gandalf the Grey, reveals the ring's history to Frodo. He explains that Frodo is in danger, and the ring must leave the Shire. Frodo enlists the help of his friends Sam, Merry, and Pippin. Thus their adventure begins.

In the meantime, Sauron's spirit has survived, and he once again rules his realm of Mordor. But he needs the One Ring to regain his full power. Minions of Sauron capture Gollum, who is desperately searching for the ring, and Sauron discovers that Bilbo Baggins now has it. Sauron sends the Ringwraiths, his terrible and almost-immortal servants, for the ring. Attracted by the ring's presence, the Ringwraiths almost catch the four young hobbits as they flee the Shire.

Cutting through the Old Forest, the hobbits meet a Ranger named Strider—who turns out to be Aragorn, long-lost heir to the throne of Gondor, the kingdom next to Mordor. Aragorn helps the hobbits escape, but the Ringwraiths wound Frodo with a poisoned knife. Aragorn explains that the Elf leader Elrond will give the hobbits refuge in Rivendell. With Frodo suffering from his wound and the Ringwraiths in pursuit, Elrond saves them by making the river to flood behind Aragorn and the hobbits.

 Analyzing Literature

In Rivendell, Frodo is nursed back to health. Elrond and his council have learned that the Dark Lord has corrupted the once-good wizard Saruman, who now works on Sauron's behalf. The threat is becoming dire: war is looming, and the One Ring must be taken to Mount Doom in Mordor, where it was forged, and tossed in the volcano's molten center to be destroyed. Frodo volunteers for this crucial task. A "fellowship of the ring" forms to accompany and protect him, consisting of the four hobbits, Aragorn, Gandalf, Gimli the Dwarf, Legolas the Elf, and the son of the ruling steward of Gondor, a man named Boromir.

The fellowship attempts to cross the Misty Mountains but is turned back by falling rocks, eerie noises, and a blinding snowstorm. So they cross underneath through the Mines of Moria, where they are attacked by orcs. There, Gandalf battles an ancient balrog demon and dies, sacrificing himself so that his friends can escape. They flee to Lothlórien, a beautiful forest realm of Elves. They meet Lady Galadriel, who gives them supplies and sends them on their way. One thing she gives them is *lembas*, a bread that sustains them like no other food can and increases their will to go on.

Along the way, Boromir is finally lured by the evil magnetism of the ring. He attempts to take it from Frodo. Frodo runs away from Boromir and decides to go on alone, feeling the pull of the ring growing stronger as he nears Mordor. Sam follows Frodo and insists on accompanying him to Mount Doom.

After Frodo and Sam depart, the orcs attack the others, killing Boromir and capturing Merry and Pippin. Aragorn, Legolas, and Gimli pursue the orcs into the kingdom of Rohan, where the resident horse-lords surprise and slay the orcs. Unseen, Merry and Pippin escape into the forest, where they are protected by the ancient walking-tree creatures called Ents.

Three days have passed. As Aragorn tracks Merry and Pippin through the forest, he meets up with Gandalf, who was resurrected and is now "Gandalf the White." Galdalf tells Aragorn that Merry and Pippin are safe, but warns they will have to take a stand. They go to Rohan, where Théoden, the king, has been bewitched by Saruman. Gandalf wakes Théoden just as orcs attack. However, Gandalf brings reinforcements to crush the orcs at last.

On another front, the peaceful Ents have learned about events from Merry and Pippin. Enraged, the tree people attack Saruman's fortress Isengard and trap the evil wizard just as armies led by Gandalf and Théoden arrive. Gandalf strips Saruman of his powers. Merry and Pippin are reunited with the remaining fellowship. Unfortunately, Pippin looks into Saruman's seeing-stone, a mystical device the wizard uses to communicate with Sauron. Sauron spies Pippin, mistaking him for the Ring-bearer. Gandalf spirits Pippin off to Gondor to protect him.

Meanwhile, Frodo and Sam approach Mordor, with Gollum trailing them. They capture him and force him to reveal his secret entrance into Mordor. But Gollum betrays them by leading them to the great spider Shelob, who bites Frodo. Sam, believing Frodo is dead, takes the ring, vowing to continue the quest. Orcs appear, and Sam hides. As they carry Frodo off, Sam overhears them say he is just unconscious. Sam follows to rescue his friend.

Chapter 4

> Meanwhile, the war for Middle-earth rages as Sauron's armies attack Gondor. But Aragorn, along with the Rohan army, defeats Sauron's forces. In Mordor, Sam rescues Frodo, and they climb to the rim of Mount Doom. Frodo, growing ever weaker, is ensnared by the power of the One Ring and refuses to throw it into the volcano—but right then, Gollum appears! He leaps upon Frodo and bites off Frodo's finger with the ring on it. Then Gollum, dancing with evil glee, slips and falls into the fiery pit, taking the ring with him. The One Ring is destroyed! Sauron's fortress crumbles, his armies retreat, and the Dark Lord is vanquished forever. Aragorn returns to Gondor and is crowned king.
>
> However, Saruman has escaped to the Shire, where he holds its citizens captive. When the victorious hobbits return, they mount a rebellion and overthrow Saruman, who is killed in the fighting. They restore the Shire and are proclaimed heroes. Sam marries the girl he has always loved. Frodo, however, remains wounded; some time later, he decides to leave the Shire. Accompanied by Bilbo and Gandalf, Frodo departs for the Undying Lands, a place removed from the realm of the world, where very few except the Elves are allowed to go.

What similarities did you notice between the biblical passages and the synopsis of The Lord of the Rings? Tolkien draws on a number of biblical images, themes, and character types to tell the story. One example is that Gandalf symbolizes Jesus Christ when he sacrifices himself for others in the Mines of Moria and is brought back to life three days later, stronger than ever. Another example is that Frodo carries the burdens of others, as depicted in Galatians, by taking the ring back to Mount Doom—a heavy burden indeed! Now answer these questions about other allusions that Tolkien makes.

5   Which is the main conflict in The Lord of the Rings?

    A   The hobbits need to find a way to save their Shire from evil outside forces.

    B   All of the races must unite in order to defeat the ghastly forces of evil.

    C   Frodo and the fellowship must resist and destroy the ring to defeat Sauron.

    D   Aragon must embrace his role as leader so the fight against Sauron can succeed.

6   How does the *lembas* that Lady Galadriel gives the fellowship relate to Jesus's bread of life?

_____

_____

7   What biblical theme is suggested by Gandalf coming back to life after being killed by the demon?

    A   Love and sacrifice can save you.

    B   Treat others like you want to be treated.

    C   Good always triumphs over evil.

    D   Justice and love are opposing values.

Analyzing Literature

8 What other biblical themes, events, or character types might Tolkien have drawn from to tell the story? Use your own paper to write your response.

ANALYZING ADAPTATIONS OF TEXTS

You have probably seen films or plays that were based on written works. These are called *adaptations* since they are works adapted from other works. An adaptation can greatly help you understand the original work of literature. To have that happen, you need to be able to **analyze how a filmed or live adaptation stays faithful or departs from a text or script**.

For example, you might read a play by William Shakespeare in school. When you see the play performed, you might notice a difference. Perhaps a character does not behave quite as you expected. You need to figure out what choices were made by the director or actors to change things. Do they make the play more entertaining to watch? Do they help you understand something in the play?

The same is true in filmed adaptations. Have you seem movies that are based on books? Some recent ones include the Twilight series based on the books by Stephenie Meyer, the Chronicles of Narnia books by C. S. Lewis, the Harry Potter series by J. K. Rowling, and an assortment of superhero films adapted from comic books and graphic novels. If you saw some of these, had you read the books first? If so, how well did you think they were adapted to film? You might often hear people complain about some aspect from a favorite book being left out of the movie. Sometimes, there is just not enough time in a film to include everything from the book. Other times, part of the plot changes, or a character is portrayed differently, to make a point. There are many ways in which elements like plot, characters, setting, and theme might be altered. The key is for you to understand what the differences are and why some elements might have changed.

In the previous section, "Analyzing How Modern Literature Draws on Tradition," you read about the ancient Roman myth of Pygmalion. You also read how it inspired a twentieth century drama. Shaw's play *Pygmalion* was based on the ancient tale, but many aspects changed in his adaptation. The setting of the play is London (in the modern day, when Shaw wrote it) rather than in the ancient Roman Empire. The characters are people who would have lived then. Shaw could have made Henry Higgins a sculptor, but he chose to give him a more modern profession as a phonetics professor. He also made Eliza Doolittle an actual woman rather than a statue. Why do you think the author changed her in this way? Perhaps this was done to make the story more believable. He focused on themes such as overcoming the roles people play in society rather than the supernatural events of the myth.

George Bernard Shaw's play was filmed several times. The most famous adaptations are *Pygmalion* in 1938 (starring Leslie Howard and Wendy Hiller) of the play itself, and *My Fair Lady* in 1964 (starring Rex Harrison and Audrey Hepburn) incorporating songs from the musical version and a "happy ending" in which Eliza stays with the professor.

Now that you know the background of this story, complete the following exercise. If you need to, ask your teacher or tutor how you can access copies of the play and the film mentioned below.

Chapter 4

Practice 4: Analyzing Adaptations of Texts
RL 7, W 1, 2

Writing Task

Read one of the following books.

- *The Outsides* by S. E. Hinton
- *The Diary of a Young Girl* by Anne Frank
- *Flowers for Algernon* by Daniel Keyes

If you can't decide, ask your teacher or tutor which book might be best for you. In the book you read, pay special attention to the characters, plot, setting, and themes. Then, watch a film adaptation of the book.

- *The Outsiders* (1983) starring C. Thomas Howell and Matt Dillon
- *The Diary of Anne Frank* (1959) starring Millie Perkins and Shelley Winters or *The Diary of Anne Frank* (1980) starring Melissa Gilbert and Maximilian Schell
- *Charly* (1968) starring Cliff Robertson and Claire Bloom or *Flowers for Algernon* (2008) starring Matthew Modine and Kelli Williams

What similarities do you see between the book and the film? What major differences are there? Why do you think the changes were made from the book to the film? Is the film faithful to the book in many details, or does the book serve as just background inspiration? Be sure to discuss various story elements (setting, characters, plot, theme) and support your ideas with evidence from the book and the movie.

CHAPTER 4 SUMMARY

Analyzing literature takes careful reading plus some thought about what is under the surface.

Sometimes authors might state clearly what they mean, but often you will need to use **inference skills**. You must read between the lines to **make inferences** and **draw conclusions** based on facts in the text and what you already know. Then, you need **support an analysis** of the text by evaluating the **evidence** left by the author.

There are several ways to **compare and contrast literature**.

The **structures of texts contribute to their meaning and style**.

Many **modern works of fiction draw on traditional stories, religious works, and mythology** for their plots, characters, or themes.

You must be able to **analyze how a filmed or live adaptation stays faithful or departs from a text or script**.

For more practice with this chapter's material, see the Literature Review on page 67.

Literature Review

This chapter covers the following eighth grade strand and standards.

> **RL** 1–7, 9–10, **W** 1–4, 7–10, **SL** 1–3, **L** 1–6

This review will give you more practice with the skills you read about in chapters 2, 3, and 4. Read the passages, and answer the questions that follow. Then, you will write about what you read.

Excerpt from *The Red Badge of Courage*

by Stephen Crane

Someone cried, "Here they come!"

There was rustling and muttering among the men. They displayed a feverish desire to have every possible cartridge ready to their hands. The boxes were pulled around into various positions, and adjusted with great care. It was as if seven hundred new bonnets were being tried on.

The tall soldier, having prepared his rifle, produced a red handkerchief of some kind. He was engaged in knotting it about his throat with exquisite attention to its position, when the cry was repeated up and down the line in a muffled roar of sound.

"Here they come! Here they come!" Gun locks clicked.

Across the smoke-infested fields came a brown swarm of running men who were giving shrill yells. They came on, stooping and swinging their rifles at all angles. A flag, tilted forward, sped near the front.

As he caught sight of them the youth was momentarily startled by a thought that perhaps his gun was not loaded. He stood trying to rally his faltering intellect so that he might recollect the moment when he had loaded, but he could not.

A hatless general pulled his dripping horse to a stand near the colonel of the 304th. He shook his fist in the other's face. "You've got to hold 'em back!" he shouted, savagely; "you've got to hold 'em back!"

In his agitation the colonel began to stammer. "A-all r-right, General, all right, by Gawd! We-we'll do our—we-we'll d-d-do-do our best, General." The general made a passionate gesture and galloped away. The colonel, perchance to relieve his feelings, began to scold like a wet parrot. The youth, turning swiftly to make sure that the rear was unmolested, saw the commander regarding his men in a highly resentful manner, as if he regretted above everything his association with them.

The man at the youth's elbow was mumbling, as if to himself: "Oh, we're in for it now! Oh, we're in for it now!"

The captain of the company had been pacing excitedly to and fro in the rear. He coaxed in schoolmistress fashion, as to a congregation of boys with primers. His talk was an endless repetition. "Reserve your fire, boys—don't shoot till I tell you—save your fire—wait till they get close up …"

Perspiration streamed down the youth's face, which was soiled like that of a weeping urchin. He frequently, with a nervous movement, wiped his eyes with his coat sleeve. His mouth was still a little ways open.

He got the one glance at the foe-swarming field in front of him, and instantly ceased to debate the question of his piece being loaded. Before he was ready to begin—before he had announced to himself that he was about to fight—he threw the obedient well-balanced rifle into position and fired a first wild shot. Directly he was working at his weapon like an automatic affair.

He suddenly lost concern for himself, and forgot to look at a menacing fate. He became not a man but a member. He felt that something of which he was a part—a regiment, an army, a cause, or a country—was in crisis. He was welded into a common personality which was dominated by a single desire. For some moments he could not flee no more than a little finger can commit a revolution from a hand.

If he had thought the regiment was about to be annihilated perhaps he could have amputated himself from it. But its noise gave him assurance. The regiment was like a firework that, once ignited, proceeds superior to circumstances until its blazing vitality fades. It wheezed and banged with a mighty power. He pictured the ground before it as strewn with the discomfited.

There was a consciousness always of the presence of his comrades about him. He felt the subtle battle brotherhood more potent even than the cause for which they were fighting. It was a mysterious fraternity born of the smoke and danger of death.

He was at a task. He was like a carpenter who has made many boxes, making still another box, only there was furious haste in his movements. He, in his thoughts, was careering off in other places, even as the carpenter who as he works whistles and thinks of his friend or his enemy, his home or a saloon. And these jolted dreams were never perfect to him afterward, but remained a mass of blurred shapes.

Presently he began to feel the effects of the war atmosphere—a blistering sweat, a sensation that his eyeballs were about to crack like hot stones. A burning roar filled his ears.

Following this came a red rage. He developed the acute exasperation of a pestered animal, a well-meaning cow worried by dogs. He had a mad feeling against his rifle, which could only be used against one life at a time. He wished to rush forward and strangle with his fingers. He craved a power that would enable him to make a world-sweeping gesture and brush all back. His impotency appeared to him, and made his rage into that of a driven beast.

Buried in the smoke of many rifles his anger was directed not so much against the men whom he knew were rushing toward him as against the swirling battle phantoms which were choking him, stuffing their smoke robes down his parched throat. He fought frantically for respite for his senses, for air, as a babe being smothered attacks the deadly blankets.

There was a blare of heated rage mingled with a certain expression of intentness on all faces. Many of the men were making low-toned noises with their mouths, and these subdued cheers, snarls, imprecations, prayers, made a wild, barbaric song that went as an undercurrent of sound, strange and chantlike with the resounding chords of the war march. The man at the youth's elbow was babbling. In it there was something soft and tender like the monologue of a babe. The tall soldier was swearing in a loud voice. From his lips came a black procession of curious oaths. Of a sudden another broke out in a querulous way like a man who has mislaid his hat. "Well, why don't they support us? Why don't they send supports? Do they think—"

The youth in his battle sleep heard this as one who dozes hears.

There was a singular absence of heroic poses. The men bending and surging in their haste and rage were in every impossible attitude. The steel ramrods clanked and clanged with incessant din as the men pounded them furiously into the hot rifle barrels. The flaps of the cartridge boxes were all unfastened, and bobbed idiotically with each movement. The rifles, once loaded, were jerked to the shoulder and fired without apparent aim into the smoke or at one of the blurred and shifting forms which upon the field before the regiment had been growing larger and larger like puppets under a magician's hand.

The officers, at their intervals, rearward, neglected to stand in picturesque attitudes. They were bobbing to and fro roaring directions and encouragements. The dimensions of their howls were extraordinary. They expended their lungs with prodigal wills. And often they nearly stood upon their heads in their anxiety to observe the enemy on the other side of the tumbling smoke.

The lieutenant of the youth's company had encountered a soldier who had fled screaming at the first volley of his comrades. Behind the lines these two were acting a little isolated scene. The man was blubbering and staring with sheeplike eyes at the lieutenant, who had seized him by the collar and was pommeling him. He drove him back into the ranks with  many blows. The soldier went mechanically, dully, with his animal-like eyes upon the officer. Perhaps there was to him a divinity expressed in the voice of the other—stern, hard, with no reflection of fear in it. He tried to reload his gun, but his shaking hands prevented. The lieutenant was obliged to assist him.

The men dropped here and there like bundles. The captain of the youth's company had been killed in an early part of the action. His body lay stretched out in the position of a tired man resting, but upon his face there was an astonished and sorrowful look, as if he thought some friend had done him an ill turn. The babbling man was grazed by a shot that made the blood stream widely down his face. He clapped both hands to his head. "Oh!" he said, and ran. Another grunted suddenly as if he had been struck by a club in the stomach. He sat down and gazed ruefully. In his eyes there was mute, indefinite reproach. Farther up the line a man, standing behind a tree, had had his knee joint splintered by a ball. Immediately he had dropped his rifle and gripped the tree with both arms. And there he remained, clinging desperately and crying for assistance that he might withdraw his hold upon the tree.

At last an exultant yell went along the quivering line. The firing dwindled from an uproar to a last vindictive popping. As the smoke slowly eddied away, the youth saw that the charge had been repulsed. The enemy were scattered into reluctant groups. He saw a man climb to the top of the fence, straddle the rail, and fire a parting shot. The waves had receded, leaving bits of dark "debris" upon the ground.

Some in the regiment began to whoop frenziedly. Many were silent. Apparently they were trying to contemplate themselves.

After the fever had left his veins, the youth thought that at last he was going to suffocate. He became aware of the foul atmosphere in which he had been struggling. He was grimy and dripping like a laborer in a foundry. He grasped his canteen and took a long swallow of the warmed water.

A sentence with variations went up and down the line. "Well, we've helt 'em back. We've helt 'em back; derned if we haven't." The men said it blissfully, leering at each other with dirty smiles.

The youth turned to look behind him and off to the right and off to the left. He experienced the joy of a man who at last finds leisure in which to look about him.

Under foot there were a few ghastly forms motionless. They lay twisted in fantastic contortions. Arms were bent and heads were turned in incredible ways. It seemed that the dead men must have fallen from some great height to get into such positions. They looked to be dumped out upon the ground from the sky.

From a position in the rear of the grove a battery was throwing shells over it. The flash of the guns startled the youth at first. He thought they were aimed directly at him. Through the trees he watched the black figures of the gunners as they worked swiftly and intently. Their labor seemed a complicated thing. He wondered how they could remember its formula in the midst of confusion.

The guns squatted in a row like savage chiefs. They argued with abrupt violence. It was a grim pow-wow. Their busy servants ran hither and thither.

A small procession of wounded men were going drearily toward the rear. It was a flow of blood from the torn body of the brigade.

To the right and to the left were the dark lines of other troops. Far in front he thought he could see lighter masses protruding in points from the forest. They were suggestive of unnumbered thousands.

Once he saw a tiny battery go dashing along the line of the horizon. The tiny riders were beating the tiny horses.

From a sloping hill came the sound of cheerings and clashes. Smoke welled slowly through the leaves.

Batteries were speaking with thunderous oratorical effort. Here and there were flags, the red in the stripes dominating. They splashed bits of warm color upon the dark lines of troops.

The youth felt the old thrill at the sight of the emblems. They were like beautiful birds strangely undaunted in a storm.

As he listened to the din from the hillside, to a deep pulsating thunder that came from afar to the left, and to the lesser clamors which came from many directions, it occurred to him that they were fighting, too, over there, and over there, and over there. Heretofore he had supposed that all the battle was directly under his nose.

As he gazed around him the youth felt a flash of astonishment at the blue, pure sky and the sun gleamings on the trees and fields. It was surprising that Nature had gone tranquilly on with her golden process in the midst of so much devilment.

Practice 1: Excerpt from *The Red Badge of Courage*

RL 1–4, 10, L 5

DIRECTIONS Answer these questions about the passage you just read.

1

How does the main character in the regiment get over his fear and begin fighting? What is the turning point for him? Support your answer with evidence from the passage.

_____
_____
_____
_____

2

The author uses analogies, metaphors, and similes throughout this passage. Choose two of these, and tell how they help the reader to understand what is happening.

_____
_____
_____
_____

Literature Review

3

What message about war does the author mostly convey in this passage?

A War is nothing more than a big, laughable joke.

B War is always a glorious and honorable endeavor.

C War is something everyone should experience.

D War is a horrifying experience for all involved.

4

If you are writing about how well Crane uses vivid language to describe the emotional state of his characters, which line from the passage would best support this claim?

A They displayed a feverish desire to have every possible cartridge ready to their hands.

B He was welded into a common personality which was dominated by a single desire.

C Immediately he had dropped his rifle and gripped the tree with both arms.

D The firing dwindled from an uproar to a last vindictive popping.

"Not to Keep"

by Robert Frost

They sent him back to her. The letter came
Saying … And she could have him. And before
She could be sure there was no hidden ill
Under the formal writing, he was in her sight,
Living. They gave him back to her alive—
How else? They are not known to send the dead—
And not disfigured visibly. His face?
His hands? She had to look, and ask,
"What was it, dear?" And she had given all
And still she had all—*they* had—they the lucky!
Wasn't she glad now? Everything seemed won,
And all the rest for them permissible ease.
She had to ask, "What was it, dear?"

"Enough,
Yet not enough. A bullet through and through,
High in the breast. Nothing but what good care
And medicine and rest, and you a week,
Can cure me of to go again." The same
Grim giving to do over for them both.
She dared no more than ask him with her eyes
How was it with him for a second trial.
And with his eyes he asked her not to ask.
They had given him back to her, but not to keep.

Literature Review

Practice 2: "Not to Keep"

RL 1, 3, 4, 6, 10, L 5

DIRECTIONS Answer these questions about the passage you just read.

1. What genre of literature is this? How do you know?

2. How might this passage be different if the husband narrated it?

3. Which phrase makes the wife realize her husband must go back to the war?

A They sent him back to her.

B And all the rest for them permissible ease.

C Can cure me of to go again.

D And with his eyes he asked her not to ask.

4. How does the tone progress from the start to the end of the passage?

A Worried – relieved – dejected

B Thrilled – depressed – shocked

C Gloomy – contented – anxious

D Outraged – unhappy – joyful

Practice 3: Write about the Passages

RL 1, 2, 5, 10, W 1–4, 10, L 1–3

DIRECTIONS On your own paper, write about these two passages.

A. Compare and Contrast the Passages

The passages you read have different structures. As you know, text structure affects meaning and style. Tell how the two passages are similar and how they differ. Then consider whether each passage could have the structure of the other? How would that work, if at all?

Use your own paper to write your essay. Make sure your writing is clear and well organized. Be sure to use support from the passages in your writing.

B. Write a Story

Think about a time in your life when what you expected changed suddenly. For example, you might have thought something scary was coming up, but then you found out it was not so bad. Or, you might have expected a fun event that turned into a disaster—though maybe you made the best of it. Consider this time in which your feelings changed drastically over a short time. Tell the story of what happened. You can tell it in first person, with you as a character, or you can use it to inspire a made-up story about characters you invent.

Use your own paper to write your story. Make sure your writing is clear and well organized. Be creative, and incorporate literary elements and devices into your writing. Be sure to check for and fix any mistakes.

Literature Review

Activity 1

RL 10, **W** 3, 4, **SL**1

Turn your narrative into a short play. Write out dialogue (what each person says) for the characters in it. Provide directions for how characters should portray the emotions they feel, and give stage directions for actions. Create some simple scenery and props. Then, get a group together to be the actors. Act out the play for other groups. Each group can produce one short play. Talk about each play after you watch it.

Activity 2

RL 7, 10

Read the entire novel, *The Red Badge of Courage*. (The paperback is less than 200 pages.) Then, watch the 1951 movie adaptation, *The Red Badge of Courage*, directed by John Huston. Take notes about what is adapted faithfully from the book and what has been changed by the director or actors. After giving it some considerations, write a brief essay about what changes the most in the adaptation, and why you think it was changed.

Practice 4: Research Project

RL 1, 2, 5, 10, **W** 1–4, 10, **SL** 4–6, **L** 1–3

Consider the effects of war, both negative and positive, throughout history. Pick a universal concept, like families losing loved ones or soldiers being changed through the experience, and do some research. Pick two or three specific times of war (this could be ancient wars, local wars, world wars, or so on), and focus on one way in which people were affected. Find writing from that time and use it to support your ideas.

Examples of Research Projects

1. Inventions that were made due to war efforts but helpful long after (resources include articles and books about medicine, equipment, architecture)

2. Families being separated (resources include books, journals, letters)

3. Nationalism and uses of propaganda (resources include articles from the time, posters)

Ask your teacher or the media specialist about the best resources to use. Take notes about what you find, and draft your essay. Make sure your writing is clear and well organized. Be sure to use support from the resources you found.

Then, use your report to give a speech. Ask your teacher to choose a day when everyone can present their research projects. Each student can talk about what he or she chose to research. Then, the audience can ask questions.

Chapter 5
Understanding Informational Texts

This chapter covers the following eighth grade strand and standards:

> **Reading: Informational Text**
> 1. Cite the textual evidence that most strongly supports an analysis of what the text says explicitly as well as inferences drawn from the text.
> 2. Determine a central idea of a text and analyze its development over the course of the text, including its relationship to supporting ideas; provide an objective summary of the text.
>
> **Craft and Structure**
> 4. Determine the meaning of words and phrases as they are used in a text, including figurative, connotative, and technical meanings; analyze the impact of specific word choices on meaning and tone, including analogies or allusions to other texts.
> 5. Analyze in detail the structure of a specific paragraph in a text, including the role of particular sentences in developing and refining a key concept.
> 6. Determine an author's point of view or purpose in a text ….

Informational texts tell facts and relate true stories. Some can be articles or essays that provide information about a topic. Others can be like stories, telling about actual events or the life of a real person.

CENTRAL IDEA AND DETAILS

The **central idea** is what a passage is all about. It is the focus of the passage. To identify a central idea, you must first read carefully. A good reader will also look for clues and use thinking questions like these:

- What is the passage mostly about?
- Is there one sentence that states the central idea?
- How can I summarize the passage in my own words?

You should be able to **analyze the development of the central idea** in the text. This means looking at how the author builds the idea and uses details to support it. It includes exploring how the author uses specific **sentence and paragraph structure** to make a point. Picking out exactly which part of the text supports an idea can help you answer questions too. When you respond to questions in class and on tests, you will need to **cite evidence that supports your analysis** of the text.

Chapter 5

Another important skill is identifying the **details** of a piece of writing. Once you have determined the central idea, you can look deeper into the text to see other details. To find details, you can ask questions like the **five Ws and one H**: *who? what? where? when? why?* and *how?* and then support your answers to these questions with information from the text.

SUMMARIZING

Summarizing is a great way to grasp the central idea and details. It involves developing a short description of what you read. It should express the central idea and major supporting details. Writing a summary is a way to increase reading comprehension. It is also useful in writing reports and essays when a large amount of information must be condensed into a few sentences. Remember that a summary is not a critique; it should provide an objective (impartial) synopsis of a text.

Read the following text. Then read the questions and explanations that follow.

Can Snakebites Be Healthy?

Bill Haast, a 100-year-old Floridian, developed a reputation as a man with an acquired immunity to snakes. Playing with a cobra was an everyday activity with Mr. Haast, who during his long life had been bitten no less than 173 times by venomous snakes.

He began his experimentation with snake venom in 1948 by injecting himself with small amounts of rattlesnake venom. Over the years, he built up the dosage. He believed the snake venom kept him healthy. He never became sick once he began injecting himself with venom.

He had his near-death experiences, though. In 1958, Haast was bitten by a blue krait, an Asian snake which has venom many times more poisonous than a cobra's. The krait's venom has been known to kill elephants. During his ordeal, Haast realized that something as powerful as venom must have something useful for medicine.

In the late 1970s, Haast produced a drug called PROven, which mirrored the effects produced by his own immunity to snakebites. The drug has been used to treat rheumatoid arthritis and MS (multiple sclerosis). Over seven thousand patients have been treated with this high-demand drug.

Because he lost a finger in 2003 due to a bite from a Malayan pit viper, Haast stopped handling venomous snakes. However, he still allowed his wife to inject venom into his veins each day. His own blood was still so full of antibodies that it could be used as an antidote for victims of snakebites. Haast credited the effects of the venom for his unusually long life span.

 **Understanding Informational Texts**

What is the central idea of this text?

A   Bill Haast lived to be one hundred thanks to snake venom.

B   Bill Haast loved all kinds of snakes better than any other animals.

C   Bill Haast nearly died several times but continued to get injected with snake venom.

D   Bill Haast realized the power of snake venom and created an immunity medicine from it.

Which answer did you pick? Answer A is not correct, even though the second paragraph does say "He believed the snake venom kept him healthy." The whole text is not just about how Haast lived so long. Answer B is incorrect because there is nothing in the article to support it. While answer C is true, it is not the central or most important idea in the text. Answer D is the correct answer. The main point of the article is that, through his activities, Haast saw that snake venom has some powerful medicinal properties. He harnessed that power for a positive purpose.

Which of the following best describes Bill Haast's motivation for creating a drug from snake venom?

A   He wanted to help snakes gain a better reputation.

B   He realized the powerful venom must have medicinal qualities.

C   He wanted to raise money so he could buy a house for his snakes.

D   He was no longer able to sell his own blood as an antidote for snakebite victims.

Did you choose B? You are correct. The third paragraph tells how Haast nearly died even though he had built up his immunity to snake venom. It made him think about the power of the poison. This led to his experiments.

On your own paper, write an objective summary of this article.

Is your summary in your own words? Does it give a brief overview of the central idea and major details? Is it objective? Here is an example of a summary written by one student.

> Bill Haast had learned to make use of snake venom. He began injecting himself with venom, and he built up immunities. He realized the venom could be used for medicine, and he produced a drug with it to treat various diseases. He continued to receive daily injections of snake venom.

Chapter 5

Practice 1: Central Idea and Details
RL 1, 2, 5

DIRECTIONS Read the following passage, and answer the questions.

William Shakespeare

Have you heard of *Romeo and Juliet*, *Hamlet*, or *Macbeth*? Maybe you've heard someone say "forgive and forget" or "all's well that ends well." These are the works and sayings of the famous poet and playwright William Shakespeare.

Shakespeare was born in England during the mid-1500s. He received a good education as a young boy. When he was eighteen years old, he married a woman named Anne Hathaway. By the time he turned thirty, Shakespeare had a career in London as a playwright. He also started writing poetry. Thus began a very productive career.

During the time that Shakespeare lived, people entertained themselves by attending and performing in plays. Shakespeare was an actor in many plays, but he is famous for the many plays and poems that he wrote. There are thirty-seven plays and over fifty sonnets credited to Shakespeare. He liked to have fun with language and invented many new phrases.

Many of Shakespeare's plays were performed at the Globe Theater. The Globe Theater was a three-story, open-air amphitheater. It was a round structure with a stage in the middle. It had no roof and could hold three thousand people. Many would gather there to watch the plays performed by Shakespeare's theater company, the Lord Chamberlain's Men.

Some skeptics believe that someone else wrote the plays that are credited to Shakespeare. There are many theories. Some scholars think a few of the plays look like the work of other playwrights at the time. Some suggest that a member of the royal family wrote the plays but needed to remain anonymous. However, there has never been reliable evidence to prove any of these ideas.

Shakespeare died in 1616. He was buried at Holy Trinity Church in England. His works have endured over many generations. They are still acted out on stage all over the world, and many have been adapted again and again.

1. When did Shakespeare write most of his plays?
   A Mid-1500s
   B Late 1500s
   C Mid-1600s
   D Late 1600s

Understanding Informational Texts

2   Which specific sentences in the text point you to the years in which Shakespeare did his writing?

   _____
   _____
   _____
   _____

3   The central idea of this passage is that —

   A   another person might have written Shakespeare's plays and poems.
   B   Shakespeare was an extremely creative poet and playwright.
   C   Shakespeare is an enormously important part of England's history.
   D   people in Shakespeare's time loved to attend outdoor plays.

4   The writer states that Shakespeare had "a very productive career." Choose three sentences from the text that best support this claim.

   _____
   _____
   _____
   _____

5   Write an objective summary of this article.

   _____
   _____
   _____
   _____
   _____

AUTHOR'S PURPOSE AND STYLE

When you read any text, remember that a real person wrote it. The words did not just appear on the page. You can see something about the author in how it is written, and this can further help you to understand the writing. Consider the author's purpose for writing the text and the way in which the author uses words and phrases to communicate.

Chapter 5

AUTHOR'S PURPOSE

Every time you write, you have a purpose or reason for doing so. The same is true for all authors. An **author's purpose** for writing may be to inform, to entertain, to motivate, to persuade, and so on. You can identify an author's purpose, or motivation, from the way the author writes. Here is an example of two different purposes in writing: Two students write articles about water for the school newsletter. One student writes about ways to conserve water at home. This author's purpose is *to inform* readers about how to save water. The second student writes an opinion-based article about the importance of conserving water. This author's purpose for writing is *to persuade* readers to accept the author's point of view on water conservation.

See if you can find out the author's purpose in writing the following two paragraphs. Remember to look at words and phrases to give you clues.

1. The border collie is known to be a reliable, friendly, and loyal breed of dog. The male can grow up to twenty-three inches in height, and the female can grow to twenty-one inches. Their coats can be long or short, and they come in many different colors and patterns. Border collies are highly intelligent and are easily trained. But be aware that these dogs need constant exercise! Border collies were bred to herd sheep and to work hard. As a result, they have boundless energy and stamina. A border collie needs a big yard to run in and enough mental stimulation to keep from getting bored. But with the right setup, a well-trained border collie can make a great pet—not to mention a future Frisbee-catching champion.

2. Uncle Tate came by our house unexpectedly last Saturday morning. He was wearing a grin that stretched from ear to ear. He was also wearing his usual flight jacket and his boots that clattered on the flagstone floor as he marched into the house past my dad. Uncle Tate stopped and, with a flourish, pulled a small black puppy, with bright chocolate eyes, out from under the jacket. As he set it on the floor, the puppy began to bounce up and down and wiggle all over at the same time. Going to our knees to stroke the puppy and to get acquainted, we could hear the growls from our father and the replies from Uncle Tate passing overhead.

"If you think you are going to leave that animal here, you've been in too many tailspins."

"And if you don't think those kids need a dog, you haven't been in enough!"

Both paragraphs above discuss dogs, but they do so in very different ways. Paragraph 1 provides basic information about a border collie. The author's tone is fact-based, with no emotion or dialogue. The author's purpose in this paragraph is *to inform*.

In paragraph 2, on the other hand, the author writes in a descriptive tone. The author describes characters, actions, and events. The author uses expressive words and dialogue. The author's purpose in paragraph 2 is *to entertain*.

Understanding Informational Texts

If you can identify the author's purpose in writing a text, it will add greatly to your understanding of the text. Become familiar with the following list. It will help you better understand and describe the reasons why an author writes.

Author's Purpose

Purpose	Definition	Sample Title
To inform	To present facts	"Life Cycle of the Armadillo"
To entertain	To offer enjoyment	"My Baby-Sitting Disasters"
To persuade	To encourage action	"The Importance of Outdoor Play"
To instruct	To teach about a subject	"How to Groom Your Dog"
To create suspense	To convey uncertainty	"Spats, the Ferret, Disappears"
To motivate	To encourage to act	"Join the Environment Club!"
To cause doubt	To question the accepted	"Are Student Lunches Healthy?"
To describe an event	To narrate	"My First Day in High School"
To teach a lesson	To relate knowledge	"Mastering Verb Phrases"
To introduce a character	To describe a person's traits	"Sue Clue, Private Eye"
To create a mood	To set up an atmosphere	"Terror in the Abandoned House"
To relate an adventure	To tell an exciting story	"Lost on a Theme Park Field Trip"
To share a personal experience	To tell about an event in your life	"The Day My Sister Became My Friend"
To describe feelings	To show emotion through words	"My Brother Left for College Today"

Remember, you cannot always sum up the author's purpose in one word: "The author's purpose is to _____." Read a passage more than once. Look not only for the author's purpose but also for statements that describe that purpose. For instance, in the previous passages about dogs, you might identify and describe the authors' motives in the following ways:

Chapter 5

Passage 1: The author's purpose is *to inform* readers about *the characteristics of a Labrador retriever.*

Passage 2: The author's purpose is *to entertain* readers with *a story about an unexpected gift.*

AUTHOR'S STYLE

You read in chapter 3 about how authors use literary devices to make their writing more interesting and to give it meaning. The same holds true for writers of informational texts. Each **author's style** comes through in the words and phrases used in a text. Just like fiction, nonfiction can contain **figurative meanings**, **allusions**, **analogies**, and so on. Authors use words with certain **connotations**  (understood meanings) to make their meaning clear. (For more about figurative language, review chapter 3; for more about denotation and connotation, review chapter 7.)

Nonfiction writing also can contain **technical vocabulary**. This might include words and phrases that are specific to a certain topic. It can also include words that take on special meaning in a certain context. For example, the terms *byte*, *integrated circuits*, and *nanometer* are specific to computer technology. But think about the term *document*. In the context of computers, the noun *document* means "a file created by a software application." In everyday language, *document* can be any written work, printed or electronic. And the verb *to document* means to record in writing or to provide with evidence (as when documenting sources). When reading, pay attention how the author is using technical vocabulary.

Now, read this excerpt from Mary Shelley's introduction to her novel *Frankenstein*. Focus on to the language she uses to describe her thoughts as she worked on the book.

> I busied myself to think of a story—a story to rival those which had excited us to this task. One which would speak to the mysterious fears of our nature and awaken thrilling horror—one to make the reader dread to look round, to curdle the blood, and quicken the beatings of the heart. If I did not accomplish these things, my ghost story would be unworthy of its name. I thought and pondered, vainly. I felt that blank incapability of invention which is the greatest misery of authorship, when dull Nothing replies to our anxious invocations, "Have you thought of a story?" I was asked each morning, and each morning I was forced to reply with a mortifying negative.

What's the author's purpose for writing this introduction? Is she trying to convince readers that her story is a good one to read at night to keep them awake with fright? Does she explain the process of writing an effective horror story? No; what she does is reveal her feelings and ideas as she started thinking about what to write. She is describing vividly the goals she had and how, at first, she missed achieving them.

Understanding Informational Texts

Of course, when you answer a question about the purpose for writing, you need to support your ideas with evidence from the text. So, what evidence shows that Shelley is describing her experience with writing this book? She begins by saying "I busied myself to think of a story." She then describes the kind of story she set out to write: "One which would speak to the mysterious fears of our nature and awaken thrilling horror—one to make the reader dread to look round, to curdle the blood, and quicken the beatings of the heart." Finally, she tells readers that story ideas were just not coming to her. "I thought and pondered, vainly. I felt that blank incapability of invention which is the greatest misery of authorship …" She makes her description vivid with words and phrases like *mysterious fears*, *thrilling horror*, *dread*, *curdle the blood*, and *quicken the beatings of the heart*. She even uses personification when she writes that "Nothing" replies to the question she asks every day about what her story will be.

Complete the following exercise to practice finding the author's purpose. Be sure to consider the author's style to support your ideas.

Practice 2: Author's Purpose and Style

RL 4, 6

DIRECTIONS Read the passages below. Then answer the questions that follow.

A Trip to Remember

My mother has crazy ideas sometimes. Now and then, she gets like a song bird that needs to fly around the room once or twice before she can settle in to the abundance and protection of the cage again. One year after having moved to Savannah, she decided it was time to visit Seattle again. We couldn't get a plane ticket to Seattle for the weekend, but that didn't stop her. She just bought tickets to San Francisco instead. "We'll wing it from there," she said. "Winging it" meant landing in San Francisco, taking a cab, and waiting in the Amtrak station until 2 a.m. for a train. Then, for twelve hours, the sleek, silver train took us north. But since we had left home, we were not able to get in touch with anyone!

In those days, we didn't have cell phones; nobody did. The station had no phone, there was no time at the airport, and the train never stopped long enough for us to find a phone booth, call home, and dash back to the train before it departed. My dad didn't know where we were for a whole day. But I knew. I remember sleeping in the passenger car and eating soup in the restaurant car. I vividly recall watching the rising sun outside the window, the passing mountains, and glimpses of the ocean. And I especially remember the feeling of secret adventure, of being aware that no one knew where I was. It was the best trip I've ever had.

Chapter 5

Read this analogy from the first paragraph.

Now and then, she gets like a song bird that needs to fly around the room once or twice before she can settle in to the abundance and protection of the cage again.

1. What is the narrator saying about her mother?

   A She dislikes her life and wants to get away from it.

   B She is frightened about losing her way of life.

   C She likes to explore but always comes back home.

   D She loves traveling more than being a mother.

2. What is the author's purpose? Include support for your idea.

_____

_____

_____

_____

Excerpt from "The Great Society" Speech (1964)

by Lyndon Baines Johnson

1   … I want to talk to you today about three places where we begin to build the Great Society—in our cities, in our countryside, and in our classrooms.

2   Many of you will live to see the day, perhaps fifty years from now, when there will be four hundred million Americans—four-fifths of them in urban areas. In the remainder of this century urban population will double, city land will double, and we will have to build homes, highways, and facilities equal to all those built since this country was first settled. So in the next forty years we must rebuild the entire urban United States.

3   Aristotle said "Men come together in cities in order to live, but they remain together in order to live the good life." It is harder and harder to live the good life in American cities today. The catalogue of ills is long: there is the decay of the centers and the despoiling of the suburbs. There is not enough housing for our people or transportation for our traffic. Open land is vanishing and old landmarks are violated.

4   Worst of all, expansion is eroding the precious and time-honored values of community with neighbors and communion with nature. The loss of these values breeds loneliness and boredom and indifference.

5   Our society will never be great until our cities are great. Today, the frontier of imagination and innovation is inside those cities and not beyond their borders. New experiments are already going on. It will be the task of your generation to make the American city a place where future generations will come, not only to live, but to live the good life.

6   I understand that if I stayed here tonight I would see that Michigan students are really doing their best to live the good life.

7   This is the place where the Peace Corps was started. It is inspiring to see how all of you, while you are in this country, are trying so hard to live at the level of the people.

8   A second place where we begin to build the Great Society is in our countryside. We have always prided ourselves on being not only America the strong and America the free, but America the beautiful. Today that beauty is in danger. The water we drink, the food we eat, the very air that we breathe, are threatened with pollution. Our parks are overcrowded, our seashores overburdened. Green fields and dense forests are disappearing.

9   A few years ago we were greatly concerned about the "Ugly American." Today we must act to prevent an ugly America. For once the battle is lost, once our natural splendor is destroyed, it can never be recaptured. And once man can no longer walk with beauty or wonder at nature his spirit will wither and his sustenance be wasted.

10   A third place to build the Great Society is in the classrooms of America. There your children's lives will be shaped. Our society will not be great until every young mind is set free to scan the farthest reaches of thought and imagination. We are still far from that goal.

3   The author's purpose is to —

A   instruct readers about places that need to be improved.

B   share a personal experience about being the president.

C   entertain readers with anecdotes about "the good life."

D   persuade readers about what can make a nation great.

Chapter 5

4   In paragraph 7, the president says "We have always prided ourselves on being not only America the strong and America the free, but America the beautiful." This sentence contains allusions to song lyrics about America. Do you know what songs are referenced here? Why does he use these words rather than simply saying we need to conserve natural resources?

_____

_____

_____

_____

In paragraph 8, the president compares two ideas. Complete the following analogy about what he compares.

   <u>Battle</u> is to <u>lost</u> as <u>nature</u> is to _____.

5   Which word belongs in the blank space?
   A   Polluted   B   Untamed   C   Grand   D   Quiet

> # Chapter 5 Summary
>
> **Informational texts** tell facts and relate true stories.
>
> The **central idea** is what a passage is all about.
>
> You should be able to **analyze the development of the central idea** and see how the author uses specific **sentence and paragraph structure** to make a point.
>
> You also need to **cite evidence that supports your analysis** of the text.
>
> Another important skill is identifying the **details** of a piece of writing.
>
> **Summarizing** is giving a short description of the central idea and major supporting details in your own words.
>
> An **author's style** comes through in the words and phrases used in a text. This includes **figurative meanings**, **allusions**, **analogies**, **connotations**, and **technical vocabulary** used to make the purpose and meaning clear.

For more practice with this chapter's material, see the Informational Texts Review on page 107.

Chapter 6
Analyzing Informational Texts

This chapter covers the following eighth grade strand and standards:

> **Reading: Informational Text**
>
> **Key Ideas and Details**
>
> 1. Cite the textual evidence that most strongly supports an analysis of what the text says explicitly as well as inferences drawn from the text.
>
> 3. Analyze how a text makes connections among and distinctions between individuals, ideas, or events (e.g., through comparisons, analogies, or categories).
>
> **Craft and Structure**
>
> 6. … analyze how the author acknowledges and responds to conflicting evidence or viewpoints.
>
> Integration of Knowledge and Ideas
>
> 7. Evaluate the advantages and disadvantages of using different mediums (e.g., print or digital text, video, multimedia) to present a particular topic or idea.
>
> 8. Delineate and evaluate the argument and specific claims in a text, assessing whether the reasoning is sound and the evidence is relevant and sufficient; recognize when irrelevant evidence is introduced.
>
> 9. Analyze a case in which two or more texts provide conflicting information on the same topic and identify where the texts disagree on matters of fact or interpretation.
>
> 10. By the end of the year, read and comprehend literary nonfiction at the high end of the grades 6–8 text complexity band independently and proficiently
>
> **Writing** (in Writing Tasks throughout chapter)
>
> **Text Types and Purposes**
>
> 1. Write arguments to support claims with clear reasons and relevant evidence.
>
> 2. Write informative/explanatory texts to examine a topic and convey ideas, concepts, and information through the selection, organization, and analysis of relevant content.
>
> **Speaking and Listening**
>
> 2. Analyze the purpose of information presented in diverse media and formats (e.g., visually, quantitatively, orally) and evaluate the motives (e.g., social, commercial, political) behind its presentation.

As you read in the last chapter, understanding informational texts is the first step. The next step is to analyze them so that you can see how to use them. For example, you need to know which texts offer the most factual or well-supported information and which ones might be best to use for a project you are doing. In this chapter, you will review how to analyze informational texts.

Chapter 6

FACTS AND INTERPRETATIONS

Facts are statements that can be proved. For example, an article in an encyclopedia is written to present facts. "Abraham Lincoln was president during the Civil War" is an example of a fact. Typically, when authors write to give information, they include facts.

An **opinion** is a personal viewpoint on a topic that not everyone agrees on. "Abraham Lincoln was the best president ever" is an example of an opinion. Authors who are writing to persuade state their opinions and then support them with evidence.

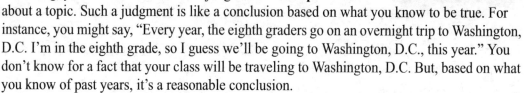

Often, by taking in all the facts and opinions from one or more pieces of writing, you can make a reasoned judgment or **interpretation** about a topic. Such a judgment is like a conclusion based on what you know to be true. For instance, you might say, "Every year, the eighth graders go on an overnight trip to Washington, D.C. I'm in the eighth grade, so I guess we'll be going to Washington, D.C., this year." You don't know for a fact that your class will be traveling to Washington, D.C. But, based on what you know of past years, it's a reasonable conclusion.

It is helpful to distinguish facts from opinions when analyzing information. When you interpret what you read, you can express any opinion you choose. But it's important to remember that valid arguments are only those that you can support with evidence.

INFERENCES AND CONCLUSIONS

You read in chapter 4 about using inference skills when it comes to analyzing literature. These skills are important in any kind of reading. When you make an **inference**, you are making an educated guess based on facts and details in a passage. By reviewing various ideas and details in a text, you can infer information that is not directly stated.

The following is a passage in which the topic must be inferred. Notice how the details in the paragraph contribute to the inference.

> These storms occur over land and are the most violent of all atmospheric disturbances. They are highly localized and, therefore, do not affect large areas at one time. The actual path of destruction of these storms is rarely more than one hundred yards in width. They take the form of a rotating column of air that extends down to the land from a thundercloud. They happen most frequently in the Great Plains states and in the southeastern part of the United States.

Can you infer the topic of this passage? If you decide that the author is describing tornadoes, you are right. The facts and details provided all of the clues. Such information included the following:

- storms occurring over land
- the violence and localized nature of the storms
- a narrow path of destruction
- a rotating column of air

Analyzing Informational Texts

You could also draw other inferences about the selection. For example, you could infer that tornadoes cause great damage to people and property. The passage also suggests another fact. Since tornadoes emerge from thunderclouds, they occur during unstable weather such as thunderstorms.

Drawing a **conclusion** is a common type of inference skill. When you draw a conclusion, you form a judgment or opinion based on the details in a passage. S. I. Hayakawa once said that conclusions are "statements about the unknown made on the basis of the known." To draw conclusions, use all the facts and clues present in the passage.

To reach a conclusion as you read, keep in mind what you already know. Try practicing with this passage.

> Roy was dreading the holidays. Usually he enjoyed the festive season; but last week, the coach had gotten upset with him about his weight. And the way his aunt June went crazy with her over-the-top holiday baking, Roy was facing torture. If he overindulged with cookies and cakes, he would lose his place on the team; if he refused to give in to the tasty treats, he would have to watch everybody else enjoying them. But when Roy returned to school after the holiday break, he was lean and fit.

Which is the most logical conclusion?

A Roy got dumped from the team, and he is sick over it.

B Roy stuck to his diet, and he is still on the team.

C Roy decided his diet wasn't worth it, and he ate like a king.

D Roy decided to take a break from football and try swimming instead.

Answer A is not a logical conclusion. The text describes Roy as "lean and fit," not sickly. B is a logical conclusion. We can conclude that Roy stayed the course and kept up with his diet, so he is no doubt still on the team. C is not a logical conclusion. There is no evidence to show that Roy ate excessively. D could be true, but nothing has been mentioned about Roy changing his choice of sport from football to swimming.

Chapter 6

Practice 1: Facts and Interpretations

RI 1, 3, 9, 10

DIRECTIONS Read the following passages. Then choose the best answer to each question.

Excerpt from *Apple Growing*

by M.C. Burritt

The apple has long been the most popular of our tree fruits, but the last few years have seen a steady growth in its appreciation and use. This is probably due in a large measure to a better knowledge of its value and to the development of new methods of preparation for consumption. Few fruits can be utilized in as many ways as can the apple. In addition to the common use of the fresh fruit out of hand and of the fresh, sweet juice as cider, this "King of Fruits" can be cooked, baked, dried, canned, and made into jellies and other appetizing dishes, to enumerate all of which would be to prepare a list pages long. Few who have tasted once want to be without their applesauce and apple pies in season, not to mention the crisp, juicy specimens to eat out of hand by the open fireplace in the long winter evenings. Apples thus served call up pleasant memories to most of us, but only recently have the culinary possibilities of the apple, especially as a dessert fruit, been fully realized.

1. Which statement based on this passage is a fact?

   A The apple has always been the most popular fruit in the country.

   B Apples bring pleasant memories to most of us who eat them.

   C Apples can be cooked, baked, canned, and made into many dishes.

   D Only a few people who have tasted apples don't like them.

2. In what way, if any, is the information in this text relevant in today's society?

   A Everyone eats apples, so it offers useful information.

   B No one has time to cook or bake these days, so it's not much use.

   C With today's focus on healthy eating, this text offers ways to use a healthy food.

   D People today have many choices of fruit, making this passage too narrow for modern audiences.

Analyzing Informational Texts

3   Which idea from the passage is an opinion?

   A   The last few years have seen a steady growth in appreciation and use of the apple.

   B   Few fruits can be utilized in as many ways as can the apple.

   C   Apples can be cooked, baked, dried, canned, and made into jellies and other appetizing dishes.

   D   Few who have tasted once want to be without their applesauce and apple pies in season.

CONNECTIONS AND DISTINCTIONS

Many informational texts make **connections and distinctions between people, ideas, and events**. The connections help you to see how people or ideas relate to one another, or how events progress in order. Distinctions help you to tell apart various items, ideas, or individuals. Authors create connections and distinctions by using certain structures. (You'll read about these in the "Organization" section that comes next.) They can also use devices like simile or metaphor, analogies, and categorizing. These devices can help them to compare and contrast.

ORGANIZATION

How a text is **organized** can also give you clues about the connections and distinctions the author is making. Writers choose the best pattern to present the information and to make a point. Here are some of the common organizational patterns.

COMPARISON AND CONTRAST

Comparison and contrast focuses on how things are similar and different. It is a way to organize and talk about information by looking for similarities and differences. Sometimes you may be asked what is similar and/or different about two or more articles or stories. What you need to find are some points to compare and contrast. Consider the central ideas and details of each text. What people and events are involved? Once you see the facts about each text, consider how the texts relate to each other.

CHRONOLOGICAL OR SEQUENTIAL ORDER

Chronological order (also called time order) means that events happen in sequence. For example, the sequence of events in a biography is typically time order from the subject's early life to later life. There may be flashbacks and foreshadowing, but how the events actually play out when examined must be logical. A related pattern is **sequential order**. This is often used for directions or the steps of a process, like making something from a recipe.

Chapter 6

CAUSE AND EFFECT

Cause and effect explores the relationships between ideas and events. This pattern makes connections about why things happen (the cause) and what happens as a result (the effect). For example, if you eat too much food and do not exercise, you will most likely gain weight.

PROBLEM AND SOLUTION

Problem and solution is closely related to cause and effect in that you need to determine the cause of the problem and identify its effects in order to suggest an effective solution. Business leaders would use this format when writing proposals to convince companies that a problem exists and a solution can be found for the right price. Editorials frequently identify a problem and suggest a solution.

Read this article, and then look at the questions and explanations that follow.

Is Venus Really Earth's Twin?

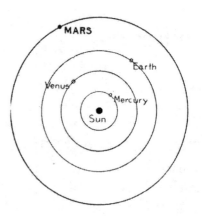

Venus, second planet from the Sun and Earth's next-door neighbor, is often called Earth's twin. But how alike are these two planets really? To begin with, the planets are similar in size. They also have similar gravity and composition. Both also have volcanic activity. However, this is where similarities end. While both planets have clouds, Venus is covered with such a thick blanket of clouds that its surface is always hidden. Venus is also closer to the Sun than Earth is. As a result of the clouds and the heat, Venus has much higher levels of carbon dioxide than Earth. In addition, Earth has one moon and Venus has none. Though Venus may be more like Earth than the other planets, the two planets are actually quite different.

What organization pattern does this text use?

If you said comparison and contrast, you are correct. The article is about how Earth and Venus are alike and different. Keep in mind that some passages just compare two things; other just contrast. This one does both. It first looks at all the things that are similar about Earth and Venus. Next, it looks at the two planets' differences. Finally, it concludes that the two do have a few similarities, but mostly they are very different.

Analyzing Informational Texts

What are two ways Venus and Earth are different?

A   Their size and the number of moons they have

B   Their volcanoes and their gravity

C   Their moons and their levels of carbon dioxide

D   Their shape and clouds

Did you choose answer C? That's correct. The other answer choices all contain at least one item that is similar about Earth and Venus. Only answer C contains two things that differ greatly on the two planets.

Practice 2: Organization

RI 1, 3, W 1

DIRECTIONS   Read the passages, and answer the questions that follow.

A Crisis in Our Schools

The community has been complaining about the lack of quality education in our schools. Parents say teachers need to be held accountable for their children's education. I don't believe the problem is with teachers. No, the problem is much broader than teacher accountability.

Teachers have to be willing to give up a lot of luxury to go into their profession. They have sacrificed high corporate salaries, cars that don't have duct tape holding them together, and the perfect nine-to-five job. Teachers have chosen to become parents to one hundred children, not just their own 2.5 children. And, they do it for fewer dollars per hour than the mechanic who keeps their cars taped together.

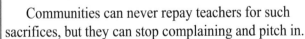

Communities can never repay teachers for such sacrifices, but they can stop complaining and pitch in. We need to quit complaining about our tax money, cut through the red tape, and get more support for our schools and teachers. You and I can do without a new set of golf clubs if it means helping our children and our neighbors' children succeed in life. In fact, we could spend less time on the golf course and more time tutoring children that need extra help in their studies. It takes a team of concerned, committed people to educate a child.

Chapter 6

1. What is the crisis in our schools?
   - A Children are not receiving free lunches.
   - B Children are not receiving a quality education.
   - C Children are not well behaved.
   - D Children are not paying for their education.

2. According to this editorial, what is the cause of that problem?
   - A Politicians are cutting education budgets.
   - B Teachers are underpaid and unappreciated.
   - C The community is complaining.
   - D The schools are understaffed.

3. What are the solutions that this author suggests to improve education?

   _____
   _____

Connecting Your New Printer

1. Shut down the computer, but leave it plugged into the surge suppressor.
2. Compare the connectors at the opposite ends of the cable. Attach the 25-pin end of the cable to the parallel, or printer, port on the computer. (The plug will go in only one way.) Tighten the hand screws securely. Connect the other end of the cable into the printer's socket. Latch the retaining clips (on most printer ports).
3. Plug the power cord into the printer and into the surge suppressor. Turn on the printer.
4. Install cartridges according to the printer manufacturer's instructions. Turn on the computer.
5. Install printer driver software according to the manufacturer's instructions.
6. Add the printer to the list of printers your computer recognizes.

---

4. Which organizational pattern does this text use? Is this the best pattern to use? Why or why not?

   _____
   _____
   _____

Analyzing Informational Texts

ARGUMENTATION

Everything you have read about so far in this chapter is important to the process of **argumentation**. In this context, arguing does not mean having a fight. It refers to making a claim and supporting it with evidence. An argument is a careful, reasoned way of presenting an idea or point of view.

An author must **make a strong claim** to begin his or her argument. Everything that comes after that must pertain to that claim and **support it with relevant evidence**. In addition, all of this information must use **logical reasoning** so that the argument makes sense to readers.

What is strong evidence? Facts and examples from credible sources are the best evidence. These include statistics, quotations, and relevant anecdotes (brief stories). These need to be logically linked to the claim. For example, say a writer claims that eating chicken is healthier than eating beef. The writer must offer some evidence for that claim. One fact that could support the claim is information about the amount of calories and fat in the same size portions of both meats. This would be a relevant fact that could be logically linked to the claim, since calorie and fat intake affect how healthy a food is for the human body. Another fact the author might offer is that it's less expensive to raise chickens than cows. The fact might be true and come from an authoritative source. However, it has nothing to do with the claim.

In chapter 9, you will review the steps to building a strong argument in your own writing. Here, you will read about how to recognize and **evaluate the author's argument** in a text. You will also review how to analyze conflicting information in two or more texts.

Read the following passages. Then look at the questions and explanations that follow.

Where's Your Order in the Family?

According to some psychologists, the order in which you were born can help determine your personality. Where you are born into the family plays a large role in determining the relationship between you and your parents and between you and your siblings. Psychologists have come to certain conclusions about behavior according to your birth order.

Oldest children tend to be responsible and obedient. They are also productive and independent. Both older and more confident than their siblings, they often take on leadership roles. Oldest children are typically well organized and precise. This can lead to them being prone to perfectionism.

Middle children are negotiators. They can be very easygoing. However, they also can feel the most stress from any sibling rivalry among their brothers or sisters. Middle children often find a place for themselves outside the family with friends or activities. Because they tend to go out on their own, they are often the most creative.

Youngest children are usually affectionate and charming. They can also be sensitive, sometimes overly so. Used to being taken care of, some are too dependent on others. Some of them become attention-seeking or manipulative.

While there are exceptions to the rule, psychologists have found these roles to play out in the majority of families. Those family relationships can also set the pattern for the way you will respond to people later in life.

What is the writer's claim?

The claim is well summed up in the second sentence: "Where you are born into the family plays a large role in determining the relationship between you and your parents and between you and your siblings." This is a good place for the claim, at the start of the text.

Is the evidence sufficient to persuade readers to agree with the claim? Why or why not?

If asked to answer this question, what would you write? Did you say that the evidence is not very strong? You are right. The author states many ideas, but they are not supported. The only evidence offered is the general idea that psychologists found these birth-order roles to be true, but specific studies are not even cited.

RESPONDING TO CONFLICTING EVIDENCE

What if authors do not agree? Naturally, this happens. When it does, you need to be able to **analyze conflicting information** and make sense of it. You should identify the basis of the disagreement. You read earlier about facts and interpretation, and the difference comes into play here as well.

One possibility is that authors disagree on **facts**. If that is the case, you can look up what the real facts are. For instance, you might have read articles about global climate change. Some provide statistics about sea levels rising or polar ice caps melting. These are measurements that can be checked. The real facts exist.

However, authors also can disagree on **interpretation**. All of the people who wrote the articles about climate change might agree about facts like how many inches of ice the North Pole loses each year. But some might say that this phenomenon is caused by humans and can be reversed through conservation. Others may argue that climate change is a natural cycle that humans can do nothing about.

Analyzing Informational Texts

As you will see in chapter 9, you must also acknowledge conflicting information when you write. You will review in that chapter how to mention and refute viewpoints that do not agree with a claim you make in your writing.

Practice 3: Argumentation

RI 1, 3, 6, 8, 9, 10, **W** 1, 2

> **DIRECTIONS** Read this passage, which is about the same topic as the sample text you read in the section above. Then answer the questions that follow.

Another Useless Theory

The topic of birth order and its effects on individuals is a controversial one. The birth-order theory holds that the particular order in which a subject was born dictates his or her personal traits. This includes social skills, academic achievement, and overall intelligence. Some people interpret the birth-order theory as a hard and fast rule. Others regard this theory as being a pseudoscience on a par with astrology.

Those who espouse this birth-order theory point to studies. Some of these statistically show that firstborn siblings outstrip the achievements of their younger siblings on many levels. Those children who follow experience a measurable decline in abilities depending on their place in the pecking order.

But how much of this is true, and how much is merely situational? The human experience is so varied and subjective that a generalization such as the birth-order theory cannot fit all instances. For example, if the rule were consistent, there would be no explanation for the existence of Mark Twain. Twain—or Samuel L. Clemens—was arguably one of the best writers the United States has ever produced. But theoretically, his intellectual abilities should not have blossomed because Samuel was the sixth child born into the Clemens family. According to the birth-order theory, he shouldn't have been able to write his own name!

Another statistic that belies this long-accepted "fact" can be illustrated in the cases of one-child families. The birth-order theory claims that the firstborn child has the advantages—but if this is so, then every only child should be a great thinker on par with Einstein. That idea is not only untrue, but in some cases is laughably wrong. How can a theory have so many exceptions, yet still be accepted by many as true?

There seems to be a human need to believe in something even if it is not a valid ideal. I say, when you hear a theory like this, ask for the proof. Look at the exceptions. Ask some actual experts. And stop believing everything you read.

Chapter 6

1. Do the authors of "Where's Your Order in the Family?" and "Another Useless Theory" disagree? If so, what do they disagree about?

   _____

   _____

   _____

2. What claim does the author of "Another Useless Theory" make about Mark Twain?

   A Twain's accomplishments prove that birth order doesn't mean much.

   B Twain would have been more successful had he been born before his siblings.

   C Twain did not like his name.

   D Twain's younger siblings were more accomplished than he was.

3. What analogy does the author of "Another Useless Theory" use to help readers understand the argument about birth-order theory?

   _____

   _____

   _____

4. Does the author use sound reasoning and offer sufficient evidence to support the claim in "Another Useless Theory"?

   _____

   _____

   _____

   _____

Writing Task

Do some additional research about birth-order theory. Incorporate your new sources with the two brief articles you just read. Now, write a well-organized report providing your conclusions about the theory. Remember to provide relevant evidence and check your writing for errors.

Analyzing Informational Texts

MEDIA

People communicate an idea or message through a medium. There are various **media** (which is the plural of *medium*). Newspapers, magazines, pamphlets, and books are examples of print media. Blogs and web content are examples of online media. Videos, commercials, and pictures are examples of visual media. Radio broadcasts and podcasts are examples of audio media.

When you do research on any topic, you might use many different kinds of sources. Some might fall into the category of media. As you analyze which sources are best to use, you must be able to **evaluate the use of media** to present a message.

People who rely on the media to share information have to choose the most appropriate medium for the audience they want to reach and for the purpose of their message. Material that requires explanation is often best suited for print media or certain online media. Information that is best shared visually, such as the impact of war or natural disasters, is often communicated most effectively through photos or video. Information or events that are best shared through audio include interviews, press conferences, political debates, and so on. Writers will often use visual images to reinforce the message. Sometimes these images are in the form of a photograph. Other times they may be an illustration, map, chart, or logo (visual image identified with a company or organization). Visual images may also be videos or slides used in presentations. Visual images may lead viewers to draw certain inferences. Viewers may understand a certain message from the image alone. For example, imagine an ad with very good-looking people all drinking a certain soft drink. The viewer is meant to infer that good-looking people prefer that beverage. If a viewer sees a picture of an athlete raising his or her hands in triumph, he or she likely infers that the athlete has been victorious.

Just like writing, media serve several purposes.

- Some media are meant *to inform*. For example, a news story reported in a paper or on a nightly newscast is an example of media that informs.
- Often, media are meant *to persuade*. A product picture in an advertisement is meant to convince people to buy the product. A political opinion expressed on a radio show is a media message meant to persuade people to agree with a position.
- Other media are meant *to entertain*. Television shows, radio broadcasts, entertaining blogs, and so on are examples of media geared toward entertainment.
- Some media are meant *to describe*. A magazine or newspaper might describe an event or process. A video might use images to describe a particular setting or the aftermath of a catastrophic event. A particular medium tries to provide an image for the reader, listener, or viewer.

Chapter 6

Practice 4: Media

RI 1, 7

> **DIRECTIONS** Read and answer the questions.

Look at this poster.

1. Its purpose is —

   A   to describe how to dunk a basketball.

   B   to explain why some shoes are better than others.

   C   to persuade people to buy a certain shoe.

   D   to inform readers about the importance of good shoes.

2. Is this the best medium for this message? Why or why not?

   _____
   _____
   _____
   _____

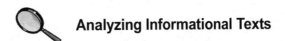

Look at this image.

3 What type of business might use this image?

    A A company that trains people how to use computer software

    B A business that sells computers, laptops, and monitors

    C A store in a mall that wants to hire people to sell computer supplies

    D A company that manufactures memory chips for computers

4 Danny wants to let other students know about the environmental group for which he is a volunteer, which needs more volunteers. He would like to describe the rewarding work, with some photos of the park he helped to clean up, and ask people to help. What is the best medium for him to use?

    A He should make an audio CD and get enough copies made for all students.

    B He should rent a billboard near school and put up a call to action.

    C He should post a blog with a link to the organization's volunteer page.

    D He should get an article published in a national newspaper.

Chapter 6 Summary

Facts are statements that can be proved.

Opinions are a personal viewpoint on a topic that not everyone agrees on.

An **inference** is an educated guess based on facts and details in a passage.

A **conclusion** is a judgment or opinion based on the details in a passage.

All the facts and opinions from one or more pieces of writing can help you make a reasoned judgment or **interpretation** about a topic.

Many informational texts make **connections and distinctions between people, ideas, and events**.

How a text is **organized** can also give you clues about the connections and distinctions the author is making.

- **Comparison and contrast** focuses on how things are similar and different.
- **Chronological order** (also called time order) means that events happen in sequence.
- **Sequential order** is often used for directions or the steps of a process.
- **Cause and effect** explores the relationships between ideas and events.
- **Problem and solution** is closely related to cause and effect in that it looks at the cause of the problem and identifies its effects in order to suggest an effective solution.

Argumentation refers to **making a claim** and **supporting it with relevant evidence**.

The author must use **sound reasoning** in presenting evidence.

When you find two or more articles on the same topic, you might need to **analyze conflicting information**.

When analyzing sources of information, you should be able to **evaluate the use of media** to present a message.

For more practice with this chapter's material, see the Informational Texts Review on page 107.

Informational Text Review

This chapter covers the following eighth grade strand and standards.

RI 1–10, W 1–10, SL 1–6, L 1–6

This review will give you more practice with the skills you read about in chapters 5 and 6. First, read the passages. Answer the questions that follow. Then, you will write about what you read.

Fall Days and Friday Night Lights

Each autumn comes the beginning of a new football season. Competitors of all ages and sizes take to the gridiron to clash on the field of battle. They begin each season with hopes of a championship. United as a team, these warriors are driven by heart, desire, and passion for the game.

For many, it starts as early as the third grade. That's the age at which kids put on their first football helmet, snap their first chin strap, bite down on their first mouthpiece, and take to the field. Even for the very young, adrenaline rises as the referee flips the coin and one team calls the toss in the air. No matter the player's age, the nerves never settle until the ball is snapped, and a young player takes his first hit.

For most of the youngest players, families play as big a role in early games as the coaches and the rest of the team. Mom or dad might even *be* the coach! The games become synonymous with pep talks with friends, group meals after practice, and weekend outings.

Eventually, there is high school football for those who really love the game. In inner cities and small country towns alike, fans pack stadiums on cool October nights. They come to watch as high school players fight and claw for every yard, striving for victory. They play with passion. Why? Many of them know that high school will be the end of their playing days.

These are the days of homecoming floats and cheerleaders. The players come to identify with the team colors and mascot, proudly sporting these on their clothes and notebooks—even if they don't know what a Spartan or a Yellowjacket is. For students associated with the team, these become identifiers and safe harbors. Being part of a team—especially a winning one—is typically a sure way to glide through challenging coming-of-age years.

For the select few, there will be college ball. Even fewer will go on to play professionally. This is where a simple game that once was all fun becomes an intense struggle. More than just a sport, college and professional football is about tradition, prestige, fame, and—ultimately—money.

The stakes get higher and the athletes more elite with each level, but the desire is still the same. Whether you're talking about pee-wee league, middle school fields, high school stadiums, college bowls, or professional teams, it all comes down to a time of year Americans wait for eagerly. Autumn is football!

Practice 1: Fall Days and Friday Night Lights

RI 1–10, W 1–2

DIRECTIONS Answer these questions about the passage you just read.

1. What is the central idea of this passage?

_____
_____
_____

2. How is this text organized?

A Problem-solution

B Chronological order

C Cause-effect

D Order of importance

DIRECTIONS **Informational Texts Review**

Read the diagram.

3

Based on the passage, what information belongs in the empty cell above?

A Fame
B Struggles
C Professional
D Possibility of injuries

4

What evidence would help make some of this writer's points stronger?

A The writer ought to choose a sport that more people like.
B The writer should provide examples from famous football movies.
C The writer could use direct quotations from actual football players of all ages.
D The writer should provide statistics about how many Americans attend football games.

People as Mascots

1   "Go! Go! Go!" scream hundreds of fans. The quarterback barrels toward the goal line. Finally, the old stadium explodes into a riot of war cries and chants. Tomahawks wave. Buckskin-clad cheerleaders wave turkey feathers and leap for joy. A war-painted mascot mimics an "Indian" dance. The scoreboard chalks up another six points for the Braves.

2   So it has been for decades on Friday nights at Centerville High School. The games and the "Indian" rituals that go along with them are a beloved tradition here—as they are in many high schools across America.

3   Meanwhile, other Americans who are not as loud or boisterous as the screaming fans, are beginning to be heard above the din. They are the descendents of the nations of America's first peoples. They look on and see cartoons of their culture used in another culture's games, and they say, "This is disrespectful."

4   In most cases, these voices are stubbornly ignored. Just as stubbornly, however, they persist. In recent years, they have been joined by the voices of other American communities. In 2004, the California Senate Education Committee began debating a bill to "eliminate racial mascots" in school sports. The Dallas School District has requested that Dallas schools not use "Indian" mascots and logos. All public schools in the district have complied with that request. Over the last thirty years, according to Jeff J. Corntassel, professor at Virginia Tech, "nearly one thousand primary and secondary schools have traded their Indian mascots for nonracist alternatives." These and other organizations have begun to reject the use of Indian-based images in sports.

5   The coach and fans of Centerville High don't understand the controversy. Why is there a problem with what they feel is a harmless tradition, they ask. How do these "Indian" mascots affect Native Americans?

6   According to Barbara E. Munson, chair of the Indian Mascot and Logo Taskforce in Wisconsin, they have many effects. One effect is that they stereotype a race of people. Mascots and logos use the most basic symbols of a people's culture. This creates stereotypes. Stereotypes, according to Munson, reduce human beings to cartoon images. Representing the various cultures of Native Americans with one image of, for example, a fierce brave, is demeaning. It is as senseless as drawing all European Americans in the image of Wall Street bankers or of Hollywood actors.

7   Another effect these logos have, says Munson, is that they lock Native Americans in the past. Native American cultures are a living part of American society. Showing them as angry warriors is like showing all European Americans as black-and-white-clad Puritan settlers.

8   "Indian" logos are blamed for making all Native Americans the same. Native Americans do not think of themselves as "Indians." They usually think of themselves first as Huron, Sioux, Cherokee, or any one of the roughly six hundred different tribes to which they belong. Secondly, they think of themselves as native, or indigenous, peoples.

9   Munson points out that mascots and logos use objects that are sacred to Native Americans. Eagle feathers, drums, and other cultural objects are part of a spiritual tradition. Using these objects in games, she says, is like waving crucifixes or menorahs to show team spirit. When Native Americans see an "Indian" medicine man used as a mascot, they feel it is humiliating. It would be like other Americans watching fans in a different culture dress up as rabbis or the pope, and dancing around at sports events.

10 Finally, according to Munson, these "Indian" sports logos use violent images. Waving tomahawks, screaming about scalping, and carrying huge pictures of scowling warriors ignores reality. Native Americans are like most other North Americans. They are peaceful, hardworking, family people.

11 "But it's all in the fun of the game," muses the Centerville coach. "No one means any harm. In fact, we are honoring the native people by using images of them. Besides, we are including another culture in public schools and sports!"

12 Like the Centerville coach, most teams mean no disrespect by using "Indian" logos. However, to this claim Native Americans reply that teams know very little about the culture they are mimicking. Therefore, they would not understand the importance these symbols hold for Native Americans.

13 As for teams meaning no harm, Munson remarks, "When someone says you are hurting them by your actions, if you persist, then the harm becomes intentional."

14 Non-native sports teams often think they are honoring Native Americans with their use of cultural symbols. However, there are no Native Americans who feel honored when teams use them as mascots. They see it as a misuse of their cultural images.

15 Finally, Native peoples say that "Indian" mascots and logos do not add to the cultural diversity in schools. They say that oversimplified images of a culture only put up barriers to understanding. Indian youths in these schools, says Professor Corntassel, "see their culture mocked and trivialized daily." As Barbara Munson says, they feel marginalized from the more common culture of the public schools.

16 Throughout its history, the United States has attempted to become a tolerant nation. In this attempt, many groups have had to fight for their right to be understood. African Americans and Asians, for example, used to be shown on television in comical and foolish ways. They had to fight against these images. They have largely succeeded, and the country has become better for it. Native Americans hope that soon, sports teams will understand the harm in using cherished symbols of a rich culture in play. When they do, they say, the United States will become much better for it.

Practice 2: People as Mascots

RI 1–10, L 4

DIRECTIONS Answer these questions about the passage you just read.

1

What is most likely the purpose of the images accompanying this article?

_____
_____
_____

2

In Paragraph 6, Barbara E. Munson accuses people who use Native American characters as mascots of —

A being intentionally cruel to Native Americans.

B painting an inaccurate image of Native Americans.

C promoting the destruction of Native American culture.

D trying to make fun of Native American culture.

3

Which of the following sentences from the article presents an opinion?

A In recent years, they have been joined by the voices of other American communities.

B The Dallas School District has requested that Dallas schools not use "Indian" mascots as logos.

C The coach and fans of Centerville High don't understand the controversy.

D Showing them as angry warriors is like showing all European Americans as black-and-white-clad Puritan settlers.

4

Are there any statements in the article that could be based on false assumptions? Find one or two pieces of evidence that might not be true. Explain how a person with an opposing viewpoint could do some research and disprove these points.

_____
_____
_____
_____

5

Explain what role paragraph 11 plays in the structure of this article.

_____
_____
_____
_____

6

Read this sentence from paragraph 15.

As Barbara Munson says, they feel marginalized from the more common culture of the public schools.

What does <u>marginalized</u> mean?

A Bullied and rejected

B Unaware of what is happening

C Made to seem unimportant

D Tricked into doing something

Practice 3: Write about the Passages

RI 1–3, 6, 9, W 1–10, L 1–6

DIRECTIONS On your own paper, write about these two passages.

A. Compare and Contrast Ideas in the Passages

Pretend that you are the author of "Fall Days and Friday Night Lights." How would you react to the article "People as Mascots"? Write a letter to the author of "People as Mascots" to express how you feel about these mascot issues.

Use your own paper to write your letter. Make sure your writing is clear and has a beginning, middle, and end. Be sure to use support from the passages in your writing.

B. Write a Narrative

What group activity have you done over the years? It might be a sports team, or a debate team, a religious group, a scouting troop, or a group that went on a camping trip. How has being a part of it affected you? Tell about your experience with this group. What did you gain? How have you changed as a result?

Use your own paper to write your narrative. Make sure your story is clear and has a beginning, middle, and end. Be creative!

DIRECTIONS | **Informational Texts Review**

Practice 4: Research Project

W 7–9

> **DIRECTIONS**
>
> Think of an athletic endeavor that you think should become an Olympic sport. Do some research about how new sports are accepted into the Olympics. Are there some now that are waiting to be accepted? Choose one of those, or create your own sport idea.
>
> Write a persuasive essay that describes the activity and tells why it should be an Olympic sport. Be sure to support your ideas with evidence. Also remember to find and fix any errors in your writing.

Activity

SL 1–6

In a group or with the entire class, share the essays you wrote for Practice 4. Choose two of the ideas to have a competition for which one should become a new Olympic sport. (Decide on a way to pick the two, such as voting or having the teacher choose them.)

Pick three students to judge the competition. Out of the remaining students, form two teams (the person who wrote the essay about each potential new sport should be on the team representing that idea). Each team should get some time to come up with a presentation for the judges. Keep in mind that you can enhance your presentation; choose the best media to help the case for your team's new sport. Be sure to set a time limit for both presentations.

Chapter 7
Vocabulary

This chapter covers the following eighth grade strand and standards:

Reading: Literature

Craft and Structure

4. Determine the meaning of words and phrases as they are used in a text, including figurative and connotative meanings; analyze the impact of specific word choices on meaning and tone, including analogies or allusions to other texts.

Reading: Informational Text

Craft and Structure

4. Determine the meaning of words and phrases as they are used in a text, including figurative, connotative, and technical meanings; analyze the impact of specific word choices on meaning and tone, including analogies or allusions to other texts.

Language

Vocabulary Acquisition and Use

4. Determine or clarify the meaning of unknown and multiple-meaning words or phrases based on *grade 8 reading and content*, choosing flexibly from a range of strategies.

    a. Use context (e.g., the overall meaning of a sentence or paragraph; a word's position or function in a sentence) as a clue to the meaning of a word or phrase.

    b. Use common, grade-appropriate Greek or Latin affixes and roots as clues to the meaning of a word (e.g., *precede, recede, secede*).

    c. Consult general and specialized reference materials (e.g., dictionaries, glossaries, thesauruses), both print and digital, to find the pronunciation of a word or determine or clarify its precise meaning or its part of speech.

    d. Verify the preliminary determination of the meaning of a word or phrase (e.g., by checking the inferred meaning in context or in a dictionary).

5. Demonstrate understanding of figurative language, word relationships, and nuances in word meanings.

    a. Interpret figures of speech (e.g. verbal irony, puns) in context.

    b. Use the relationship between particular words to better understand each of the words.

    c. Distinguish among the connotations (associations) of words with similar denotations (definitions) (e.g., *bullheaded, willful, firm, persistent, resolute*).

6. Acquire and use accurately grade-appropriate general academic and domain-specific words and phrases; gather vocabulary knowledge when considering a word or phrase important to comprehension or expression.

Chapter 7

To learn new words in any language, you need skills to decode what the letters symbolize and what the words mean. There are many methods for finding word meaning. The most basic method is what you are doing now—reading. As you read, you are putting these words together to make sense of their meaning in this sentence. When you understand all the words, you can understand the ideas that the words express.

Building Vocabulary

Building vocabulary by adding new words will add pleasure and reward to your reading and writing. Reading daily will build your confidence in using language and will increase your vocabulary. In this chapter, you will review the skills needed to build and use a rich vocabulary.

Context Clues

Sometimes you can determine the meaning of a new word by looking at **context clues**—the relationships between words and their surroundings. Context is the words and ideas in the text surrounding a word you don't know yet. They offer clues to the meaning of unfamiliar words.

For example, if you read an essay about the beauty of national parks in the fall, you might see the word *fulgent* in a sentence describing the leaves of an aspen tree:

The <u>fulgent</u> leaves made a glowing contrast to the dreary clouds.

What does <u>fulgent</u> mean from the context?

   A   Dark and scary

   B   Bright and dazzling

   C   Hateful and sad

   D   Happy and cheerful

The word *contrast* is a signal word that directs you to the meaning of the unfamiliar word. Since *contrast* means "something opposite," then the meaning of *fulgent* must be the opposite of *dreary*. Yes, *fulgent* means "bright and dazzling."

Vocabulary

By studying the phrases and signal words that come before or after an unfamiliar word, you can often figure out its meaning. Below you will find a list of the main types of context clues and their signal words.

Context Clues	Signal Words	Example
Comparison	*also, like, resembling, too, both, than*	Look for clues that indicate an unfamiliar word is similar to a familiar word or phrase. Rodney is like a field mouse gathering seeds when it comes to <u>accumulating</u> compact disks.
Contrast	*but, however, while, instead of, yet, unlike*	Look for clues that indicate an unfamiliar word is opposite in meaning to a familiar word or phrase. Lyn has an <u>aesthetic</u> sense in room decor, while her sister Amelie has no artistic tendencies at all.
Definition or Restatement	*is, or, that is, in other words, which*	Look for words that define the term or restate it in other words. The rich appearance of the neighborhood indicated a degree of <u>opulence</u> that was far beyond the couple's budget.
Example	*for example, for instance, such as*	Look for examples used in context that reveal the meaning of an unfamiliar word. Several facts pointed to the man's <u>culpability</u>; for example, he was caught with the weapon in his hand.

WORDS WITH MULTIPLE MEANINGS IN CONTEXT

You read in chapter 3 how words and phrases can have **nuances of meaning**. In addition, some **words with multiple meanings** actually denote different things in different contexts. Their meaning can change based on their position or function in a sentence. These include simple examples that you already know, like the word *bat*. Sometimes this word refers to a nocturnal flying mammal; sometimes it means a piece of equipment used in baseball. Words that change in context include those with **technical meanings** in different subject areas. Here are some examples. Look at the underlined words in this passage.

Chapter 7

Was there ever life on Mars? New discoveries make scientists think there may have been. Evidence <u>suggests</u> that Mars did have water on it at one time, and that it could have <u>supported</u> some sort of life. Scientists have found many clues that this is true. One of the most important was the discovery of an <u>ancient</u> shoreline of a large Martian sea. The area where the sea would have been is <u>level</u> where mud and silt may have built up. There are also gullies (deep ruts or ditches) on the surface of the planet that were most likely created by water. Scientists think that rushing water may have carved away the soil into large crater walls. Scientists have also discovered that Martian rocks have a different <u>composition</u> because of the presence of water.

This is a brief article that you might find in a science book or magazine. Notice how each word takes on a specific meaning based on the topic being discussed.

Here, *suggests* means "gives clues" or "imply." It does not mean "give advice" as it would in a sentence like this: "My teacher suggests that I read more poetry."

Similarly, *supported* in this context means "made possible" or "sustained." It does not mean "held up" as it would in an article about architecture, or "encouraged" as in a passage about fans attending a sporting event.

Now you try some. Look up the words if you need to.

Activity	
L 4.a	
Ancient Meaning in this article:	
Other meanings:	
Level Meaning in this article:	
Other meanings:	
Composition Meaning in this article:	
Other meanings:	

Vocabulary

GREEK AND LATIN ROOTS AND AFFIXES

Many words are made up of smaller parts. Breaking them down into their smallest units is one way to determine word meaning. Different words can be formed, or derived, from one root word. This is called *derivation*. Greek and Latin were two of the first influences on the English language, so Greek and Latin roots and affixes are widespread in our language today. You can determine the meaning of words by analyzing the meanings of their smaller parts called **roots** (the main parts of a word), **prefixes** (the beginnings of words), and **suffixes** (the endings of words). Prefixes and suffixes together are called **affixes**, as they are affixed to a root word.

For example, in the word *extraterrestrial*, "extra-" is a prefix that means outside or beyond. The root "terra" comes from the Latin word for earth. The letters "-ial" at the end of a word form a suffix that means act of, like, or as. By dividing extraterrestrial into its smallest units, you discover that it means "as beyond the earth." You can use the same process for other words. The root "dorm" found in *dormant* and *dormitory* comes from the Latin word for sleep. Dormant means inactive, as in sleep, and dormitory refers to a building with sleeping quarters.

Learning the word parts in the following lists will unlock the meanings of countless words in your reading. Mark the ones you do not know, and then learn their meanings.

\multicolumn{6}{c}{Prefixes}					
Prefix	Meaning	Example	Prefix	Meaning	Example
ab-	away from	absent	inter-	between	interstate
ad-	near, at	adhere	intra-	within	intramural
anti-	against	antigravity	mis-	incorrect	mistaken
bi-	twice, two	bimonthly	non-	negative	nonathletic
com-	with	community	post-	after	postnatal
de-	reverse remove	deregulate	pre-	before, in front of in	premix
dis-	to cause to be	dishonest	pro-	support of	proclaim
en-	out, not	endear	re-	again	review
ex-	not	extinguish	semi-	partial, somewhat	semicircle
il-	not	illegal	sub-	under, beneath	submarine
in-		insecure	un-	not	unknown

Chapter 7

Roots

Root	Meaning	Example	Root	Meaning	Example
ann	year	annual	micro	small	microscope
aqua	water	aquarium	multi	many	multiply
aud	hear	auditorium	ped	foot	pedestrian
biblio	book	bibliography	path	feeling	sympathy
bio	life	biography	phon	sound	telephone
cent	hundred	century	port	convey	transport
chrono	time	chronological	rad	light	radiation
dic	to speak	diction	scope	see	microscope
gen	race, kind	genetic	scribe	to write	scripture
ject	put	injection	tele	distance	television
magni	large, great	magnify	ven	to come	convene
med	middle	medium	viv, vit	life	vital

Suffixes

Suffix	Meaning	Example	Suffix	Meaning	Example
-able	capable of being	lovable	-itive	having the nature of	talkative
-age	related to	marriage	-ly	in a like manner	easily, quietly
-al, -ial	act of, of, like	industrial	-less	without	thoughtless
-ance	state or quality of	acceptance	-logy	study of	biology
-dom	general condition	freedom	-ment	condition of	contentment
-en	made of, to become	wooden, redden	-ness	quality, degree	neatness
-er, -or	one who	employer, actor	-ous	condition	nervous
			-ship	full of	relationship
			-tion	action, process	construction
-ful	full of	cheerful	-ure	state of being	venture
-hood	state of	childhood	-ward	to a given destination	forward, homeward
-ify	to make	magnify			
-ish	having quality of	foolish, childish			
-itis	inflammation	arthritis			

Vocabulary

DICTIONARY SKILLS

There are several resources for finding word meaning. They include a dictionary, thesaurus, or glossary. When you master the use of each of these resources, you can easily find information about new words.

The **dictionary** provides pronunciation, synonyms, antonyms, parts of speech, and the definitions for the word. It is a broad resource for acquiring full knowledge of an unfamiliar word. Some dictionaries even provide the etymology (origin and history) of a word. There are specialized dictionaries by subject, such as a medical dictionary.

In the entry that follows, you have the main entry word broken into syllables on the first line. The second line gives you a key as to the correct pronunciation for the word. The third line tells you the part of speech for the word, and the fourth line gives you the correct plural form. The remaining lines are dedicated to the various definitions for the word. The dictionary may also give sample sentences. The dictionary is alphabetized with guide words across the top of the page to show which word is the beginning entry on the page and which word is the last entry on the page.

Read all of the definitions of a dictionary entry. Suppose that the underlined word in the following sample sentence is unfamiliar to you.

The course the captain chose would take the ship dangerously close to the icebergs.

You would look up *course* in the dictionary and read the following multiple definitions.

Dictionary Entry

course (kôrs) *n.* **1a.** The act or action of moving in a path from point to point. **b.** Movement in time; duration. **2.** Accustomed procedure or normal action: *the illness ran its course.* **3.** An ordered process or succession: *a course of medical treatments.* **4.** A part of a meal served at one time. *v.* **coursed, cours·ing, cours·es 1.** To move quickly through or over. **2a.** To hunt or pursue with hounds. b. To set off hounds to hunt game. **Idiom:** At the proper or right time: *of course.* [Middle English, from Old French *cours,* from Latin *cursus,* past participle of *currere,* to run.]

Look at the next page for an explanation of the entry.

Chapter 7

1. If the word can be more than one part of speech (noun, verb, adjective, and so on), decide which part of speech the word is in the sentence. Then concentrate on the definitions for that part of speech. In a dictionary entry, the part-of-speech abbreviation (such as *v.* for verb) is usually italicized and comes before the definitions. In the sample sentenc, *course* is a noun and the subject of the sentence. Of the noun definitions in the entry, only one is appropriate.

2. Read the sentence to yourself, substituting each correct part-of-speech definition for the word. Decide which one best fits the sentence. The appropriate definition for *course*, as it is used in the sentence, is the first; "the act or action of moving in a path from point to point" the captain chose would take the ship dangerously close to the icebergs.

3. If there is more than one entry for a word, read each entry completely. Some words are homographs; they are spelled alike but have different origins and meanings. For example, the words *board* meaning "a piece of wood" and board meaning "to get on to" are homographs. Homographs are given separate entries in the dictionary. Be sure to choose the correct meaning for your sentence.

4. Notice that under the verb part of speech, there are related words listed. *Courses, coursed, coursing* are the present, past, and present participle derivations (forms) of the verb *to course*.

5. At the end of the entry, you can see the etymology of the word in brackets.

A **thesaurus** is a book containing lists of synonyms (*Syn.*) and antonyms (*Ant.*) in alphabetical order. Remember that not all words have the exact same meaning. Some words may be similar in meaning but have different connotations. The best way to find the most appropriate synonyms is also to look up their meanings.

Thesaurus Entry

height

n. **1.** [altitude] *Syn.* altitude, elevation, prominence, loftiness, highness, tallness, stature

Ant. depth, breadth, width

2. [culmination] *Syn.* end, crisis, climax

3. [eminence] *Syn.* hill, knoll, peak, apex, tip, crest

Vocabulary

A **glossary** is an alphabetical list of specialized words with their definitions. The glossary is placed at the end of a book. Glossaries are found in science, social studies, literature, math, and many other books.

Sample Glossary Page

monopoly – one company dominating a particular market such as cars or telephones

mores – standards of conduct that are held by a particular culture

multiculturalism – respecting and accepting many cultures

national health service – health care for all citizens regardless of income

nationalism – devotion to the interests and rights of one's nation

occupation – a job for pay

Practice 1: Building Vocabulary

RL 4, RI 4, L 4.a–c, 6

Concrete Setting

There are few <u>endeavors</u> in life more unforgiving than concrete setting. It's absolutely true! You are not allowed much <u>leeway</u> for errors in either <u>measurements</u> or location. Once you have a solid mass of concrete set in place, it is going to stay there. You have a <u>strenuous</u> job ahead of you if you try to <u>remedy</u> a mistake. Make very sure before you fill the form (with freshly mixed concrete), that everything is where and how you want it.

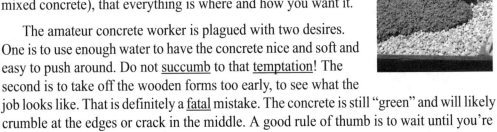

The amateur concrete worker is plagued with two desires. One is to use enough water to have the concrete nice and soft and easy to push around. Do not <u>succumb</u> to that <u>temptation</u>! The second is to take off the wooden forms too early, to see what the job looks like. That is definitely a <u>fatal</u> mistake. The concrete is still "green" and will likely crumble at the edges or crack in the middle. A good rule of thumb is to wait until you're sure that the concrete is good and hardened, and then wait one day more. Then you may remove the forms to reveal your creation in breathtaking concrete!

---

1 In the context of this passage, what does the word <u>endeavors</u> mean?

    A Expectations   **B** Efforts   **C** Stories   **D** Mixtures

Chapter 7

2. Define the word <u>leeway</u>.

_____

_____

3. Which of these would be the most appropriate substitute for the word <u>measurements</u>?
   A Dimensions
   B Volumes
   C Features
   D Components

4. What does the word <u>strenuous</u> mean?
   A Irritating
   B Easy
   C Slippery
   D Difficult

5. Which of the following is the meaning of <u>remedy</u>?
   A Hide
   B Correct
   C Heal
   D Depose

6. Which of the following is the meaning of the word <u>succumb</u>?
   A Forget about
   B Think about
   C Give in to
   D Say no to

7. Based on your knowledge of the suffix -tion, what does the word <u>temptation</u> mean?
   A Being attractive
   B Wanting to become attractive
   C Having the quality of being attractive
   D The process of being attracted to something

8. In the context of the passage, what does <u>fatal</u> mean?

_____

_____

Vocabulary

> **DIRECTIONS** **B.** On your own paper, divide each of the following words into prefixes, suffixes, and roots (when possible), and explain how these parts make up the meaning of the word. If you need help, consult a dictionary.
>
> Example:
>
> **illegible: il (not) + leg(ere) (to read) + able (capable of being) = not capable of being read**

1. argument

2. unqualified

3. illiterate

4. expel

5. bilateral

Activity

RL 4, RI 4, L 4.a–e, 6

Select a page from your literature book or from a novel you've read. Find ten words with three or more syllables. List these words, and next to each one, define any prefixes, suffixes and roots in each word. If you need help, use a dictionary. Explain the meaning of each word.

ANALYZING WORD MEANING

As you know, a word or phrase can be used in different ways. An author may choose words to tell plain facts, or an author may choose words to give the text shades of meaning and to add imagery. The choice of words and phrases has deep impact on the meaning and tone of writing. Some words also have additional meanings when used in certain technical contexts.

Chapter 7

DENOTATIONS AND CONNOTATIONS

You know that word choice can affect meaning and mood in writing. Sometimes, a word is used to stand for a specific dictionary meaning (denotation), and sometimes, the word has a more emotional association (connotation).

- The **denotation** of a word is its exact meaning as found in the dictionary.
- A **connotation** of a word, on the other hand, is meaning that is implied, or suggested.

For example, think about what it means to call someone cheap. How about frugal? If you were to look up the words *cheap* and *frugal*, you would find similar definitions:

cheap: costing very little

frugal: entailing little expense

However, the connotations assigned to the words over the years are very different. You have to know current understandings of a word to see this difference. Calling someone cheap is derogatory; it means you think the person is stingy or miserly. Being frugal, on the other hand, implies spending wisely and saving prudently.

Activity

L 4.c, 5.c

Here are some examples of word pairs that have similar denotations but different connotations. Look up each word. Then, use each one correctly in a sentence according to its connotative meaning.

- Loyal versus stubborn
- Paunchy versus chubby
- Gaunt versus slender
- Bold versus reckless

LITERAL AND FIGURATIVE MEANINGS

The **literal meaning** of a word or phrase is a factual way to use it. It provides a statement that is understood in just one way. For example, consider "This math problem is difficult to figure out." This sentence is factual: the speaker is having trouble with a math problem.

On the other hand, the **figurative meaning** has an element of fantasy or exaggeration. It paints word pictures and allows us to "see" a point. Here are some examples of figurative language. (You can read more about other kinds of figurative language in chapter 3.)

An **allusion** is a reference to a well-known place, literary or art work, famous person, or historical event.

Example: If the politicians continue with these plans, we'll have another civil war on our hands. (The remark refers to the great battle among states and likens it to some present-day issues that are likely to divide Americans.)

Vocabulary

An **analogy** usually shows the relationship between two pairs of words. For instance, the relationship between the pair of words *up* and *down* is one of opposites. Therefore, another pair of words in an analogy with *up* and *down* would also need to have the same relationship; they would have to be opposites. A word analogy is usually given in this form: Word **A** is to Word **B** as Word **C** is to Word **D**. The symbol **:** means "is to," while the symbol **::** means "as." Therefore, the analogy **man : boy :: woman : girl** can be read: **man is to boy as woman is to girl**. In literature, however, analogies are taken to another level. Rather than presenting pairs of words, an author might suggest a similar relationship to draw a picture in the minds of readers.

> **Example:** In a speech he gave, Oliver Wendell Holmes Jr. said "Many people die with their music still in them." The analogy likens unplayed musical instruments to lives that have not been lived to the fullest.

An **idiom** is a phrase or expression in which the real meaning is different from the literal or stated meaning.

> **Examples:** I'm pulling my hair out over this math problem! (Does it mean that the speaker is literally pulling strands of hair from his head? No; it just means that the math problem is very difficult.)
>
> You're driving me up the wall. (This doesn't mean you are literally maneuvering a car up a wall. It just means someone is irritating you.)

A **metaphor** compares without using the words *like* or *as*. It is a direct comparison, saying that one thing IS another.

> **Examples:** All the world's a stage.
>
> And all the men and women merely players.
>
> They have their exits and their entrances.
>
> – William Shakespeare, *As You Like It*

A **pun** uses easily confused words to make a point in a humorous way.

> **Example:** You can tune a guitar, but you can't tuna fish. Unless of course, you play bass. – Douglas Adams

A **simile** is a comparison of one thing to another, using the words *like* or *as*:

> **Example:** Talking to him is like taking sleeping pills.

Verbal irony is a contrast between what is said or written and what is meant.

Example: A person standing at a curb is splashed by water from the wheels of a passing car and mutters sarcastically, "Thanks so much. You just made my day."

Chapter 7

Practice 2: Word Meaning
RL 4, RI 4, L 4–6

DIRECTIONS — A. Read the sentences below, and decide the meaning of the underlined phrases. Think about how you came up with those meanings. Write out the meaning of each phrase and explain how you decided on this meaning.

1. Our landlord is mean, but <u>his bark is worse than his bite</u>.

2. The coach told the team to <u>rise above</u> the loss.

3. <u>Yesterday was a week long</u>.

4. <u>Knock it off</u>, or I'll tell Dad!

5. Stop <u>beating around the bush</u>.

6. Mr. Sanchez <u>picked up the tab</u> for our class party.

DIRECTIONS — B. For each pair of words, write the common denotation for the pair. Then, fill in the blanks in each sentence pair with the appropriate word choice. On the line below each sentence, write the connotation of each word to explain your choice. Use a dictionary or a thesaurus to check your choices.

1

variable, inconsistency

Denotation: _____

A. The missing _____ needed to solve the mystery was the time of the crime.

Connotation: _____

B. The _____ of the musician kept the orchestra from playing in tune.

Connotation: _____

Vocabulary

2

forceful, assertive

Denotation: _____

A. The hockey player was penalized for his _____ check of the opposing left winger.

Connotation: _____

B. Kyle is very _____ of his right to be at the meeting.

Connotation: _____

3

senior, veteran

Denotation: _____

A. The _____ player taught the rookie a few lessons.

Connotation: _____

B. The _____ couple lived on a ranch near Tyler.

Connotation: _____

Chapter 7

> **DIRECTIONS** C. Read the description below of Sherlock Holmes as he is seen by his trusted companion, Dr. Watson, from "A Study in Scarlet" by Sir Arthur Conan Doyle. Using your own paper, list five or six words with connotations that give a vivid description of Sherlock Holmes. Look up any words that are new to you. Which words in the description are more neutral, having only denotations? Share your findings with the class or your teacher.

His very person and appearance were such as to strike the attention of the most casual observer. In height he was rather over six feet, and so excessively lean that he seemed to be considerably taller. His eyes were sharp and piercing, save during those intervals of torpor to which I have alluded; and his thin, hawk-like nose gave his whole expression an air of alertness and decision. His chin, too, had the prominence and squareness which mark the man of determination. His hands were invariably blotted with ink and stained with chemicals, yet he was possessed of extraordinary delicacy of touch, as I frequently had occasion to observe when I watched him manipulating his fragile philosophical instruments.

Vocabulary

CHAPTER 7 SUMMARY

Building vocabulary adds pleasure and reward to your reading and develops your confidence in using language.

To determine the meaning of an unfamiliar word through **context clues**, look at the words around it.

Words and phrases can have **nuances of meaning** and some **words with multiple meanings** actually denote different things in different contexts. This includes **technical meanings** in different subject areas.

You can analyze word **roots**, **prefixes**, and **suffixes** to determine the meaning of words. Prefixes and suffixes are called **affixes**, as they are affixed to a root word.

Mastering the use of resources like a **dictionary**, **thesaurus**, and **glossary** will help you easily find information about new words.

Remember that words can be chosen for their **denotation** (dictionary meaning) or **connotation** (implied meaning).

The **literal meaning** of a word or phrase is a factual way to use it; the **figurative meaning** of a word or phrase has an element of fantasy or exaggeration. Some techniques of figurative language that authors use include **allusion**, **analogy**, **idiom**, **metaphor**, **pun**, **simile**, and **verbal irony**.

Chapter 7 Review

RL 4, RI 4, L 4–6

DIRECTIONS: Read the following passage, and answer the questions.

Shy Shadows: Octopus and Squid

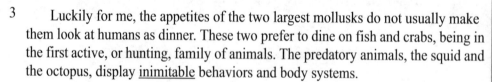

Octopus

1   As I watch, a shadow glides toward the ocean floor where it disappears into rocks which are pockmarked with holes and craters. I have had a close encounter with the world's first carnivorous predator. No, it is not the shark. My encounter has been with an octopus.

2   Biologists have <u>identified</u> a class of the *Phylum mollusca* (mollusks) as the first active, carnivorous predatory animals. The class is named *cephalopoda* (Latin and Greek for "head-foots"). The class *cephalopoda* is limited to marine animals and has six hundred living species including those of the octopus and the squid.

3   Luckily for me, the appetites of the two largest mollusks do not usually make them look at humans as dinner. These two prefer to dine on fish and crabs, being in the first active, or hunting, family of animals. The predatory animals, the squid and the octopus, display <u>inimitable</u> behaviors and body systems.

4   Both of these marine animals are shy and choose to stalk their prey quietly. When threatened, the octopus has been observed actually growing pale in color. This behavior provides an <u>illusion</u> of greater size and is a defensive action for the octopus. The octopus can also change colors to blend into its surroundings. A different defensive behavior or strategy that the octopus and the squid share with cephalopods is the ability to squirt a cloudy fluid which cuts down on the ability of possible attackers to see them.

5   These strategies, as well as the tendency of the octopus to hide in enclosed spaces (rocks, sunken ships, or reefs), are necessary for survival. Cephalopods may have either an external shell, an internal shell, or as in the case of the octopus—no protective shell at all. So the brain, the stomach, the arms, and all the other soft tissues are exposed and <u>vulnerable</u> to injury. The squid has an internal shell which gives it the <u>distinctive</u> streamline shape. The unprotected octopus has a rounded almost undefined shape, undefined, that is except for the body feature that people think of when they think of an octopus or squid: the arms or tentacles.

Vocabulary

6   The arms are the most recognizable features of the octopus and the squid. The octopus gets its name partly from its number of arms: *octo* is the Latin word for "eight." Both the octopus and squid use their arms for capturing and eating food. They bring the food to their beaklike jaws to cut it into smaller pieces. The octopus also uses its arms to move along the ocean floor as well as using a flow of water through its body to <u>propel</u> it along. It can take water into its body and then squirt the water out, propelling itself at a rapid pace. The squid differs only in that it does not use its arms to move. Instead, the squid stays <u>suspended</u> between the ocean floor and surface and moves only by water propulsion. In fact, since the squid has no other means of movement, its body shape and muscles have become well suited to the water-propulsion method, making it one of the fastest invertebrate (animal with no backbone) marine animals.

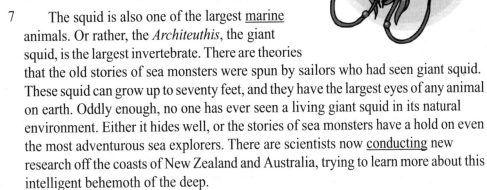

Squid

7   The squid is also one of the largest <u>marine</u> animals. Or rather, the *Architeuthis*, the giant squid, is the largest invertebrate. There are theories that the old stories of sea monsters were spun by sailors who had seen giant squid. These squid can grow up to seventy feet, and they have the largest eyes of any animal on earth. Oddly enough, no one has ever seen a living giant squid in its natural environment. Either it hides well, or the stories of sea monsters have a hold on even the most adventurous sea explorers. There are scientists now <u>conducting</u> new research off the coasts of New Zealand and Australia, trying to learn more about this intelligent behemoth of the deep.

8   Keeping an eye out for the marine creatures that do not turn down humans for lunch, I slowly head toward the rocks where the shadow has hidden. My time is running short, along with the air in my oxygen tanks. I must go back to my own world, away from the hushed, dim world of the cephalopods. Before I go, I catch a last glimpse of the creature, turned a reddish color to match the rocks behind it. The <u>fragile</u> octopus has every reason to be shy. It has no shell to retreat into…

---

1   What does the word <u>identified</u> mean in paragraph 2?

    A Destroyed   **B** Provided   **C** Labeled   **D** Conducted

Chapter 7

2. How would the figurative phrase "the old stories of sea monsters were spun by sailors" best be written in a literal sentence?

    A   The old stories of sea monsters were told by sailors.

    B   The old stories of sea monsters were sewn together by sailors.

    C   The old stories of sea monsters were circled by sailors.

    D   The old stories of sea monsters were laughed at by sailors.

3. What does the word inimitable mean in paragraph 3?

_____

4. What does the word illusion mean in paragraph 4?

    A   Raw power   C   Safety net

    B   Good excuse   D   False image

5. What does the word distinctive mean in paragraph 5?

    A   Noticeable   B   Indescribable   C   Spherical   D   Measurable

6. What does the word propel mean in paragraph 6?

_____

7. What does the word suspended mean in paragraph 6?

    A   Hung   B   Twisted   C   Bent   D   Sewn

8. The word marine comes from Latin marīnus, meaning "sea." Knowing this, what other word came from the same Latin root?

    A   Marriage   B   Maritime   C   Marsupial   D   Marsh

9. What does the word conducting mean in paragraph 7?

    A   Speaking of   C   Writing about

    B   Leaving   D   Directing

Read this sentence from the passage.

My time is running short, along with the air in my oxygen tanks.

10. How would its figurative meaning best be written in a literal sentence?

    A   The time I have to breathe with the oxygen tanks is brief.

    B   My time is speeding away and taking the air with it.

    C   The time is too quick for me and my full oxygen tanks.

    D   My time is flying by and is using the air from my tanks.

Chapter 8
Research

This chapter covers the following eighth grade strand and standards:

> **Writing**
>
> **Research to Build and Present Knowledge**
>
> 7. Conduct short research projects to answer a question (including a self-generated question), drawing on several sources and generating additional related, focused questions that allow for multiple avenues of exploration.
>
> 8. Gather relevant information from multiple print and digital sources, using search terms effectively; assess the credibility and accuracy of each source; and quote or paraphrase the data and conclusions of others while avoiding plagiarism and following a standard format for citation.
>
> 9. Draw evidence from literary or informational texts to support analysis, reflection, and research.
>
> a. Apply *grade 8 Reading standards* to literature (e.g., "Analyze how a modern work of fiction draws on themes, patterns of events, or character types from myths, traditional stories, or religious works such as the Bible, including describing how the material is rendered new").
>
> b. Apply *grade 8 Reading standards* to literary nonfiction (e.g., "Delineate and evaluate the argument and specific claims in a text, assessing whether the reasoning is sound and the evidence is relevant and sufficient; recognize when irrelevant evidence is introduced").

RESEARCH SOURCES

You may need to do **research** for many reasons. You do research every day to find products, services, and places. In school, research helps you find information for essays, reports, and presentations. Whatever the reason for your research, the first thing you must do is to **find sources**. These are materials that help you get what you need. Then, you must analyze which ones are the best to use for a given purpose. Finally, you need to synthesize them all to get the best result, whether that's shopping at the right store or handing in a well-crafted paper.

Chapter 8

PRIMARY AND SECONDARY SOURCES

One of the ideas about sources that you want to keep in mind is their perspective in relation to your topic. A **primary source** is one that has a firsthand relationship to the topic. In other words, if you are writing about an event, primary sources would be journals or letters written by people who were actually there. A **secondary source** might include documents written years later about the same event. They include encyclopedia articles, books, or journal articles written by experts, among others. Secondary sources have the advantages of hindsight, historical perspective, analysis, and possible later revelations that shed new light on the event.

Primary Sources	Secondary Sources
Public speeches	Encyclopedias
Letters	Journals and magazines
Diaries	Newspapers
Private journals	Computer software
Eyewitness accounts	Internet

You also will use the **literary and informational texts** you read for class as sources. Most of the time, they will be primary sources that you will analyze in some way. For example, your teacher might ask you to write about how a modern story uses themes or character types from myths or traditional stories. This would mean using the modern story as a primary source and then doing research to find myths, traditional stories, or religious works to which you can compare it.

ELECTRONIC SOURCES

Using the Internet can challenge your research skills. There are many databases, software programs, and websites on the Internet. These are called **electronic sources**. Today, many sources are available electronically using a computer. However, some still are not, so it is important to use several methods of research rather than relying solely on electronic sources.

The Internet can be one of your greatest resources for information or the biggest waste of time. There are so many sites to explore that you can easily lose track of your original topic. You have to know how to find the right information and how to evaluate it for accuracy and value. Using the Internet requires some specific skills.

Research

Search engines can help you find the sites you need for information. The Internet has many different search engines to aid you in your research. Some of the most common ones are Google, Yahoo!, and Ask.

Search terms (also known as **key words**) attract information on the web the way a baited hook lures fish when cast into the water. A long list of information links will appear on your computer screen in a split second (a little more quickly than fish). The results of your search depend entirely on the effectiveness of the key words you enter.

Tips for Using Key Words

1. Create a list of words describing the type of information you are looking for.

2. Use more than one key word to narrow your search. For example, instead of searching for tigers, you could search for Siberian tigers.

3. To narrow your search even more, put your key words inside quotation marks. This type of search will show only sites that have that exact phrase.

ORGANIZATIONAL FEATURES

There are many sources that can give you a large amount of information. Most sources contain **organizational features** to help you locate and organize information. If you are familiar with these features, you can use them to find even more relevant sources that will aid in your research questioning.

Organizational Features of Research Sources	
Feature	**Description**
Appendix	This is additional material located at the end of a book or other source. An **appendix** contains information that is related to the text but not crucial enough to include within the body of the text, such as supporting documents, maps, a glossary or index, and so on. A source can have one or more appendices, or none at all.
Bibliography	This is a list of books and other works used as references for what you are reading. When you find a relevant source, its **bibliography** or works-cited list can provide a treasure trove of other sources to check. It is a way to credit sources you use in an essay or research paper.
Footnote	A **footnote** is placed at the bottom of a page or at the end of a document. It provides an added explanation or detail about something in the text.

Chapter 8

\	Organizational Features of Research Sources (continued)
Feature	Description
Graphic features	This includes **graphics** like tables, maps, and illustrations as well as **type styles** that draw attention to certain information. For example, headings might be in boldface, unfamiliar or foreign language words may be in italic type, lists may have bullets to separate items, and other important information may be underlined.
Headings	**Headings** are titles of sections within a text that set them apart from other sections. The major heading is usually the document's main title. All sections after that may have equally sized headings or may have smaller subheadings depending on the importance of the information.
Table of contents	The **table of contents** is a list of chapters, headings, subheadings, and any supplemental sections of the text, as well as the page numbers where they can be found. It is written to show the order of information from the beginning to the end.

Practice 1: Research Sources

W 8–9

DIRECTIONS Choose the best answer for each question.

1. Malik is looking for information about how many ships were destroyed in the 1941 attack on Pearl Harbor. What is the best source to look in?

   A A website about Navy ships

   B A book about the development of warships

   C An encyclopedia article about the attack

   D An almanac for the year 1941

2. Teri finds some useful information in an article and wants to look at the book where the facts originally came from. What feature will provide the name of the book?

   _____

3. Which of the following is an example of a print resource?

   A A search engine   C A documentary film

   B A television show   D A magazine article

 **Research**

4 Ricky is using a search engine to research swimmer Michael Phelps' Olympic career. Which search term would be most likely to aid in his search?

    A Olympic Games Michael Phelps   C Beijing Olympics medals

    B Michael Phelps endorsements   D swimming Michael Phelps

5 Louis is researching Neptune for a science paper. All of these questions would be helpful in his research except which one?

    A How big is Neptune?

    B What are the other planets?

    C Does Neptune have any moons?

    D How far away is Neptune from the sun?

6 If Julianne is researching Edgar Allan Poe's "The Raven," which search term entry will give her best results from a search engine?

    _____

7 Which would be the most reliable source for a classroom presentation on "Women in the Workplace during World War II"?

    A A novel about a woman who survived the war by working in a factory

    B A recent report from the Bureau of Labor Statistics about women who work

    C A photograph of a woman working in a factory alongside male workers

    D A journal article about women who joined the workforce during the war

EVALUATING SOURCES

In the first section you read about how to find what you are looking for. Now, you need to compile what you find to figure out the best way to use it.

DEVELOPING RESEARCH QUESTIONS

After you choose a topic, you need to decide how you will approach it. For most kinds of papers, asking **research questions** will help you focus on what exactly you will write about. For example, say your topic is the Transcendental Poetry movement. Well, that is a very broad topic! An effective research question helps to narrow it.

    Example: What is the role of nature in Transcendental poetry?

As you can see, this question provides a direction for your research. A strong research question passes the "So what?" test. In other words, it asks an interesting question that invites discussion. It is not so broad that it cannot be answered in an essay.

Chapter 8

CHOOSING THE BEST SOURCES

Once you develop your research question, you need to **analyze and evaluate** the sources you found to see how they relate to your topic and to each other. You also need to organize them so you can easily locate what is in each source. Highlight what is important in each source. Make notes in the margins. Or, keep a set of note cards with brief summaries.

Two qualities of research sources that you must assess are **credibility and accuracy**. Credibility refers to the reliability. It means a source is trustworthiness. Accuracy refers to how factual a source's information is.

Keep in mind that sources are written by people, and people have different viewpoints. For example, an advertisement for fur coats will portray fur as a must-have luxury. An article by an animal rights group will portray a fur coat as a product that results from the cruel killing of animals. In the same way, you will want to be aware of different perspectives when researching literary topics. Some critics (scholars who analyze and comment on literary works) will interpret an author's writing in a variety of ways. Keep different perspectives in mind and be aware of any bias (having a preference for a particular point of view) that a source may have.

A source is most credible if is it written by an expert on that the topic. It is also more trustworthy if the information is balanced. If the author shows a significant bias (slant) toward one side or the other, it might mean that information is weighted. If there is research involved, you should also check whether the organization that conducted it has a bias. Finally, check that the source is published by a reputable company or organization.

Credibility can lead to accuracy. Chances are that the most credible source will provide the most accurate, and therefore best, information. When evaluating how accurate sources are, the best approach is to find at least three sources that agree about facts or statistics. Also look at when the information was gathered and published. Updated information, even about older events or works, could have the advantage of pertinent information that has come to light in recent times.

Here are some questions to ask about material that you might use as a source:

- Is the writer an expert?
- Does the writer have a bias that comes across in the writing?
- Who wrote it or funded the research?
- How old is this information?
- How many other sources verify this information?

Research

USING SOURCES

Now that you have reviewed how to find and evaluate sources, it's time to use them. There are many ways for you to incorporate what you've learned into a research project.

CITING SOURCES

As you use research materials in your work, you must **cite sources** (give credit to the original authors). Using someone else's work, ideas, or words as your own is called **plagiarism**, and it is a form of cheating. It is not accepted in any school.

There are two places in which you give credit. The first place is in your text. After a quote, you place a short note in parentheses. You can see examples of this in the next section on "Ways to Incorporate Sources."

The second place in which you cite sources is the **bibliography**. Depending on the style guide you use, this section might be called the bibliography, references, or works-cited page. The bibliography gives all the details about each source that you used in your research. This information allows readers to check the research sources that are named in your paper. A reader may also want to read more about your topic in the materials on your works-cited page.

A bibliography is always separate from the rest of your research document. All information on this page must be written in a very specific format, according to the style guide you use. Ask your teacher about the guide you should be using.

To demonstrate a style in this book, you will read about MLA style. The guidelines for citing sources and writing a bibliography are explained in the MLA style guide, titled *MLA Handbook for Writers of Research Papers*. In this style, the page is called "Works Cited" and contains sources that you used in your research report. Entries are listed in alphabetical order by the author's last name. Here are examples of several bibliographical entries, using MLA style.

Book

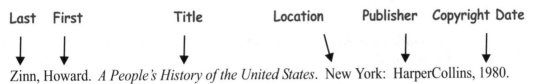

Zinn, Howard. *A People's History of the United States.* New York: HarperCollins, 1980.

Magazine or Article

Du Bois, W. E. B. "The African Roots of War." *Atlantic Monthly* 15 May 1915: 17–27.

Chapter 8

Internet Website

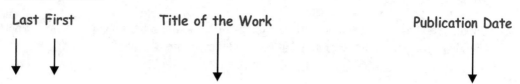

Perman, Anna. "Why Are We So Good at Recognizing Our Own Facial Expresssion?" 3 August 2011. 15 August 2011. <http://www.annaperman.wordpress.com>.

[**Note:** Instead of the Web address, you might be asked to list the source medium at the end. Ask your teacher the preferred way to list Internet sites.]

Encyclopedia Article

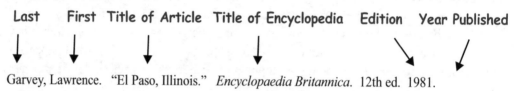

Garvey, Lawrence. "El Paso, Illinois." *Encyclopaedia Britannica.* 12th ed. 1981.

WAYS TO INCORPORATE SOURCES

Direct quotations are the exact words of the original author or speaker. Use quotation marks around these words and attribute them to the person who said or wrote them. The **in-text citation** goes in parentheses after the quoted material.

> **Example:** At the beginning of "The Masque of the Red Death," Prince Prospero is "happy, dauntless, and sagacious" (Poe 1).

Notice that the author's last name comes first, followed by the page number. In MLA style, there is no comma in between.

Paraphrasing (also called an **indirect quote**) is restating the words of another person in your own words. Paraphrasing does not need quotation marks, but it does require giving credit to the person who originally said or wrote it.

Original material:

William Seward, Lincoln's Secretary of State, commented on the limitations of the Emancipation Proclamation. He said, "We show our sympathy with slavery by emancipating slaves where we cannot reach them and holding them in bondage where we can set them free."

Paraphrase:

Lincoln's Secretary of State, William Seward, recognized that the Emancipation Proclamation created no actual change for slaves at the time.

 **Research**

Summarizing is used for longer passages or entire works. It involves putting the original author's main idea into your own words. When you summarize, you only include the author's main point. Summaries are much shorter than the original material and simply provide a broad overview.

Example: The Declaration of Independence states the reasons that the colonists sought independence from England.

Practice 2: Evaluating and Using Sources

W 7–9

DIRECTIONS Choose the best answer for each question.

1. Which is the best research question for a paper about chocolate?

    A. Who discovered chocolate?

    B. What percentage of people like chocolate?

    C. How is chocolate made?

    D. Does chocolate cause acne?

Paul Revere was more than a messenger riding on a horse, shouting and warning Americans about a British attack. He gave back to his country many talents and is one of our greatest heroes. When he died, many mourned his passing. Today he lives on in his famous silver art pieces, and his many acts of bravery will always be remembered. Over a thousand descendants now carry on the Revere name in the United States.

2. Which phrases from the passage reveal the author's bias?

    A. Shouting and warning Americans … British attack

    B. One of our greatest heroes … will always be remembered

    C. Messenger riding on a horse … carry on the Revere name

    D. Famous silver art pieces … thousand descendants

3. What is the best source to use to find information about the invention of the jet airplane?

    A. A website called inventors.com

    B. A book about the development of the jet engine

    C. An encyclopedia entry about Orville and Wilbur Wright

    D. The official Internet site of the National Aeronautic Association

Chapter 8

4   Sheryl finds a long article about marine life in a biology magazine. She needs to find out whether it is a good source for her paper about shellfish. What is the best way for her to do this?

_____

_____

5   You are writing a paper on pollution in the Gulf of Mexico. Your key word search finds several websites on the subject. Write at least three questions you can ask yourself about each site to determine if you can trust the information on that site.

_____

_____

_____

_____

6   You are preparing to write a paper on the Vietnam War. On April 23, 2011, you interviewed your uncle Roderick Bacon about his experience on the Landing Ship Tank boats that cruised the Mekong Delta during the war. How would you cite this source in your bibliography?

_____

_____

7   While writing a paper on the Holocaust, you read a book by Nobel Prize–winning author Elie Wiesel called *Night*. The book was published by Bantam Books of New York in 1960. How would you cite this book in your bibliography?

_____

_____

8   For a literary research paper about author Betsy Byars, you read three of her novels: *Pinball*, *The Summer of the Swans*, and *Tornado*. The edition of *The Summer of the Swans* that you read was published by Scholastic Inc. of New York. Its copyright is 1970. How would you write a bibliographic entry for this book?

_____

_____

 **Research**

CHAPTER 8 SUMMARY

You may need to do **research** for many reasons. Whatever the reason for your research, the first thing you must do is **find sources**.

A **primary source** is one that has a firsthand relationship to the topic. In other words, if you are writing about an event, primary sources would be journals or letters written by people who were actually there.

A **secondary source** might include documents written years later about the same event. They include encyclopedia articles, books, or journal articles written by **experts**, among others.

You also will use the **literary and informational texts** you read for class as sources.

There are many databases, software programs, and websites on the Internet called **electronic sources**. To search the Internet, you need to know how to use **search engines** and **search terms (key words)**.

Most sources use **organizational features** to help you locate and organize information. These include the following:

- Appendix
- Bibliography
- Footnote
- Graphic features
- Headings
- Table of contents

Asking **research questions** will help you focus on what exactly you will write about.

You need to **analyze and evaluate** materials to see how they relate to your topic and to each other. Two qualities of research sources that you must assess are **credibility and accuracy**.

You must **cite sources** that you use and avoid **plagiarism**.

Chapter 8

CHAPTER 8 REVIEW

W 7–9

> **DIRECTIONS** Suppose you want to write a report about different ways people have developed to tell time. You will need to learn about how the concept of time is tracked during a single day, a year, and within history. Three different sources of information about telling time are included in this review section. Read them, and then answer the related questions.

Source 1

Keeping Track of Time

When you want to plan a holiday or event, what is the first thing you consult? Chances are it's a calendar. Calendars allow us to plan the future and remember the past. Without using a calendar, imagine trying to plan a summer vacation, remember your friend's birthday, or even describe when you were born. There was a time, though, when days followed each other, unnamed and unnumbered. How did the ancient peoples come up with formulas for naming and counting the days in this nebulous flow of time?

The calendar followed today in most Western countries has taken on some peculiar incarnations in the past. Rulers, priests, and mathematicians molded, twisted, added, and deleted days and months, trying to get them to fit into patterns of whole numbers that could be counted. The problem, though, is that days, months, and years are not that simple. Their life spans are measured in the very awkward realm of numbers with up to ten decimal places. For instance, one year, from the beginning of spring to the end of winter, lasts approximately 365.25 days (rounding out several decimal places).

In ancient Greece, farmers and rulers alike noticed that time was divided into patterns. So it seemed natural to count using those patterns. One of the most obvious patterns was the rising and setting of the sun. Another pattern the ancient Greeks knew well was the waxing and waning of the moon. In addition to these cycles, they also knew the cycle of the seasons.

The ancient Greek calendars measured the changes of the moon. It takes about twenty-nine days for the moon to complete its cycle. This is known as a "lunar month." In one year, there are twelve lunar months—minus approximately ten days. In other words, a lunar year of twelve lunar months would end on December 21. Therefore, in order for the lunar months to fit the cycle of seasons, the Greeks would simply add a number of calendar days to the end of each year.

Research

Unlike the Greeks, the ancient Egyptians ignored the phases of the moon. They based their calendar on the sun. They divided the year into twelve months of thirty days each. That made 360 days. They were still a little over five days short of a complete cycle of seasons, otherwise known as a "tropical year." This posed little problem to the Egyptians, however. They simply added five party days to the end of each year. For five days, they celebrated the birthdays of important gods. Then they began their next calendar year.

Of course, the "whole number" problem remained. Remember, a year is 365 *and a quarter* (rounding out the several decimal places) days long, not simply 365 days long. Do the math. Under this scheme, every four years the calendar year would end a day earlier. Did the Egyptians party for an extra day in those years? Apparently not. They were content to let the timely order of days slide—by about one day every four years.

Meanwhile, in ancient Rome, the calendar was being organized around the phases of the moon, as it had been in ancient Greece. There were twelve lunar months to the year. But, since twelve lunar months only add up to a year minus ten days (approximately), the Romans would throw in an extra month when needed. (It would be a short month.)

With all the adding and subtracting of months and days, the Roman calendar still went out of rhythm with the seasons. To correct this in 46 BC, Julius Caesar gave his people a gift of three months of extra time in their year. Back in step with nature, Julius Caesar made a further change of adding a "leap day" to February every four years—an idea we still use today.

The Julian calendar, as Caesar's invention is called, still measured about eleven minutes more than the exact length of a solar year. Therefore, spring would begin eleven minutes earlier each year. In 1582, Pope Gregory XIII designed a new calendar. He wanted the date of the spring equinox to be on March 21 each year. The only solution was to remove some days from the calendar so that it would catch up with the seasons and equinoxes. That is exactly what he did. On October 4, 1582, people went to sleep only to wake up on October 16, 1582. Ten days had disappeared overnight by papal order!

Once the pope's Gregorian calendar had performed an overnight catch-up with the solar year, the pope made other minor changes to keep the calendar year and the solar year in synch. His new calendar was adopted by most European countries. Both England and France, however, were reluctant to accept a system designed by the Catholic Church. England, in fact, kept the Julian calendar for another 170 years. England also broke away from the Roman Catholic Church in the sixteenth century and formed the Church of England.

The Gregorian calendar is used by most Western nations today. However, it is not the only calendar in use. Muslim countries, which account for one-fifth of the world's population, use the Islamic calendar, which is based on the phases of the moon. Like the ancient Greek calendar, the Islamic calendar consists of twelve lunar months, each about twenty-nine days long. Each month begins with the new crescent moon. That moon must be *visually sighted* by a respected witness before the month can officially begin.

Chapter 8

The Islamic calendar measures time from the year the Prophet Mohammed traveled to Medina. This journey was called the Hegira, and every year after it is classified AH, or *anno Hegira*, meaning the year of the Hegira. The year the actual Hegira took place was AD 622, as measured by the Gregorian calendar. Therefore, the year 2003 of the Gregorian calendar is the year AH 1424 for Muslim countries. That is because it is 1,424 years after the Hegira.

The calendar is one of our most useful cultural tools. Yet, over the last many centuries and through many modifications, it still has flaws. Today, proposals are still being made for a more perfect system for measuring time. Meanwhile, nations who follow the Gregorian calendar continue their best efforts in imposing order on the changing patterns of nature. If that means having days appear and disappear from the picture, it may just serve to add an intriguing counterbeat to the inevitable rhythm of days.

Source 2

World Time

Helsinki	12:00 a.m.	Honolulu	12:00 p.m.
Moscow	1:00 a.m.	Anchorage	1:00 p.m.
Abu Dhabi	2:00 a.m.	San Francisco	2:00 p.m.
Islamabad	3:00 a.m.	Phoenix	3:00 p.m.
Dhaka	4:00 a.m.	New Orleans	4:00 p.m.
Jakarta	5:00 a.m.	New York	5:00 p.m.
Hong Kong	6:00 a.m.	San Juan	6:00 p.m.
Seoul	7:00 a.m.	Sao Paulo	7:00 p.m.
Brisbane	8:00 a.m.	Montevideo	8:00 p.m.
Sydney	9:00 a.m.	Azores	9:00 p.m.
Suva	10:00 a.m.	Casablanca	10:00 p.m.
Wellington	11:00 a.m.	Paris	11:00 p.m.

Research

Source 3

Table of Contents	
Preface	1
A Brief History of the Clock	4
Sundials	7
Shadow Clocks	9
Equatorial	12
Horizontal	13
Diptych	15
Equiangular	16
Capuchin	19
Water Clocks	23
Hourglasses	35
Candle Clocks	46
Eastern Mechanized Astrological Clocks	52
Modern Clocks	61
Pendulum Clocks	72
Quartz Clocks	80
Atomic Clocks	95
Information for Collectors	104
Clock Repairs	122
Illustrations	145
Bibliography	159
Index	167

1 When it is 7 a.m. in Seoul, what time is it in Casablanca?

   A 9 p.m.

   B 10 p.m.

   C 7 a.m.

   D 6 a.m.

Chapter 8

2. What is the central idea of the information in the article "Keeping Track of Time"?

   A The article traces the development of the calendar.

   B The article describes the purpose of the calendar.

   C The article convinces the reader to use a particular calendar.

   D The article informs the reader about inventors of the calendar.

3. Which calendar is most similar to the Greek calendar? Where did you find this information?

   _____

   _____

   _____

   _____

4. Which of the entries below is an example of a correct bibliographic entry for a magazine article?

   A Martins, Linda. "Correctly Positioning a Sundial in Your Garden." *Gardening Life* 12 June 2002: 14–16.

   B "Correctly Positioning a Sundial in Your Garden," *Gardening Life*, by Martins, Linda. June, 12, 2002, pp. 14–16.

   C Linda Martins. "Correctly Positioning a Sundial in Your Garden." *Gardening Life*. 12 June, 2002: 14–16.

   D Martins. "Correctly Positioning a Sundial in Your Garden." *Gardening Life*. 12 June 2002: 14–16.

5. To locate additional sources with information about clocks, where should you look?

   _____

   _____

6. How can you check the credibility and accuracy of these sources?

   _____

   _____

   _____

   _____

 **Research**

7 Which of these statements from "Keeping Track of Time" is irrelevant evidence?

   A Rulers, priests, and mathematicians molded, twisted, added, and deleted days and months, trying to get them to fit into patterns of whole numbers that could be counted.

   B Therefore, in order for the lunar months to fit the cycle of seasons, the Greeks would simply add a number of calendar days to the end of each year.

   C England also broke away from the Roman Catholic Church in the sixteenth century and formed the Church of England.

   D The Islamic calendar measures time from the year the Prophet Mohammed traveled to Medina.

8 Say that you want to write about how important the moon is to the creation of certain calendars. Which civilizations relied on the moon? Use evidence from the sources to support your answer.

_____

_____

_____

_____

9 Which of the following should be checked to assess the credibility of each source?

   A Authority

   B Length

   C Complexity

   D Graphics

Chapter 8

Chapter 9
The Writing Process

This chapter covers the following eighth grade strand and standards:

> **Writing**
>
> **Production and Distribution of Writing**
>
> 4. Produce clear and coherent writing in which the development, organization, and style are appropriate to task, purpose, and audience. (Grade-specific expectations for writing types are defined in standards RL 1–3.)
>
> 5. With some guidance and support from peers and adults, develop and strengthen writing as needed by planning, revising, editing, rewriting, or trying a new approach, focusing on how well purpose and audience have been addressed.
>
> 6. Use technology, including the Internet, to produce and publish writing and present the relationships between information and ideas efficiently as well as to interact and collaborate with others.
>
> **Range of Writing**
>
> 10. Write routinely over extended time frames (time for research, reflection, and revision) and shorter time frames (a single sitting or a day or two).
>
> **Language** (1–2 in proofreading reference)

No matter why you write, there are some good habits you need to cultivate. Some of the main challenges to focus on include using strong evidence, organizing your thoughts, and having ideas flow smoothly from one to the next. This chapter reviews the steps of the writing process. In the next chapter, you will review types of writing.

STEP 1: PLANNING

When you write for class assignments or tests, you will score highest if you follow certain guidelines. These include addressing the topic or question clearly, organizing your ideas well, and using style and language expressively. All of this begins with **planning**, the first step in the writing process.

Chapter 9

PURPOSE FOR WRITING

You must first focus on what you need to write. So as you begin planning, make certain you understand your **purpose for writing**. For class and on tests, you will have a specific **writing task** to complete. The task is the assigned topic or the question in a writing prompt. Be sure to read the assignment or prompt carefully. Ask questions if you do not understand it completely.

How you choose to organize your essay will depend on the writing task. For example, if you are asked to write a report about the similarities and differences in two styles of painting, such as Impressionism and Realism, you should write a comparison and contrast essay. This is the pattern that best fits the purpose and task. You will read more about organization in "STEP 2: Drafting."

AUDIENCE

Another important consideration during the planning phase is to identify the **audience** for which you will write. Of course, in school and on tests, you are writing for your teacher or other education professionals who will score your essay. However, sometimes the prompt will ask you to write as though you are talking to someone else. For example, you might get an assignment to write a letter to the editor of a magazine or newspaper. Or a writing task might ask you to write an essay for publication in the school newspaper, which means the audience would be other students at your school.

Knowing your audience gives you important information including the following:

- **The audience's interest:** what topic or information is of interest to the audience (so you can capture the interest of your readers)
- **The audience's prior knowledge:** what the audience already knows (so you don't tell the readers something they already know, and you can draw on that prior knowledge)
- **The audience's vocabulary:** words that the readers understand (so you don't use words that are too easy or too difficult)
- **What the audience needs to know:** information or explanations that you want the audience to know (so you can make a unique presentation for each audience)

This valuable information helps you write more effectively. You might use slightly different vocabulary, examples, or style based on the audience. But keep in mind that your work will be graded, so in the end, you should always write in a **formal style** that is appropriate to academic text. That means using complete sentences with varied sentence structure, precise language, correct spelling, and very few or no slang terms. You can read more about conventions in chapter 11.

The Writing Process

Here is a sample writing prompt that you might see on a test. Following are some questions to ask yourself about it. Study the explanations.

> A recent survey showed that teens watch an average of 11 hours of television each week. However, children between the ages of 2 and 5 watch an average of 13 hours of television each week. Your teacher has given you an assignment to discuss with your family the amount of TV watched by children. Decide what you think about young children watching an average of 2 hours of television each day. To introduce the topic, you will write an essay answering this question: "Does TV affect young children positively or negatively? Explain your answer." Once you finish the essay, your parents will read it, and this will start your family's discussion.

Question	Answer	Explanation
What question does this writing prompt ask?	"Does television affect young children positively or negatively?"	The writing prompt does not ask you to address whether your family watches too much television, or why teens watch less television than younger children. The prompt asks whether television affects young children positively or negatively. Stick to this issue.
What writing mode should be used?	Persuasive writing	Watching television may affect young children in both positive and negative ways. You must decide if, overall, the effects are positive *or* negative. In persuasive writing, it is important to choose one side of an issue. Though it is helpful for you to acknowledge and/or answer possible objections to your position, don't try to argue both sides of the issue at the same time. Since your purpose is to persuade readers, you must first be clear about your position.
Who is the audience?	Your parents	Of course, the teacher will be reading this sample essay, but the task is to write as though you will share it with your parents. This is similar to testing situations or writing homework assignments in which you are asked to address a certain audience, but the essay will be graded by a teacher or professional reader. In response to this sample writing prompt, you must use more formal language and tone for your teacher, while at the same time being aware of comments or objections your parents (as the assigned audience) might have.

DEVELOPING IDEAS

As you prepare to write, make some notes to **develop ideas** based on the writing task. You can use a variety of graphic organizers to help categorize your ideas. Here are just a few examples, and you can ask your teacher for additional ideas.

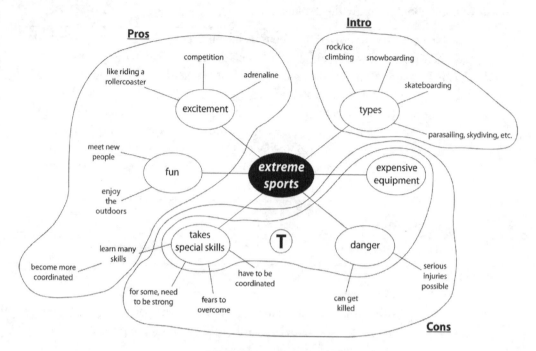

Mapping and Clustering

Mapping can be used for most topics. To create a map, make a circle on your note paper and write the topic inside it. Then draw lines to other circles in which you write the main supporting points. Details can be added in circles around those points. You can group ideas by **clustering**, which means drawing larger circles around related ideas. In the examples, a student grouped ideas for the topic (marked with a capital T), the introduction, and pros and cons to address in the essay.

Spiders and Beetles

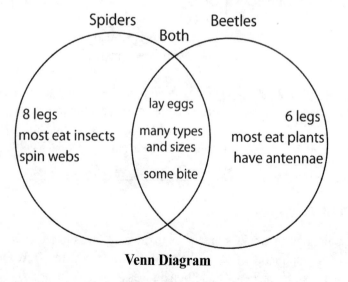

Venn Diagram

The Writing Process

A **Venn diagram** is useful when comparing and contrasting ideas. It is a quick, visual way to see points that are alike and those that are different. Draw two circles that overlap, labeling one for each of the items or ideas that you are comparing. Write the points that are unique to each item in its own circle. In the overlapping part of the circles write the similarities between the two. To compare and contrast three items, add a third circle.

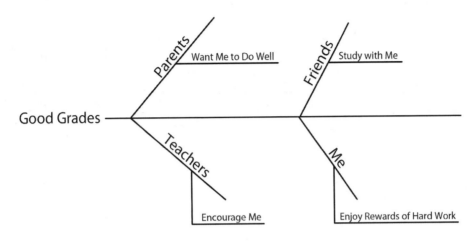

Fishbone Map

A **fishbone map** is helpful when thinking about causes and effects. In this example, you can see that a student has written an effect, "Good Grades," on the main line. The various causes that contribute to the effect are written on the diagonal lines (the ribs), and supporting details on smaller lines attached to each. For topics that deal with a cause and many effects, you can write the cause on the main line and the effects on the ribs.

In addition to using graphic organizers, you can also make a **brainstorming** list or do some **free writing**. Free writing involves writing for a set period of time (say 30 minutes), without regard to grammar or punctuation, in order to collect initial thoughts that you can refine and focus at a later time. You might also make a traditional **outline** to organize your ideas.

I. Art
A. Drawing
B. Painting
II. New ways of seeing things
A. Colors
B. Shapes
C. Textures
III. Art in my life
A. Carry sketch book
B. Paint pictures as gifts
C. Will pursue art career

Outline

Whichever method you use to develop your ideas, keep the goal in mind. You want to be able to use whatever notes you made as a road map to follow as you begin to write. Once you have your ideas in a usable list or organizer, it's time to begin drafting.

STEP 2: DRAFTING

When you begin **drafting**, remember what you are working on—your first draft. It does not need to be perfect. You will make improvements later, in the revision stage, and you will correct errors as a last step. Drafting is the time to get your ideas on paper, put them in the right order, and make sure they address the writing task and specified audience. Here are some things to keep in mind as you draft.

ORGANIZATION AND COHERENCE

Think about the **organization** of your essay. The organizational pattern you choose should be best for the writing task. You read about these patterns in chapter 6. They include comparison and contrast, chronological or sequential order, cause and effect, and problem and solution. Each pattern is best for certain topics or writing tasks. Keep in mind that you can combine them.

In addition to the writing mode, you need to put your information into an **essay structure**. This includes the following parts.

The **introduction** is the first paragraph of your essay. This is where you introduce your topic by writing your central idea. A good introductory paragraph also captures the readers' attention, so that they will want to continue reading.

The **body** of the essay is the supporting paragraphs. Depending on the topic and the number of main supporting ideas, there may be two, three, or more body paragraphs. Remember that each paragraph is about one idea. This is expressed in a topic sentence, and all other sentences in the paragraph support it. In turn, all body paragraphs should support the central idea or thesis statement of the essay.

The **conclusion** is the last paragraph. This paragraph restates your central idea and summarizes your main points. It can also leave readers with a final thought or an action to take. No new information should be written in a conclusion.

Coherence means sticking together. You want the ideas of your essay to "stick together," that is, connect and to lead from one to the next. Tying your ideas together is important to help readers understand your writing. Three ways to improve the coherence (to link the ideas and paragraphs in your essay) are planning an order, using transitions, and repeating key words and phrases.

1. Planning an Order

Organizing your ideas in an effective order is the first step in developing a coherent essay. Remember to choose the pattern that best suits your topic or writing task.

2. Using Transitions

Transitional words and phrases link ideas from one sentence to another. They also link ideas between paragraphs. Without them, the writing becomes less interesting and even less understandable.

3. Repeating Key Words and Phrases

While you don't want to say the same thing over and over, repeating certain key words and phrases can improve readers' understanding of the topic. By including key words or ideas from your controlling idea or thesis, you will make it easier for the reader to follow your train of thought. These repeated words are like landmarks along the road of your essay, reminding the reader where you have been and where you are going.

Look at the following plan for an essay in which the topic sentences repeat key words from the thesis statement:

Controlling Idea: Citizens of the United States could greatly improve the country by obeying the law, protecting the environment, and being kind to other people.

Paragraph 1 Topic Sentence: The first and most basic step to improving the country is to obey the law.

Paragraph 2 Topic Sentence: In addition to obeying the law, citizens can make this country even more beautiful by protecting the environment.

Paragraph 3 Topic Sentence: A third way to make the United States a better place to live is for citizens to reach beyond their own self-interest and be kind to one another.

In addition to the repetition of key words found in the thesis, you can see that this student has used transitions at the beginning of each topic sentence. They include "The first and most basic step," "In addition," and "A third way."

Chapter 9

CLARITY AND STYLE

When your writing has **clarity**, it is easy for readers to understand. That does not mean the ideas need to be simple. It means that, no matter how complex the ideas may be, they are clearly stated using precise language, vivid explanation, and logical reasoning. Descriptive language and natural flow of ideas create clarity.

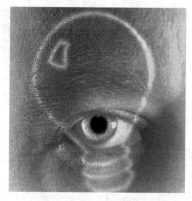

Writing **style** refers to how an author uses language to express his or her own unique voice. It is a combination of word choice, sentence formation, and tone. These all work together to give personality to the writing that others can recognize. Have you ever read something and thought, "I can tell who wrote this"? Many writers—including Ernest Hemingway, Edgar Allen Poe, Jack London, and many others—have their own styles which make their work easy to recognize. Over time, you will develop your own style. For now, focus on making sure your word choice, sentence structure, and tone, are suited to the writing task.

Look at this sample writing prompt and one student's response to it. Then review the questions and explanations that come after it.

> **Sample Writing Prompt**
>
> Your school newspaper has requested brief articles that offer advice to other students about back-to-school supplies. Write about something that you would recommend.

Sample Response

    There are many things to consider as you shop for back-to-school supplies—other than your favorite brand of snacks. One of the newest alerts being sent out, along with that school supply list that you are clutching in your sweaty palm, is the warning about oversized and overstuffed backpacks. Manufacturers are making backpacks bigger, and everyone knows that bigger is better, right?

    Well, in this case, it's not. Both parents and teachers have noted the increased complaints about carrying loads that would bring a buffalo to its hairy knees. Kids are struggling through hallways banging into each other and their empty lockers. (What? You thought that's where the books would go? So uncool!) The backpacks, on average, weigh about twenty pounds, 20 percent or more of the total body weight of many school kids. That is a serious load.

    So, when you go out looking for the perfect way to lug all those books around, don't ask your big sister to shoulder the weight. Look for a smaller backpack—or a bookcase on wheels.

Does the response address the writing task?

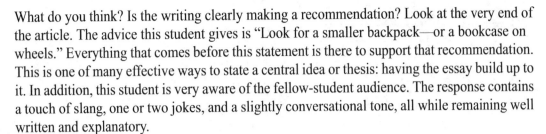

The Writing Process

What do you think? Is the writing clearly making a recommendation? Look at the very end of the article. The advice this student gives is "Look for a smaller backpack—or a bookcase on wheels." Everything that comes before this statement is there to support that recommendation. This is one of many effective ways to state a central idea or thesis: having the essay build up to it. In addition, this student is very aware of the fellow-student audience. The response contains a touch of slang, one or two jokes, and a slightly conversational tone, all while remaining well written and explanatory.

Is the writing clear and coherent?

At the beginning, the writer captures readers' attention by bringing up something all students think about—getting ready for school. The introductory paragraph also ends with a leading question, making students want to read on.

The body paragraph gives some details about the problem of heavy backpacks. The response loses some of its coherence here. For example, the writer could have explained better why students do not place their books in lockers but carry most of them around all day. It also lacks support for why all the extra weight is such a serious issue. What problems result from kids carrying that weight?

The conclusion is brief and issues a call to action. It advises students to buy smaller backpacks (but those would not carry all their books) or a bookcase on wheels (as a joke). However, it offers no serious alternative solution for all the books that students feel they need to carry.

With some feedback, this student could make the needed revisions and additions to polish this essay. If this response was written based on a test writing prompt, however, it would likely receive a high score. It addresses the prompt, is well organized, and uses expressive language.

Practice 1: Planning and Drafting

W 4

> **DIRECTIONS**   Read the writing prompt. Then follow the directions for the planning and drafting steps of the writing process.

> Inventions such as the telephone, television, cars, and computers have changed the way people live. Some people feel the changes have been for the better, while others think the changes have been for the worse. If you had the power to eliminate any invention in the world, what would it be?
>
> Using this prompt, begin your planning. Decide how you should address the topic for the audience and what mode of writing to use. Then, develop some ideas about the topic, and write a first draft. Review the "Drafting" section of this chapter for important concepts to keep in mind while drafting.
>
> Save your work. You will further develop this essay later in the chapter.

Chapter 9

STEP 3: REVISING

Even if you plan your essay carefully and write your draft precisely, you will still need to improve it. Even seasoned, professional writers need to revise. Remember that writing is a process, and this is the next step in that process. **Revising** means reading through the draft of your essay with the intention of making changes to improve it. Revising involves making such changes as adding details where needed, taking out unrelated information, and combining sentences for interest and variety.

There is one other possibility that you should be prepared for. Once in a while, you may need to **try a new approach**. As you revise, you might see that the improvements you can make just don't work. They may not fulfill the major criteria of an appropriate essay—one that addresses the topic or prompt, is well developed and organized, and uses language correctly and expressively. When that happens, consider starting over. If you have the time to do so, go back to the planning stage and try a different way to approach the task.

GUIDANCE AND SUPPORT

After you draft your composition, you can get **guidance and support** by collaborating with others. For example, you can conference with your teacher or a tutor about how to improve your writing. You can also work with other students to peer review each other's writing.

When you ask others to look at your draft and offer suggestions on how to improve it, be sure to tell them what advice you need. For example, as they read your draft, have them consider the following questions:

- Did the essay grab audience attention?
- Is the central idea or thesis clearly stated?
- Are the supporting ideas easy to understand?
- Is each paragraph clearly about one idea?
- Does your essay flow logically from beginning to end?
- Does the essay have a strong conclusion?

The Writing Process

MAKING IMPROVEMENTS

Once you have gathered ideas for what needs to improve, you need to **make improvements** by rewriting. It's time to write your final draft. (When you are completing a writing task on a test, you might not be able to rewrite your entire draft, so be sure to make clean, understandable corrections. Clearly cross out what you want to delete, and write what you want to add above the line or in the margin.)

Read your draft as if you were a member of the audience for whom you wrote it. Are the ideas clear and well stated? Do they flow logically? Are there any problems with the sentence structure or word choice? To practice, read this student essay and study the questions that follow.

On the top of an extinct volcano on the Big Island of Hawaii, there is a wonderland for astronomers. The world's largest astronomical observatory is perched there on the highest point in Hawaii. The modern scientists who work there share the mountain with ancient, sacred grounds of the native islanders.

Mauna Kea is a fascinating place for many reasons. The summit is 13,796 feet above sea level, but the base of the mountain sits about 35,000 feet below on the floor of the Pacific Ocean. The top of the mountain is so high that even in the tropical location of Hawaii the daytime summer temperature reaches only about 60 degrees Fahrenheit. It can also drop below 32 degrees. Large amounts of snow sometimes fall. The upper elevations often keep some snow on the ground year-round.

The Mauna Kea Observatory site boasts many telescopes. There are thirteen telescopes from eleven countries. The University of Hawaii built the first telescope in 1968. It also owns a second telescope at the observatory. The other telescopes are jointly owned by various universities and countries.

The summit is above 40 percent of Earth's atmosphere, and it has one of the highest proportions of clear nights of any location in the world, about 300 out of 365. Mauna Kea is considered to have better conditions for observing space than any other developed site. The atmosphere is extremely dry, which is important for the measurements scientists are taking.

Does the essay have a clear central idea or thesis statement?

Chapter 9

Probably the closest statement is the first sentence in paragraph 2, "Mauna Kea is a fascinating place for many reasons." It is rather brief and vague. It might be clearer and more interesting to state the topic right in the first paragraph:

> On the top of an extinct volcano on the Big Island of Hawaii, there is a wonderland for astronomers. <u>Mauna Kea, the world's largest astronomical observatory, is perched there on the highest point in Hawaii.</u> The modern scientists who work there share the mountain with ancient, sacred grounds of the native islanders.

Is the information in the best order? Do any details need to be added or deleted?

The writer did a commendable job of providing many details about the observatory and its location. A few places could use some clarification, though. In paragraph 2, the writer describes summer temperatures. Then some low temperatures and snowfall are mentioned, but readers are not told in what season these happen. This could be a point of confusion. In paragraph 3, a reasonable addition would be to explain why other countries have telescopes at Mauna Kea. You may have found other places where you might recommend that this writer add something to clarify meaning.

The main issue with all the facts is that they may not all be needed. If the essay is about the observatory and all of its advantages to astronomers, do readers really need to read so much about the year-round weather? Instead, perhaps the writer should develop a paragraph about discoveries made at the observatory or more about its history.

Is there anything else this essay needs?

Do you see anything missing? How about a strong conclusion? An appropriate conclusion is the most commonly missing piece of written responses. Don't forget that it's very important!

Another aspect that can be improved is sentence variety. Notice paragraph 3, for instance, which contains a string of simple sentences. Here is a revised version of the paragraph with some improvements in sentence structure, which involved moving some information around:

> The Mauna Kea Observatory site boasts many telescopes. In fact, there are thirteen from eleven countries. In 1968, the University of Hawaii built the first telescope and now owns two at the observatory. The other telescopes are jointly owned by various universities and countries.

Activity

W 4, 5

Write a strong conclusion for the essay about the Mauna Kea observatory.

The Writing Process

Practice 2: Revising

W 5

> **DIRECTIONS**
>
> Take out the draft you wrote for Practice 1. You will now revise it.
>
> If possible, get guidance and support from a teacher or tutor. You can also work with other students using peer review. Read over your own paper, and make improvements to it. Be sure it is clear, coherent, and descriptive.
>
> Save your work. You will work on this essay again in Practice 3.

STEP 4: PROOFREADING AND EDITING

You've written and revised your essay, and now you are ready to hand it in to your teacher, right? Well, almost. Not even the best writers turn in a piece of writing before they do careful **proofreading and editing**. Proofreading is the process of checking your essay for errors in conventions such as capitalization, punctuation, spelling, and grammar as well as for repeated words or omitted words. Editing is the process of correcting those mistakes.

Before turning in the final copy of your essay, take time to look for these small but costly errors. Proofreading the final copy of your essays will help you demonstrate knowledge of Standard American English through grammar and usage. More importantly, using the correct conventions will ensure that readers understand what you write.

Practice 3: Proofreading and Editing

W 5, L 1–2

> **DIRECTIONS**
>
> Take out the draft you revised for Practice 2. You will now proofread it.
>
> Chapter 11 covers the conventions to which you need to pay most attention at this time. Review that chapter, and then proofread your essay. Then, come back to this chapter to take the final step in the writing process and to complete the chapter review.
>
> Save your work. You will have one final step to take with your essay in Practice 4.

Chapter 9

STEP 5: PUBLISHING

If you are writing for class, the final step might be **publishing** your work. After revising your essay and completing your final draft, you can share it with others. Publishing allows others to view and read what you have written. You might want to print out a clean copy of your essay for your classmates to read. You could post your essay to a blog or website using the Internet. However you choose to publish your work, you are allowing others to read and comment about what you have accomplished.

A great thing about today's technology is that it allows multimedia interaction. Whether you print you paper in hard copy or post it online, you can add graphics to enhance it. These can help your readers to better understand what you have written. Keep in mind that images, just like texts, have creators and owners. You must give credit (use citations) for these just as you do for quoted text.

Practice 4: Publishing

W 6

DIRECTIONS	Take out the essay that you wrote, revised, proofread, and edited. You are now ready to publish it. Choose a medium (print or electronic). Print or upload your essay with any accompanying graphics or other media. Ask your teachers, tutor, and/or classmates to read it and give you their feedback. As a final step, make notes about what you would do differently in the writing process next time.

CHAPTER 9 SUMMARY

Creating a well-developed and organized essay begins with **planning**, the first step in the writing process.

You must be clear about your **purpose for writing**, which is based on a **writing task** and the **audience** for which you will write.

Always write in a **formal style** that is appropriate to academic text.

Make notes to **develop ideas** based on the writing task, or use graphic organizers like **mapping and clustering**, a **Venn diagram**, or a **fishbone map**.

The next step is **drafting**. This is the time to get your ideas down on paper—you will correct errors later.

Think about the **organization** of your essay, choosing an organizational pattern that works best for the writing task. Remember that your essay should have an **introduction**, **body**, and **conclusion**.

Work on **coherence** in your essay by planning an order, including transitions, and repeating key words and phrases.

Ensure **clarity** by using precise language, vivid explanation, and logical reasoning.

Focus on making sure your **style** (word choice, sentence structure, and tone) matches the writing task.

The next step, **revising**, involves reading your draft and making improvements such as adding details, deleting unrelated information, and combining sentences for interest and variety.

Occasionally, you may need to restart your efforts at planning and **try a new approach**.

After you write your draft, you can get **guidance and support** by collaborating with others.

Make improvements in your essay by rewriting.

The next step is **proofreading and editing**. Proofreading is the process of checking your essay for errors in conventions such as capitalization, punctuation, spelling, and grammar; editing is the process of correcting those mistakes.

The final step is **publishing** your work on paper or online.

Chapter 9

CHAPTER 9 REVIEW

W 4–6, 10, L 1–2

> **DIRECTIONS**
>
> 1. Practice reviewing an essay by another student.
>
> Chad's assignment was to write a comparison and/or contrast essay about himself and another member of his family. He decided to write about himself and his father. Read and evaluate Chad's essay. Rate the essay on a scale of one to four, with one being the lowest rating and four being the highest. See chapter 1 for more about rating. Use the material in this chapter to develop reasons for the rating that you choose. Share your results with the class or with your teacher.

Like Father, Like Son

My father and I are very close. He has always been the one to teach me the importance of life, and what it has to offer. My dad knows a great deal about life, and for that reason he is the best teacher a son could ever have. My father and I are much alike, but our most comparable attributes are those of being friendly, and being honest.

My father and I share many of the same characteristics, but the most notable one is that of being friendly. Dad has always been the one who starts a conversation. I have tried to followed in his footsteps, and often find myself making the first attempt to start a conversation with all those around me. Joking around is a trait my father has mastered. I find myself coming to school and telling the same jokes, and being the same "class Clown" that my father is. He has always taught me to treat everyone the same, this teaching has become a motto for me. I find myself helping those who are less fortunate. Helping others is a trait my father is famous for, and I hope I can carry on this tradition. Being friendly is a notable characteristic that my father and I both share, and so is that of being honest.

Being honest is a very important attribute in life, and it is one that my father and I both have. My father has spent many hours trying to teach our family about the importance of being honest. Ever since I was a small child my father has taught me to tell the truth. Telling the truth has now become a habit to me. My father would not lie to anyone. He is the most honest man I know. His honesty has effected me greatly. I now find it hard not to tell the truth. I dislike it very much when people lie to me, and I feel that this is a peeve that my father and I both share. I recall when I was a child I accidently broke a lamp. I lied to my father, and did not tell him the real reason why I had done it. He knew that I was lying, and took the opportunity to teach me. From that day on I knew not to tell lies. I am glad that my father has taught me to be honest. I know that being honest is a great attribute that my father and I both posses.

In summary, I know that my father and I are comparable in many ways, but the most notable characteristics are those of being friendly, and being honest. I know that by his example he has taught me a great deal. I hope that one day I can be even more like my father. I pray that one day I can be as good to my future children as he has been to our family.

The Writing Process

DIRECTIONS 2. Work further on your own essays.

Take out some of the essays that you wrote for the chapter 9 review. Consider these essays as drafts only. Take them through the rest of the writing process by applying the revision, proofreading, and publishing steps.

DIRECTIONS 3. Choose one of the following writing prompts.

Carefully follow the steps of the writing process to complete an essay based on the prompt. Share your essay with your teacher, tutor, or classmates. For more practice, complete essays based on the other prompts.

- Pick a sport, game, or hobby that you enjoy. Say that a friend has come to you and asked you for help to join in. Write an essay that explains how your friend can become familiar with the activity.
- There is a proposal before the school board to make school days shorter and the school year longer in order to make up for it. Do you think that's a good idea? Why or why not? In your opinion, what is the ideal length of both school days and the school year?
- Think about the books you have read over the past school year. Choose one, and provide a detailed review. Tell whether or not you would recommend it, and why.
- Write a story based on one of these ideas:

    The day I became famous

    A very unselfish act

    The newest form of transportation

    A place where no one grows old

Chapter 9

Chapter 10
Types of Writing

This chapter covers the following eighth grade strand and standards:

> **Writing**
> **Text Types and Purposes**
> 1. Write arguments to support claims with clear reasons and relevant evidence.
>   a. Introduce claim(s), acknowledge and distinguish the claim(s) from alternate or opposing claims, and organize the reasons and evidence logically.
>   b. Support claim(s) with logical reasoning and relevant evidence, using accurate, credible sources and demonstrating an understanding of the topic or text.
>   c. Use words, phrases, and clauses to create cohesion and clarify the relationships among claim(s), counterclaims, reasons, and evidence.
>   d. Establish and maintain a formal style.
>   e. Provide a concluding statement or section that follows from and supports the argument presented.
> 2. Write informative/explanatory texts to examine a topic and convey ideas, concepts, and information through the selection, organization, and analysis of relevant content.
>   a. Introduce a topic clearly, previewing what is to follow; organize ideas, concepts, and information into broader categories; include formatting (e.g., headings), graphics (e.g., charts, tables), and multimedia when useful to aiding comprehension.
>   b. Develop the topic with relevant, well-chosen facts, definitions, concrete details, quotations, or other information and examples.
>   c. Use appropriate and varied transitions to create cohesion and clarify the relationships among ideas and concepts.
>   d. Use precise language and domain-specific vocabulary to inform about or explain the topic.
>   e. Establish and maintain a formal style.
>   f. Provide a concluding statement or section that follows from and supports the information or explanation presented.
> 3. Write narratives to develop real or imagined experiences or events using effective technique, relevant descriptive details, and well-structured event sequences.
>   a. Engage and orient the reader by establishing a context and point of view and introducing a narrator and/or characters; organize an event sequence that unfolds naturally and logically.
>   b. Use narrative techniques, such as dialogue, pacing, description, and reflection, to develop experiences, events, and/or characters.
>   c. Use a variety of transition words, phrases, and clauses to convey sequence, signal shifts from one time frame or setting to another, and show the relationships among experiences and events.
>   d. Use precise words and phrases, relevant descriptive details, and sensory language to capture the action and convey experiences and events.
>   e. Provide a conclusion that follows from and reflects on the narrated experiences or events.
>
> **Range of Writing**
> 10. Write routinely over extended time frames (time for research, reflection, and revision) and shorter time frames (a single sitting or a day or two).

Chapter 10

By grade 8, you have done plenty of writing in school. Now, you will do even more as you prepare for high school. You will need to write routinely for extended time periods. Your essays might be based on research that you conduct, reactions you have to texts and performances, and your own reflection about ideas and issues. For all essays that you compose, you will focus on writing in a formal style that is appropriate for school assignments.

There are three basic types of essays that you are expected to compose well at this point: **persuasive**, **informative**, and **narrative**. In grade 8, you will mostly write essays to analyze topics, but you might also write some stories. This chapter will help you review the key concepts for creating a well-developed essay in each mode.

PERSUASIVE WRITING

You need to be able to **write arguments** (known as **persuasive writing**) that convince readers about your thoughts or viewpoints. To do this, you must clearly state your position, support it with relevant evidence, and use logical reasoning.

You will write an argument anytime you are making a point that you must support. Say that you read a novel for your English class. Your teacher has asked you to write an essay about which character in the story you thought changed the most. You will need to choose a character and then make a case for why you believe he or she changed most. The same concept is true if you are asked to respond to informational texts. For example, if you read several articles about an issue, you might be asked to give your viewpoint and defend it. In both cases, you will use the same techniques to write an effective argument. Let's review the steps now.

MAKING A CLAIM

The first step in building a good argument is to make a **claim**. A claim is the position taken on a particular issue. It needs to be expressed as a strong controlling idea. The claim lets a reader know the position of the text. By its nature, a claim can be argued; others can disagree with it. So, it must be well supported. Read the following statements, and decide which one is a claim that might make a good starting point for an argument.

1. Over the past three decades, there has been increasing public interest in self-help books, including the maintenance of health through self-regulated programs of exercise and diet.

2. We ought to be increasing programs that help the hungry children in our country rather than giving more money to an already well-financed program like the military.

Statement 1 presents information in a factual, nonpersuasive way. The information could be used to persuade, but neither statement encourages one belief over another. Statement 2 urges the reader to agree. In other words, it makes a claim. It can be argued. Claims use words like *must*, *should*, *ought to*, *demand*, *only*, and *best*. These key words often indicate that the author is encouraging the reader to take a side.

Types of Writing

PROVIDING EVIDENCE

The claim must be supported with **relevant evidence**. Building a strong argument includes arranging supporting details, reasons, and examples in a way that makes sense and persuades. All of this shows that you fully understand the topic you are writing about.

In presenting evidence, it is important to use **logical reasoning**. For example, a person could say, "I refuse to get a flu shot because some people have bad reactions to it." It might be true that a small percentage of people who get flu shots experience flu-like symptoms. However, most do not, and they are protected from the actual flu virus, which can lead to a very serious illness. The speaker's reasoning is faulty because it does not balance pros and cons. It simply uses an uncommon event (some people having a bad reaction to flu shots) as a reason for a decision.

Look at this example.

Do you like arts classes? Have you ever studied drama, music, or dance? What if these were not part of the curriculum? Arts classes are sometimes seen as extras on top of the core classes like English, math, science, and social studies. Some people say that students shouldn't be wasting time in public school with anything but the core subjects, but arts classes are just as important and should be supported in the same way. Those who support the arts being taught in public schools make the excellent point that such classes promote expression, creativity, and ways of using core knowledge that open up the minds of students. For example, you can apply math in music (meter and rhythm) as well as in fine art (geometry of perspective). Even though I play an instrument, I still don't like math. You can apply psychology and historical perspective in drama class. And all of the theory and history learned in arts classes also applies to interpretation of today's world. Studies have found that arts classes promote higher attendance. One study even found that students active in arts curricula did better in core subjects than those who were not. So I ask: Where's the waste of time in that?

This author begins by asking questions to capture reader interest. Next, she uses strong language (*wasting time*) in presenting an objection to her claim, which is that arts classes are just as important as core classes and should be supported in the same way. She then provides support (example, studies) for how valuable arts classes are. She presents a counterclaim (*Some people say that students shouldn't be wasting time in public school with anything but the core subjects*) and refutes it using examples and evidence. With a final question (*So I ask: Where's the waste of time in that?*), the writer invites readers to give more thought to the topic. The writer uses sound reasoning throughout.

Chapter 10

There is one piece of irrelevant evidence included that does not support the claim. Can you pick it out? It is the sentence "Even though I play an instrument, I still don't like math." It does not support the argument and should be removed.

RESPONDING TO COUNTERCLAIMS

Readers have their own views. They may already have strong opinions about the claim that the author is making. Effective authors know this and do some research about contrasting opinions, also known as **counterclaims**. Knowing about an opposing viewpoint and incorporating it into an argument is a good way to convince an audience that the argument is well researched. The most effective way to handle an opposing viewpoint is to acknowledge it, then refute (disprove) it.

Read this passage. Then look at the questions and explanations after it.

Concentrating on the Road

Today's drivers are more reckless than ever. Thousands of people are ticketed every year for various violations, but many more should be. Tired drivers and those with road rage can make the highway a scary and dangerous place. Many drivers obey the rules of the road and drive carefully, so they may think the actions of other motorists don't affect them. However, they can all too easily become victims of those who drive recklessly.

Drivers behind the wheel have been caught writing notes, reading newspapers, and even applying their make-up or brushing their teeth. Americans lead busy lifestyles, so they think of driving as an opportunity to multitask. Some believe they can easily eat, talk on the phone, or do other things while driving. But studies show that drivers busying themselves with other things while driving are far more cause an accident than those who concentrate on the road. According to the National Highway Traffic Safety Administration, 80 percent of automobile accidents and 65 percent of near-accidents involve at least some form of driver distraction within three seconds of the crash or near-miss.

This is why we need stricter driving laws to hold distracted drivers accountable. Accidents could easily be prevented if people realize that their car is not an office. People need to put down their phones and keep their eyes on the road. Don't scroll through your iPod while making a turn. Put your lipstick on after you park your car. Eat your sandwich after you're safely seated back at your office.

If more states started ticketing people for driving distractions, there would be far fewer accidents on our roads and highways.

Types of Writing

What is the writer's claim?

Did you say it is that drivers should be more careful on the road? That's *almost* it. The author actually claims that drivers who are distracted should be ticketed more often.

What counterclaims does the author address?

One opinion the author refutes is that safe drivers do not need to worry about distracted drivers. Another counterclaim is that some people believe they can do other things while driving and remain safe. The writer refutes this by citing statistics that prove distracted drivers cause more accidents.

ANALYZING CONFLICTING VIEWPOINTS

In your reading, you will often come across two or more texts that present information differently. In some, the authors might not agree with each other. When this happens, you need to **analyze conflicting information**.

First, you have to discover whether the disagreement is about facts or about interpretation. Facts can be checked; opinions and interpretations are subject to the strength of the argument.

Next, you should look carefully at each author's assumptions. What is each one taking for granted, and is it something that might be false? If so, then the claim might not be accurate.

Finally, evaluate the relevance and strength of each claim.

The next three articles all present information about the same topic: canine soldiers. The first is unbiased. It presents facts. This can serve as a "control" when you read the other two passages. Read all three passages. Then, review the questions and explanations that follow.

Uncommon Soldiers

Every year, thousands of young Americans go into training for the US military. And every year, over 300 of these "troops" are dogs: German shepherds and Dobermans. Dogs have been part of the US military for decades. They have played a role in most American wars. These special soldiers are trained at Lackland Air Force Base in San Antonio, Texas. It takes about 100 days to train the dogs to work in the military.

After graduation, the dogs serve in all branches of the military: Army, Navy, Marines, and Special Forces. They serve at home and at war. Some are scout dogs. They sniff out explosives, booby-traps, and dangerous chemicals. Others are sentry dogs. They walk the battle line with their handlers to watch for enemies. Dogs are a definite part of national security.

Chapter 10

Now that you have some background information on canine troops, read the two persuasive passages.

Animal Sacrifices

Every year, the US military sends shoppers to Europe. These shoppers are looking for a very special product: well-bred, intelligent German shepherds or other dogs, suitable for use by US armed forces. These government shoppers have a lot of money to spend, money that comes from the taxes that each American citizen pays.

They need plenty of money. They have to spend at least $3,000 for each dog. And they buy hundreds at once. These canine prizes are shipped back to the United States and further trained in military camps for 100 days. After they graduate, they take on some of the most dangerous work any soldier can do. Often they are in the line of fire, along with their trainers. Many dogs suffer terribly and die on duty. In Vietnam alone, hundreds of dogs were killed in battle. Most military dogs brought to Vietnam never returned.

Here at home, you would not want your pet to be put in harm's way on purpose. We have animal protection laws to prevent that. However, these laws don't seem to apply to all dogs.

Unsung Heroes

The brisk May wind blows through the crowds along the Memorial Day parade route. Flags fly and soldiers march, but all is not celebration. People's thoughts turn to lost heroes of past wars. They ponder the fact that they are safe and free today because of these fallen heroes.

But at a time like this, how many Americans think about dogs? Dogs have played a very important part in the safety of American troops in all wars. They are loyal, intelligent, courageous, and obedient. A dog is as good a soldier as anyone could hope to fight with. Many dogs have died bravely while saving the lives of other soldiers in their units. The United States War Dogs Association estimates that canine soldiers saved over 10,000 lives in Vietnam alone. Most did not make it out of the war zone, but some made it possible for their human comrades to make it home safely.

Some soldiers who have worked with war dogs have created memorials to these outstanding war heroes. You may be sure they remember their lost companions very well on Memorial Day.

Types of Writing

What conflicting information do these two passages contain?

The main conflict between the passages is viewpoint. The author of "Animal Sacrifices" clearly does not support the use of dogs in war. Meanwhile, the author of "Unsung Heroes" praises the war dog program and applauds the fallen canine soldiers as heroes.

Is the disagreement about facts or about interpretation?

Did you notice that many of the facts are the same? The authors do not really dispute how the dogs are trained, where they are sent, what they do, or the fact that many do not come back. What they disagree about is whether the program for training dogs to serve in the military should even exist.

What assumptions does each author make? Are they valid?

The author of "Animal Sacrifices" assumes that readers will agree that the military spends too much money on the program. This may be a valid assumption for some readers but not for others. At the end, there is also some faulty reasoning used when the author compares specially trained dogs serving in the military to household pets.

The author of "Unsung Heroes" assumes what people are thinking on Memorial Day. What is written may be true for many but, of course, not all.

Is strong and relevant evidence used to support each claim?

Which of the two articles do you think presents better evidence to support its argument? Look at each passage. Highlight or underline the evidence. Compare the evidence from both passages. Have a discussion in class about how well supported each passage is.

PROVIDING A STRONG CONCLUSION

The final piece of your argument is a strong **concluding statement**. Keep in mind that the ending of an essay is just as important as the beginning. You don't want to end by running out of ideas. You want to bring your essay to a logical conclusion. The concluding paragraph should let the reader know that he or she has reached the end of the essay. You can remind the reader about the points you have discussed along the way, but do not simply repeat the controlling idea word for word. Instead, you can summarize how you have proved your point throughout the essay. You can also leave the reader with a thought to ponder. This provides a sense of closure to your writing.

Chapter 10

Practice 1: Persuasive Writing

W 1.a–e, 10

DIRECTIONS Read the passages, and answer the questions that follow.

Letters to the Editor

Dear Editor:

I am writing in regard to your recent article on genetic engineering. I believe you presented a lopsided view of the issue by omitting key points. Since the middle of the twentieth century, genetic engineering has had an impact on society. Scientists apply the process, which changes the genetic makeup of plants and animals, to agriculture and medical research.

Scientists use genetic engineering to modify plants. The modified plants are stronger than naturally grown plants. They produce more fruits, grains, and vegetables. The result is an increase in world food production to help support the growing population.

Cloning is only one aspect of genetic engineering. Cloning uses a cell from one organism to create a second organism. The second organism is identical to the original. Over the last decade, cloning, especially the prospect of reproductive human cloning, has gained worldwide attention.

Scientists have cloned many different animals. The first recognized clone was a tadpole. The cloning took place in 1952. Forty-five years later, the world heard about a sheep named Dolly. Born in Scotland, Dolly was the first mammal ever created by cloning. Her creation sparked worldwide interest and concern. Your article used that concern and fed into the belief that tomorrow we will be creating our own twins.

There is still much to be learned about cloning and no thinking person would deny the ethical questions involved in the issue. However, data learned from cloning could lead to the development of healthier livestock. Cell cloning also has a major impact on medical research. Scientists use the process to develop new medicines. Research in cloning may lead to cures for life-altering diseases like diabetes and Alzheimer's disease.

I hope in the future, your paper will strive to present both sides of the issue.

Mary E. Cooper

Types of Writing

> Dear Editor:
>
> I am writing in response to Mary Cooper's letter regarding your article on genetic engineering.
>
> Ms. Cooper wrote about the positive impact of modifying plant life. However, she failed to cite the negative impact it has on poor farmers. The special fertilizers and pesticides used on modified plants make this type of plant too costly for many farmers to grow. If the financial stress it causes farmers isn't enough to make Ms. Cooper think again, the health effects of these chemicals on both farmers and consumers should be cause to reevaluate her judgment.
>
> As far as the cloning process is concerned, Ms. Cooper should consider the lack of balance found in her letter. I agree cloning lacks sufficient research, and the issue opens many ethical questions. However, Ms. Cooper seems to be advocating going forth blindly without first finding solutions to these issues.
>
> The facts she failed to include show cloning is inefficient and has produced a large proportion of unhealthy offspring. More than 90 percent of cloning attempts result in failure. Those clones that survive to birth have a high chance of dying early in life and experience very high rates of birth defects. The animals show increased tumor growth and disease. Dolly survived only to the age of six, though her life expectancy was eleven to twelve years.
>
> Cloning and genetic engineering are issues that go to the core of our value systems. Individuality as well as family and religious values are factors that can't be ignored.
>
> *Kevin M. Rogers*

1. If you were to compare and contrast these two letters, what would your analysis focus on?

   _____
   _____
   _____

Chapter 10

2 Based on Ms. Cooper's letter, readers can infer that Dolly's creation caused concern over —

    A the possibility of human cloning.

    B the gap in research between countries.

    C the time span between the tadpole and sheep cloning.

    D the financial investment in genetic engineering research.

Dolly and Her Offspring

Read the following sentence from Kevin Rogers' letter.

Those clones that survive to birth have a high chance of dying early in life and experience very high rates of birth defects.

3 Mr. Rogers included this information to show —

    A more experimentation is needed.

    B the cloning process is very risky.

    C sheep are not good subjects for cloning.

    D cloning has no scientific documentation.

4 What assumptions do the authors make in their respective letters? Are they valid? Why or why not?

Cooper letter

Assumption 1 _____

Valid? _____

Assumption 2 _____

Valid? _____

Rogers letter

Assumption 1 _____

Valid? _____

Assumption 2 _____

Valid? _____

Types of Writing

5 What idea is found in both Ms. Cooper's letter and Mr. Rogers' letter?

   A The quality of life for farmers increased with the creation of modified plants.

   B The results of genetic engineering research have received very little publicity.

   C The cloning of Dolly was successful.

   D Cloning involves many ethical issues.

Writing Task

A. Write an essay that evaluates Ms. Cooper's and Mr. Rogers' viewpoints and draws a conclusion about which of them offers better supporting evidence. Choose an organization pattern for your essay that best helps to supports your claim. Use some of the tips in this chapter to make a strong argument about which letter contains better support. Be sure to check your essay for errors and fix any you find.

B. Develop a persuasive essay for one of the topics below. Conduct some brief research to find out about the topic and to gather evidence for your viewpoint. Remember to make a strong claim, support your claim, maintain a formal style, provide coherence and transitions, respond to counterclaims, and close with a strong conclusion. As always, check your essay for errors and fix any you find. For more practice, write essays for additional topics from this list or from ideas that you develop on your own.

- Bumper stickers that some people find offensive
- "No homework" policy for middle school students
- Raising the driving age to 18
- Punishment for school bullies
- Using cell phones while driving
- Voting on the Internet

Activity

W1.a–e, 10

Look through newspapers and magazines. Find three examples of persuasive language and determine the author's purpose. Then, find three examples of nonpersuasive articles, and rewrite them in order to persuade the reader to take a stand on one side of an issue.

Chapter 10

INFORMATIVE WRITING

Another mode of writing that you will need to master is **informative writing** (also called **expository writing**). It involves writing texts that inform or explain. This is the mode you will use to write research reports about topics that you explore or to provide instructions for a process or task.

The **introduction** is an important part of the essay. It presents your topic. You should preview what you will talk about in the essay. This will compel your audience to keep reading. For example, if your essay is about the reasons for the growth of the British Empire, you might begin by offering clues about what you will say: "The British Empire expanded over several hundred years due to Britain's limited resources, growing population, and political goals."

As with crafting arguments, you must organize informative writing logically. Your essay needs to be **cohesive**, which means ideas flow well from one to the next. To help achieve this, remember to use appropriate **transitions** for your chosen organizational pattern. As you write, be sure to focus on **precise language** to convey your ideas.

Be sure to explain your ideas clearly. Remember that you have several tools at your disposal to help do this. Organizational features like **headings** and subheadings can quickly direct your readers to particular information. M**ultimedia** features like **graphics** can further illustrate the points you make in your writing. You can read more about these in chapter 5 and 6 where you reviewed how authors organize and support informational writing.

Developing an effective informational essay means providing plenty of information, but only information that supports your claim. Use concrete **details**, well-chosen **facts**, and authoritative support such as **quotations**. You may want to present general information by answering questions like "who, what, when, where, why, and how" about a subject. These key questions are sometimes called the five W's and H.

Look at the following example of an informative essay written by Ricardo. Then, read the questions and explanations after it.

The Labrador Retriever

Dogs come in many sizes, shapes, and colors. Some dogs are large while others are small. I own a Labrador retriever. Learning about this dog can help anyone who wants a Lab for a pet.

Types of Writing

My veterinarian, Dorothy Howe, says Labrador retrievers originally came from Canada. These dogs stand about 2 feet tall and weigh between 60 and 75 pounds. They come in black, yellow, or chocolate, and they are sometimes used for bird hunting. Howe says the personality of a Lab should match that of the dog's owner, so before choosing a Lab, a person should observe its personality and behavior. Labrador retrievers can live eight to twelve years or longer depending on the owner's attention to their health.

Care of the Labrador retriever involves regular feeding, usually two cups of food each day with plenty of fresh water. Dog experts recommend a high-quality dog food with a few nutritious snacks now and then. Labs should never be allowed to overeat. Labrador retrievers love to play fetch, so always keep a Frisbee or rubber bone handy. Labs are also very strong dogs that will drag you along on their leash unless they are trained to walk with you. They also must learn not to chase other dogs or cars.

I learned that Labrador retrievers can get diarrhea, worms, especially heartworm, and distemper. They can also go blind and suffer from hip diseases and skin infections. They need checkups and shots on a regular basis. As puppies, Labs can die quickly if they become too cold. Both puppies and adult Labs are fun-loving, affectionate, and protective of their owners.

Most people enjoy Labrador retrievers. They're playful, loyal, and good hunting dogs too. When I look into my Lab's eyes, I see a smart and lovable dog. That's what makes him interesting to me.

How strong is the introduction?

The writer begins in a vague way that does not grab the attention of readers. The introduction should invite people to read further and want to find out what comes next.

How well organized and supported is the topic?

Ricardo does present relevant facts and details about Labs in his essay. An excellent addition is the use of information from an expert, the veterinarian. The essay talks first about the dog's background and disposition, then about caring for Labs, and finally about specific health issues. For clarity, Ricardo could add more transitions such as *likewise*, *first*, *finally*, and so on in appropriate places. The conclusion is appropriate for the essay.

Chapter 10

What multimedia component would be the most effective to help people understand this essay?

Did you say pictures or videos of Labs? Since this essay reports what Labs are like, the only thing missing is seeing what they look like. Photographs would be helpful to readers to add that understanding.

Practice 2: Informative Writing

W 2.a–f, 10

> **DIRECTIONS** Read the sample essay, and answer the questions that follow.

How to Sink a Free Throw Every Time

A basketball free throw is just what it sounds like: an opportunity to toss the ball through the hoop while you are free from other players trying to distract you. When making a free throw, you stand at the free throw line (fifteen feet from the basket), with no other players defending you, and take a shot. It should be easy to make every free throw, but many players miss because they don't practice the essential elements of free throw shooting.

The first thing you want to do is relax. As you practice your shot, set your feet shoulder-width apart with your shooting foot slightly forward of the other foot. In other words, if you shoot with your right hand, put your right foot slightly forward. Then, you should look at the hoop to let your eyes register the distance. This lets your brain know where you want the ball to go.

After you bounce the ball a few times to relax your shooting muscles, hold the ball gently but with confidence. Make sure your shooting hand is directly under the ball and your elbow is pointing down at your knee. Then, look again at the hoop, take a deep relaxing breath, bend your knees, and take your shot. After you release the ball, remember to follow through with your fingers pointing toward the hoop, and watch the ball "swish" through the net.

Finally, repeat these steps to establish a routine that works for you, and practice it regularly. Stand in the same place on the free throw line. Bounce the ball the same number of times. Take your breath at the same time. Keep your routine the same. In this way, every time you step up to the free throw line, you don't have to think. Your body goes on automatic pilot, and you sink the free throw every time.

Types of Writing

1. What organization does this essay use?

   _____

2. Which of these statements would be best to add to the introduction?

   A The sure-fire way to sink a free throw every time is to practice using the steps outlined here.

   B Getting distracted can cause even the best players to miss when they get a chance at free throws.

   C Free throws are the easiest shots in the game, so just take it easy and let your practice pay off.

   D Missing a free throw can be an unpleasant and disappointing moment for a player and the entire team.

3. What type of support could this writer add to make this essay more credible?

   _____
   _____
   _____

4. What is this essay missing?

   A A strong introduction
   B Precise details
   C Transitions
   D A strong conclusion

5. Which of these graphics would best support understanding of this essay?

   A A table showing the average free throws sunk by various athletes
   B Photographs of unusual free throw stances
   C Drawings of each of the positions a player should take
   D A video of a professional basketball game

Page 187

> **Writing Task**
>
> Write an essay about one of the following topics. Be sure to organize your ideas logically. Use well-chosen facts and concrete details to describe your topic. As always, check you essay for errors and fix any you find. For more practice, write essays for additional topics from this list or from ideas that you develop on your own.
>
> - An unusual musical instrument
> - The official dish of a specific country
> - A recently discovered animal species
> - A fad from the past that seems odd today
> - A strange law that remains on the books
> - How to make a milkshake or a smoothie
> - How to play a game (choose one)
> - How a time clock works
> - How to catch a fish
> - Ways to become healthier

NARRATIVE WRITING

Narrative writing tells a story. It might be about a real experience or an imagined series of events. To write an effective story, you need to use a variety of **narrative techniques**. This includes the **literary devices and elements** that writers of fiction and literary nonfiction use. You can read about these in chapters 2 and 3.

A story needs to have the basic elements of story: **plot**, **characters**, and **setting**. You also need to establish a **point of view** and decide who the narrator will be. Remember that it can be a character in the story or an unknown third-person narrator. Even if you are writing from your own life, you do not necessarily need to tell the story in first person. You do not have to be the narrator.

As with any essay, a story needs an **introduction** in which you orient readers to where and when the story takes place. **Descriptive details** and **sensory language** (words and phrases that appeal to the senses) are very important. They help readers to experience the action and feelings in the story. The events should unfold in a **logical and natural order**. Using appropriate **transitions** and **pacing** help to achieve this.

Finally, the **conclusion** should wrap up the story in a logical way. Some stories do end on an open note, with no clear resolution for the main character. But even these have some final thought or idea that readers take away. Most stories have an ending that provides some final outcome of everything that has happened.

Types of Writing

Read this example of a brief narrative that a student wrote for an assignment. Then study the questions and explanations after it.

Trial by Lava

I wished that I were sitting under the frigid waters of Lake Michigan. But I wasn't so lucky. I was standing in front of my class about to begin a presentation. I remember gazing at the school calendar up on the wall. September's photo featured the autumn colors of red, orange, and yellow. That same yellow ran in a stripe up my back giving me chills. I suffered from a fear: public speaking. I wished I could have fled like a yellow rabbit to the lake.

My partner and I were leading a talk about 1960s culture. Matt brought music and a CD player, and I chipped in sunflower cookies and a lava lamp. The PowerPoint presentation was my idea. Our table was filled with '60s stuff. It was also draped with wires for the CD player and lava lamp. Folk rock music played softly. The lava lamp glowed dimly as Matt delivered his speech, and then I was on.

Matt was waving his hand at me to start. The Rolling Stones came on next and the music blared. Mick Jagger was making me ill. The lava lamp was all warmed up and bubbling faster now. My throat closed in panic; my heart was a jackhammer. I looked out at the faces—they were all looking back! I shuffled nervously—and that's when it happened. I accidentally stepped on an electrical cord. I looked on, helpless, as the lava lamp rose with a quick jerk and then crashed down, shattering glass and splashing waxy, red lava. No one moved or spoke, except me. "Anybody got a mop?"

Matt bolted to fetch the janitor while everyone eyed me with a mixture of surprise and alarm. And so I began. I don't remember a word of my talk, and others claim I was as white as a ghost. They sympathized with the disaster. But a strange thing happened though. It cured my phobia. When I give presentations in front of the class now, I never wish I were sitting in the icy waters of Lake Michigan.

What is the purpose of this narrative?

The purpose is not stated right at the beginning, as it would be in persuasive of informative writing. In narratives, authors can hold back their purpose, central idea, or theme to be revealed later. In fact, the purpose in this story is provided in the last paragraph when the narrator says, "But a strange thing happened though. It cured my phobia."

Chapter 10

Does the writer describe the setting well?

In the first paragraph, the author describes the story's setting: a school room. The description is adequately developed, but a few words could be more specific. Additional details would be helpful, such as describing some of the contents of the table instead of saying "Our table was filled with '60s stuff." You may or may not feel that the description is detailed enough, but in either case, you should cite specific examples to support the claim you make.

What organization pattern does the story use? List the key events in the narrative.

Did you say that this narrative is chronological? You are correct. The key events include these: waiting for the presentation to start, the lava-lamp disaster before the narrator's turn to speak, the presentation, and the conclusion.

Describe the main character. What details are missing that would help you better know this character?

The main character, who narrates this story, is a student who was afraid to make a presentation, had a disastrous accident happen, saw that it wasn't the end of the world, and now is no longer afraid to present in front of class. You can see all of these things in the description of this person. However, there are many things you do not know. Is the narrator a boy or a girl? What does he or she look like? Details about physical appearance and additional actions the narrator takes would help readers get to know the character.

Give two examples of literary devices that the author uses in this story.

Did you find the literary devices? The first paragraph has a reference to an idiom when the narrator says, "That same yellow ran in a stripe up my back giving me chills." Being yellow or having a yellow streak run down your back is an idiom for being a coward. In the third paragraph, the writer uses the metaphor "my heart was a jackhammer." This figurative language drives home the point that the narrators heart was beating hard and fast. Do you see any other literary devices?

Practice 3: Narrative Writing

W 3.a–e, 10

DIRECTIONS Read this story. Then, answer the questions that follow.

Hawk-Eye

Whenever Ryan sees a hawk swoop and dive over a fog-shrouded meadow, hunting dinner, he thinks of his first boss.

Types of Writing

He was the director of student volunteers for the nature center, where Ryan applied one summer. Way over six feet tall, dressed in muddy, forest green coveralls and a floppy-brimmed camouflage hat, the man looked like a giant poacher. His face was solemn as Ryan asked for the director. Maybe his shaggy, silvered eyebrows twitched, but he led Ryan to an office.

Abruptly, he traded the camo hat for a black top hat and sat behind a canoe-sized desk. When he spoke, his voice rumbled low but had melody and rhythm, like Johnny Cash reciting the verse of a song. They shook hands over Ryan's application. Ryan would never forget that handshake. It was as rough yet gentle as shaking hands with an elephant, if it had hands. Two fingers were missing from the man's gnarled hand, which was crisscrossed with violet scars and pitted with the wounds wild things cause. He clasped Ryan's hand carefully, lifting and dropping his arm with great deliberation.

As Ryan looked up, he caught a whiff of corn kernels, field mice, and bat guano from the man's clothes. Meeting his gaze, he saw the grizzled face relaxed into a sunny expression. Suddenly, he was out the door with a crashing bang, hoarsely calling for Ryan to come back and start the next day.

His name is Mr. Travis, and he often can be spotted striding along cool, shaded paths with a hawk perched securely on one broad shoulder and his hands full of feed sacks. But no one ventures to ask him what is in those sacks.

1. How does the writer capture reader attention early on?

_____
_____
_____
_____

2. What is the setting of the main character's encounter?
   A An unemployment office
   B The edge of a foggy meadow
   C The office of a nature center
   D A shaded path in a nature center

Chapter 10

3. What is the organization of the plot?

   A It jumps from the present to the past and back to the present.

   B It begins in the far past and moves forward to the present.

   C It starts in the present and then moves back in time to the past.

   D It switches from the past to the present and back to the past.

4. What is the purpose of the conclusion?

   _____

   _____

   _____

   _____

5. Give an example of sensory language that the author uses to appeal to each of the senses. If there isn't an example for a sense, write "None."

Sight: _____

Sound: _____

Touch: _____

Taste: _____

Smell: _____

Writing Task

Using what you have reviewed about writing an effective narrative, write two or three stories for practice. Remember to organize your story well and include literary elements and devices. Provide vivid details and sensory language. Be sure to check for and fix any errors you find. Choose your own narrative ideas, or select some of the following topics:

Tell a story about a time you were really afraid. What made your experience so frightening? How did you feel when it was over? Develop your story with details.

Write an imaginary story about meeting an alien from another planet. Tell the reader about the experience. Develop your story with details.

Write about an experience you had that taught you a valuable lesson about life. Tell about the main events of that experience. Develop your story with details.

Tell a story about a friend or family member who made everyone laugh. Write a narrative about the experience. Develop your story with details.

Chapter 10 Summary

There are three basic types of essays that you are expected to write: **persuasive**, **informative**, and **narrative**.

You need to be able to **write arguments** (known as **persuasive writing**) that convince readers about your thoughts or viewpoints.

The first step in building a good argument is to make a **claim**.

The claim must be supported with **relevant evidence**.

It is important to use **logical reasoning** and respond to **counterclaims**. To do this, you must know how to **analyze conflicting information** in your sources.

The final step is to provide a strong **concluding statement**.

Informative writing (also called **expository writing**) involves explaining a topic or process.

The **introduction** should preview what you will say in the essay.

Your essay needs to be **cohesive**, with appropriate **transitions** and **precise language** that conveys your ideas.

You can use organizational features like **headings** and support the text with **multimedia** features like **graphics**.

To support your ideas, use concrete **details**, well-chosen **facts**, and authoritative support such as **quotations**.

Narrative writing tells a story.

You can use a variety of **narrative techniques** in your stories, including **literary devices and elements** such as **plot**, **characters**, **setting**, and an appropriate **point of view**.

Use the **introduction** to familiarize readers with your characters and setting.

Descriptive details and **sensory language** help readers to experience the action and feelings in the story.

The right **transitions** and **pacing** help events unfold in a **logical and natural order**.

The **conclusion** should wrap up the story in a logical way.

Chapter 10

CHAPTER 10 REVIEW

W 1–3, 10

> **DIRECTIONS** On your own paper, practice writing persuasive, informative, and narrative essays. Keep your writing in a portfolio to work on again in the future.

Read this poem. Then read the writing prompt, and write a response.

The Debt

by Paul Laurence Dunbar

This is the debt I pay
Just for one riotous day,
Years of regret and grief,
Sorrow without relief.

Pay it I will to the end—
Until the grave, my friend,
Gives me a true release—
Gives me the clasp of peace.

Slight was the thing I bought,
Small was the debt I thought,
Poor was the loan at best—
God! but the interest!

---

1. Write an essay to explain the meaning and message of this poem. Make sure to clearly define your claims about what the poem means and support these with evidence from the poem. Organize your essay in a logical way, and use descriptive language. Finally, find and fix any errors you might make.

Types of Writing

2. Choose one of the prompts below, and write a well-organized persuasive essay. Be sure to clearly state your claim, logically support your ideas with relevant evidence, and use language to create cohesion among claims and counterclaims.

- Suppose that the current laws in your community permit citizens to cite other residents for disturbing the peace if their dog barks excessively. These citations can lead to fines and court hearings. However, people reporting the disturbance can do so anonymously and do not have to provide proof that the dog has, in fact, even barked. Is this law appropriate or not? Why?

- One of your relatives tells you that parents are ultimately responsible for your success. Think about this statement, and form an opinion. Are parents or their children more responsible for success in school? Explain your viewpoint clearly, and make certain to address counterclaims to strengthen your argument.

- You are entering a competition to get an article published in *New World Journal*. The editors of the magazine are asking contestants to write a paper convincing the readers to pick one exercise as the healthiest physical activity for their New Year's resolutions. What physical activity do you think is the healthiest? Make sure to support your claim with strong evidence as to why the activity you picked is the healthiest.

- Confucius once said: "Choose a job you love, and you will never have to work a day in your life." However, many people feel that they can't make enough money at the job they would really like to do. What do you consider more important in a job: work satisfaction or a high salary? Be sure to address counterclaims to strengthen your position.

- The wonders of modern medicine have made it possible for more people to live longer than ever before. Many consider the added years a blessing that allows people to do more with their lives than they thought possible. Others, however, feel that the poor quality of life that elderly people experience is a curse more than a blessing. How do you feel about people living to be 90 or 100 years old?

- The impact of video games on culture in the United States has received much attention. The issue has acquired even more importance as a local radio station this week asks listeners to respond to the following question: "Is playing video games harmful or beneficial for human beings?" How would you answer this question? Be careful not to base your argument on a false premise.

3. Choose one of the topics below, and write a well-organized informational essay. Clearly introduce your topic, develop it with well-chosen details, and provide a strong conclusion.

- Preparing for a new school year
- Why your town or state is an interesting place to live
- Saving money for the future
- Characteristics of a successful student
- Why it is important to know math in everyday life
- How to be on time for important events

Chapter 10

4. Choose one of the prompts below, and write a well-developed narrative. Engage the reader, use a variety of narrative techniques, include vivid description and sensory details, and provide an appropriate conclusion.

- Listen to a favorite song or musical composition. Can you picture a story to go with the music? Even if the song doesn't contain a narrative itself, the lyrics might speak to you on an emotional level that brings a particular story or experience to mind. Make notes about your story. Write your story, and give it a title like "The Story in [Title of Song or Musical Composition.]"

- Think of a memorable conversation you had with a friend or family member. Write down what you remember about the conversation, particularly things that might have struck you in some profound way. Then write a dialogue between you and the other person. Include details. Skim through one or two of your favorite novels to see how professional authors write effective dialogue.

- An autobiography is a story you write about your own life. Make a timeline of the key events in your life. Include details about each event. Then write your autobiography from the time you were born to the present. Include significant events only—ones that have heavily influenced your life. Use vivid details to help your readers experience the world as you have.

- Who is the most remarkable teacher you have ever had? Recall a time when this teacher made an impression on you. Relate the details of the experience and how it might have changed you in some way.

- Write about the worst weather you have ever experienced. Perhaps it was a thunderstorm, tornado, hurricane, tidal wave, avalanche, monsoon, or a snowstorm. Write a narrative about that experience. Were you frightened? Excited? Or perhaps both? Try to engage the various senses and emotions of your readers to help them experience the storm as you did.

- What is the most amazing sports event you have experienced? Tell about it.

Chapter 11
Conventions

This chapter covers the following eighth grade strand and standards:

> **Language**
>
> **Conventions of Standard English**
>
> 1. Demonstrate command of the conventions of standard English grammar and usage when writing or speaking.
>   a. Explain the function of verbals (gerunds, participles, infinitives) in general and their function in particular sentences.
>   b. Form and use verbs in the active and passive voice.
>   c. Form and use verbs in the indicative, imperative, interrogative, conditional, and subjunctive mood.
>   d. Recognize and correct inappropriate shifts in verb voice and mood.
> 2. Demonstrate command of the conventions of standard English capitalization, punctuation, and spelling when writing.
>   a. Use punctuation (comma, ellipsis, dash) to indicate a pause or break.
>   b. Use an ellipsis to indicate an omission.
>   c. Spell correctly.
>
> **Knowledge of Language**
>
> 3. Use knowledge of language and its conventions when writing, speaking, reading, or listening.
>   a. Use verbs in the active and passive voice and in the conditional and subjunctive mood to achieve particular effects (e.g., emphasizing the actor or the action; expressing uncertainty or describing a state contrary to fact).

By this time in the eighth grade, you have learned many **conventions** of Standard American English and are expected to use them in your writing. Conventions include using language correctly in the following areas:

- Capitalization
- Punctuation
- Sentence structure
- Complete sentences
- Subject-verb agreement
- Spelling
- Verb tense

Chapter 11

There are many rules for all of these conventions. You can use a style guide or grammar book to review these rules. In this chapter, you will review some specific conventions that you are adding to what you use when you write and speak.

VERBS: VOICES AND MOODS

You know what **verbs** are. You use them every day. You probably know all about the different kinds of verbs—action verbs, state-of-being verbs, linking verbs, helping verbs, transitive and intransitive verbs, and so on. Of course, you know about verb tenses like past, present, and future! If you need to brush up on any of these facts about verbs, review a grammar book or ask your teacher for the best way to review.

In this section, you will review some facts about **verb voices and moods** that you are adding to your stock of skills in relation to verbs.

ACTIVE AND PASSIVE VOICE

Active voice is the arrangement of a sentence so that the subject performs an action. An example is, "Lara wore a red sweater." Here, Lara is the subject, and she performed the action of wearing a sweater. **Passive voice** is when the subject has some action done to it, as in, "A red sweater was worn by Lara." In this sentence, the sweater is the subject.

As you can see, passive voice can be awkward, and it is harder to read. An easy way to spot most passive-voice constructions is to look for various forms of the verb *to be* followed by a past participle. For example, consider this passive-voice sentence: "The room was painted yellow." The verb *was* is a past tense form of the verb *to be* and *painted* is the past participle of the verb *to paint*.

Most of the time, you will use active voice in your writing and speaking. However, there are instances in which passive voice is necessary, as when you don't know who or what did something. An example is "The road was closed, so we had to take the long way around."

Another instance when passive voice is useful, though not necessary, is when you want to place emphasis on the "receiver" and not the "doer" of an action. For example, "Mary was struck by the speeding car" is more forceful than "The speeding car struck Mary."

But remember: Passive voice is generally considered lazy writing and should be used sparingly and with great care.

Activity

L 1.b, d

Find several magazine articles that you like. Read them carefully and pay attention to sentence structure. Highlight or underline any passive-voice sentences that you find. On your own paper, rewrite each passive sentence in active voice. If you spot an instance of passive voice that you think is appropriate, write an explanation of why you think the sentence needs to be in passive voice.

Verb Moods

Did you know that there are **verb moods**? They are also called grammatical moods, and writers use them to achieve certain effects. Each mood gives a sentence a different purpose. For example, look at the difference between these two sentences:

When Holly brings the rolls to the table, we can eat.

If Holly were to bring the rolls to the table, we could eat.

Read on to look closer at these moods, how they are used, and how they change the meaning and intent of a sentence.

Here are five common verb moods and the effects they can have.

Mood	Description	Examples
Indicative	The simplest mood is called **indicative** or declarative. It is used to make statements.	I like to ride my bike.
Interrogative	The **interrogative** mood is used when asking questions.	Do you have a bicycle?
Imperative	The **imperative** mood uses present tense, second-person (*you*) verb tense, though the pronoun *you* is often implied. This mood is used for commands, instructions, or requests.	Listen! Get your bike. Meet me at my house.
Subjunctive	The **subjunctive** mood is used to show a condition or an imagined situation. You will often see it in "if ... then" statements or hypothetical questions. The present tense of a verb is often used to show an action that has not happened. The verb *to be* is used in the form *were* instead of *was*.	I suggest you ride your bike. What if we were to ride bikes together?
Conditional	The **conditional** mood is used when one event is dependent on another event happening. You will often see the auxiliary verbs *could*, *would*, and *should* in these statements.	If you want, I would ride bikes with you. When should we go?

Chapter 11

USING VOICES AND MOODS

You need to know how to use all of these voices and moods when you write. By creating certain effects, they can help you achieve more clarity of meaning.

Sometimes you will have **shifts in voice and mood**. This will happen when one particular phrase or sentence needs the effect of a specific verb voice or mood that is unlike the text around it. Here is an example of shifts in voice and mood that are used to create certain effects.

> Do you think you lie perfectly still when you sleep? Think again. Studies show that everyone moves at least eight to twelve times a night. People who have trouble sleeping move around even more. Twenty to thirty position changes a night are not unusual.

The first sentence uses interrogative mood, as it asks a question. The second uses imperative mood to give an instruction. Sentences three and four are in indicative mood and active voice, but the last sentence changes to passive voice. Why? This structure highlights the number of position changes rather than the sleepers making them.

As you can see, there are time when shifts in voice and mood work well. However, you should avoid inappropriate shifts. Make sure you have a good reason to change the voice or mood.

Practice 1: Verb Voices and Moods

L 1.b–d, 3.a

DIRECTIONS Read the passage, and answer the questions that follow.

Excerpt from *Adventures of Huckleberry Finn*

by Mark Twain

Sometimes we'd have that whole river all to ourselves for the longest time. Yonder was the banks and the islands, across the water; and maybe a spark—which was a candle in a cabin window; and sometimes on the water you could see a spark or two—on a raft or a scow, you know; and maybe you could hear a fiddle or a song coming over from one of them crafts. It's lovely to live on a raft. We had the sky, up there, all speckled with stars and we used to lay on our backs and look up at them, and discuss about whether they was made, or only just happened—Jim he allowed they was made, but I allowed they happened; I judged it would have took too long to *make* so many. Jim said the moon could a laid them; well, that looked kind of reasonable, so I didn't say nothing against it, because I've seen a frog lay most as many, so of course it could be done. We use to watch the stars that fell, too, and see them streak down.

Once or twice of a night we would see a steamboat slipping along in the dark, and now and then she would belch a whole world of sparks up out of her chimneys, and they would rain down in the river and look awful pretty; then she would turn a corner and her lights would wink out and her powwow shut off and leave the river still again; and by and by her waves would get to us, a long time after she was gone, and joggle the raft a bit, and after that you wouldn't hear nothing for you couldn't tell how long, except maybe frogs or something.

1. Mark Twain often writes using characters who speak in dialect. That is the case with Huck, who narrates this passage. If Huck spoke correct Standard American English, in which phrase from the passage should he have used the subjunctive *were*?

   A   … and maybe a spark—which was a candle in a cabin window …

   B   … and we used to lay on our backs and look up at them …

   C   … discuss about whether they was made …

   D   … a long time after she was gone …

Read this sentence from the passage.

   I judged it would have took too long to make *so many.*

2. Which verb mood does this sentence use? Why is it used here?

   _____

   _____

Excerpt from "The Daisy"

by Hans Christian Andersen

Now listen! In the country, close by the high road, stood a farmhouse; perhaps you have passed by and seen it yourself. There was a little flower garden with painted wooden palings in front of it; close by was a ditch, on its fresh green bank grew a little daisy; the sun shone as warmly and brightly upon it as on the magnificent garden flowers, and therefore it thrived well.

Chapter 11

> One morning it had quite opened, and its little snow-white petals stood round the yellow center, like the rays of the sun. It did not mind that nobody saw it in the grass, and that it was a poor despised flower; on the contrary, it was quite happy, and turned toward the sun, looking upward and listening to the song of the lark high up in the air.

3 The first sentence, "Now listen!" is an example of —
   A passive voice.
   B subjunctive mood.
   C conditional mood.
   D imperative mood.

Skiing

(1) In spite of warnings against climbing the snowy mountain, Calvin and his friends made the ascent. (2) They were willing to risk it so they could ski down the pristine powder on the slopes. (3) For nearly three hours, they climbed steadily to the top due to an approaching storm, quickening their pace as they went. (4) On top of the mountain, they saw a beautiful panorama unfold before their eyes. (5) Instead of resting very long, they began their descent along the frozen slope. (6) They arrived at the bottom, a frozen tundra, and gathered together. (7) At the foot of the hill, they looked up. (8) They admired the pattern of the tracks their skis had made in the snow. (9) Because of the waning light, another run could not be made. (10) They agreed they would come back soon so they could ski this wonderful mountain again.

4 Sentence 2 uses which verb mood?
   A Indicative mood
   B Interrogative mood
   C Conditional mood
   D Subjunctive mood

5 Is Sentence 9 written correctly? Why or why not? If not, how should it be written?

   _____
   _____

6 Sentence 10 uses which verb mood?
   A Interrogative mood
   B Conditional mood
   C Subjunctive mood
   D Imperative mood

Rules — Conventions

VERBALS

Verbals are verbs used as other parts of speech. There are three kinds of verbals: gerunds, infinitives, and participles.

GERUNDS

A **gerund** is a verbal ending in *-ing* that functions as a noun.

Example: Reading is my favorite pastime on a rainy day.

Reading is used as a noun referring to an activity.

Gerund phrases consist of a gerund and any objects and/or modifiers.

Example: I dream of traveling the world.

I is the subject, *dream* is the verb, *traveling* is the gerund, and *the world* is its direct object.

INFINITIVES

An **infinitive** is formed by placing the word *to* in front of the base form of a verb. The infinitive can be used as a noun, adjective, or adverb. Because of its versatility, the infinitive is often used when constructing sentences. You will need to ask yourself what the purpose of the infinitive is in each sentence in order to distinguish it as a noun, an adjective, or an adverb.

Noun Example: I need to time the cooking of the meat for exactly thirty minutes.

In this sentence, the infinitive *to time* is used as the object of the sentence. Even though they are used as nouns, infinitives are rarely used as subjects of sentences. But it does happen, as in this example: "To err is human, to forgive divine" – Alexander Pope

Adjective Example: She needed a house to call her own.

In this sentence, the infinitive *to call* is an adjective describing the noun *house*.

Adverb Example: The poker player showed his cards to prove he wasn't cheating.

The infinitive *to prove* in this sentence acts as an adverb by answering the question, "Why did he show his cards?" Thus the infinitive acts as an adverb modifying the verb *showed*.

An infinitive phrase is an infinitive followed by any object(s) and/or modifier(s).

Example: Everyone wanted to see clearly.

Everyone is the subject, *wanted* is the verb, *to see* is the infinitive, and *clearly* is an adverb modifying the infinitive.

PARTICIPLES

A **participle** is a verb form used as an adjective. There are four different kinds of participles: past participle, present participle, perfect participle, and passive participle.

Chapter 11

Past participle—to form a past participle, simply add *-en* or *-ed* to the base form of the verb or use a special spelling for irregular verbs.

    Example: eat = eaten, starve = starved, bleed = bled, read = read

    Example: The sunken living room looks great in your house.

Here, the word *sunken* acts as an adjective describing *living room*.

Present participle—to form a present participle, add *-ing* to the verb.

    Example: skate = skating, fly = flying, drive = driving

    Example: Growing restless, the travelers left the airport.

Here, the word *growing* acts as an adjective describing the noun *travelers*.

Perfect participle—to form a perfect participle, place the word *having* in front of the past participle form of the verb.

    Example: "say" becomes "having said," "yell" becomes "having yelled," and "crawl" becomes "having crawled"

    Example: Having flown to Paris, Billy felt lost because he couldn't speak French.

Here, the words *having flown* act as an adjective modifying *Billy*.

Passive participle—to form a passive participle, place the words *having been* in front of the past participle form of the verb.

    Example: "make" becomes "having been made," "solve" becomes "having been solved," and "write" becomes "having been written"

    Example: Having been carved out of onyx, the statues were shiny and smooth.

Here, the words *having been carved* act as an adjective modifying *statues*.

Participial phrases are made up of a past or a present participle plus any objects and/or modifiers. Participial phrases always function as adjectives within a sentence.

    Example: The woman <u>carefully arranging the flowers</u> is my wife.

Woman is the subject, *is* is the verb, *arranging* is the present participle, with *the flowers* being the direct object and *carefully* being a modifying adverb within the participial phrase.

The participial phrase and the gerund phrase can look deceivingly similar. After all, a gerund takes the same form as a present participle. Just remember that a <u>participial phrase serves as an adjective</u> in a sentence, and a <u>gerund phrase functions as a noun</u> (just as a gerund itself does).

Practice 2: Verbals

L 1.a

DIRECTIONS Read this passage based on *The Sketch Book of Geoffrey Crayon, Gent.*, by Washington Irving. Then answer the questions that follow.

(1) Further reading and thinking made me more decided. (2) I visited various parts of my own country; and had I been merely a lover of fine scenery, I should have felt little desire to see the sights anywhere else, for on no country had the charms of nature been more lavished. (3) Her oceans of liquid silver; her mountains, with their bright colors; her valleys, with afternoon storms thundering in their solitudes; her boundless plains, waving with green; her broad, deep rivers, rolling in solemn silence to the ocean; her trackless forests, where vegetation puts forth all its magnificence; her skies, with the magic of summer clouds and glorious sunshine—no, never need an American look beyond his own country for the beauty of natural scenery …. (4) A great man of Europe, thought I, must therefore be as superior to a great man of America, as a peak of the Alps to a highland of the Hudson; and this idea I confirmed by observing the swelling importance of many English travelers among us, who, I was assured, were very little people in their own country. (5) I will visit this land of wonders, thought I, and see the gigantic race from which I come.

1. What type of verbal is used in Sentence 1? How does it function in this sentence?

2. In Sentence 2, what type of phrase is "to see the sights," and how does it function?

Chapter 11

3 What type of verbal is used in "afternoon storms thundering in their solitudes" from Sentence 3? How does it function in this sentence?

_____

_____

4 In Sentence 4, what type of verbal is used in "I confirmed by observing the swelling importance of many English travelers," and how does it function?

_____

_____

Punctuation

The appropriate use of **punctuation** is an important key to understanding written or spoken words. Punctuation signals how words, phrases, and sentences relate to one another and when a reader should pause, express emotion, see that a sentence asks questions, and so on. As you know, there are many punctuation rules. In this section, we will look at how to indicate a pause or break in text. There are three punctuation marks that help to do this: commas, ellipses, and dashes. Let's review how each is used.

Comma

A **comma** is typically used to signal a slight pause between parts of a sentence. Here are some of the rules for using commas.

Commas help separate items in a list containing three or more elements.

Example: Remember that we need to get crepe paper, glue, paint, and some glitter.

Note that the choice of whether to use a serial comma, the final comma before the conjunction, depends on what style guide a writer is using. For example, American Book Company uses the *Chicago Manual of Style*, which enforces use of the final comma because it adds clarity. Ask your teacher what style you should be using.

Commas also show the relationship between related independent clauses (complete sentences) when joined by a conjunction. When two complete sentences are joined by a comma and a conjunction, they form one compound sentence.

Example: They wanted to take a vacation at the beach, but they didn't schedule far enough ahead for a good hotel near the shore.

Commas also set off nonrestrictive elements (not essential to the meaning of a sentence) from the rest of the sentence. A *nonrestrictive element* is a phrase or clause that adds something but is not necessary to understanding a sentence, while a *restrictive element* is essential and not set off by commas.

Example, Nonrestrictive: We knew something was up when Larry, who has a sense of style, came to the club wearing plaid and stripes!

Example, Restrictive: Anyone with style sense knows that plaids and stripes don't mix.

Commas are also used to set apart appositives. An **appositive** is a word or group of words that renames another word in the sentence.

Example: Dr. McKey, the hospital's leading surgeon, was the only one capable of performing the operation.

A comma usually follows an introductory word, phrase, or clause.

Examples: Furthermore, the way that you enunciated made your speech easy to follow. After giving concrete examples, you finished with a strong conclusion. Given your well-prepared presentations, you've earned an A in Speech.

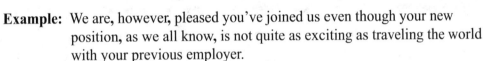

Commas are used to separate added comments or information as well as transitional elements such as conjunctive adverbs.

Example: We are, however, pleased you've joined us even though your new position, as we all know, is not quite as exciting as traveling the world with your previous employer.

Commas are used to set off direct address, tag questions, interjections, and opposing elements.

Example 1, Direct Address: Sabrina, please come here.

Example 2, Tag Question: You're not going to eat that, are you?

Example 3, Interjection: We grabbed our bikes and, wow, did we pedal fast!

Example 4, Opposing Element: Rudy said to go right, not left, when you get to the corner.

DASH

Dashes create pauses or add emphasis in your writing. They are like super-commas to place a pause before a statement where a colon would be too formal. They are also useful to set off an explanatory statement or appositive.

Example 1: Kayla was good friend—honest, optimistic, and fun to be around.

Example 2: He was late to class again—this was the seventh time in a row—but Ms. McKendrick paid no attention.

Example 3: Six of the ten poorest countries in the world—Malawi, Somalia, Comoros, Congo, Burundi, and Tanzania—are located in Africa.

Chapter 11

ELLIPSIS

Ellipsis (plural *ellipses*) means "omission" in Greek. An ellipsis appears as three dots (…) in Standard American English. Understandably, ellipses are used when something is being omitted, usually from quoted material. For instance, when you write a paper, you may want to cite a passage from a piece of literature but omit a lengthy section between two portions you want to include; you would use an ellipsis to indicate the omission.

> **Example:** "He was prodigiously pleased by her outspoken heartiness … The speech made him her friend; it couldn't well help it." (excerpted from *The American Claimant*, by Mark Twain)

Additionally, an ellipsis is sometimes used to indicate a pause or an unfinished thought.

> **Example:** Dracula never drinks … wine.

Practice 3: Punctuation

L 2.a–b

DIRECTIONS Insert the correct punctuation in this paragraph.

Growing up to ten feet long Komodo dragons are the largest living reptiles in the world. They are agile climbers and can run very fast for short stretches. These voracious eaters are carnivores meat eaters who love to dine on deer and wild boar. They typically eat animals that are already dead but they will attack live prey. If you ever meet one, beware even one bite is deadly. Komodos carry poisonous bacteria in their mouths. Long forked tongues help them track fallen prey. Like all reptiles though, they eat much less often than mammals of their size. The largest monitor lizards they spend their days sunning and their nights in shallow burrows. Found on the islands of the Indonesian archipelago at the start of the twentieth century Komodos are endangered with only a few thousand left. The islands of Padar and Rinca now serve as nature reserves to protect them.

Komodo Dragon

SPELLING

Spelling is the process of arranging letters to form words. This may seem simple, but spelling English words can be difficult. The English language has a history of taking words from other languages and trying to make the spelling of them fit into the rules of Standard American English. These rules are rather inconsistent in the first place, so it makes spelling twice as difficult.

Proper spelling is an essential part of effective writing. Incorrect spellings can make your writing sloppy, confusing, or even incomprehensible. Because so many words in English have irregular spellings, it is important to memorize commonly misspelled words. It is also helpful to follow a plan when proofreading for spelling errors.

- Consider the spelling errors that are typical for you, and look for those types of errors.
- Think about the basic structure of forming words and correct any words that do not follow the structure.
- In a notebook, make a list of words that you frequently misspell. Write them ten times each for practice.
- Use your sight memory—the memory that tells you when something just does not look right—and correct the word so it looks right.

Using this plan, your proofreading for spelling should be successful. Complete the following exercise to get some practice with catching spelling errors. If you see words that you are not sure how to spell, look them up in a dictionary.

Chapter 11

Practice 4: Spelling
L 2.c

> **DIRECTIONS:** Correct the spelling errors in the following passage. Use your dictionary to find words if you are not sure about them. The first sentence is done for you.

In addition to brushing, ~~useing~~ using dental floss helps you clean between teeth. Flossing is important, but it may feel unatural at first. Be sure to wrap the floss securly around your fingers so it doesn't slip. Another vital step is seing a dentist regularly. Once a year is sufficient, unless you are experienceing problems. What you eat should support the effectivness of your cleaning routine. A healthy diet, includeing plenty of calcium, helps build strong teeth. Chewing hard candy or ice can crack teeth, and by the time cracks are noticable, the teeth need fillings. Avoid candy altogether; even when you let it disolve in your mouth, the sugar can attack tooth enamel. The more you take care of your pearly whites, the longer you can keep smileing!

CHAPTER 11 SUMMARY

You have learned many **conventions** of Standard American English and are expected to use them in your writing. Conventions include using language correctly in areas such as punctuation, sentence structure, and spelling:

You should add knowledge of **verb voices and moods** to your stock of skills in relation to verbs.

Active voice is the arrangement of a sentence so that the subject performs an action; **passive voice** is when the subject has some action done to it. You will usually use active voice when writing, as it is clearer and easier to read. But passive voice may be used for specific purposes, as when the performer of an action is unknown.

There are also **verb moods** that you can use to achieve certain effects.

- Use the **indicative** mood to make statements.
- Use the **interrogative** mood when asking questions.
- Use the **imperative** mood for commands, instructions, or requests.
- Use the **subjunctive** mood to show a condition or an imagined situation.
- Use the **conditional** mood is to write about an event that is dependent on another event happening.

Sometimes you employ **shifts in voice and mood**, but you should avoid inappropriate shifts.

Verbals are verbs used as other parts of speech in a sentence.

- A **gerund** is a verbal ending in *-ing* that functions as a noun.
- An **infinitive** is formed by placing the word *to* in front of the base form of a verb, and it can be used as a noun, adjective, or adverb.
- A **participle** is formed from a past, present, or perfect tense verb and is used as an adjective.

Using correct **punctuation** is an important key to understanding. There are many punctuation rules; three punctuation marks that are used to indicated a pause or break include these:

- **Commas** separate the parts of a list, show relationships between clauses, separate additional information from the rest of a sentence, and so on.
- **Dashes** create pauses or add emphasis in your writing.
- **Ellipses** are used when something is being omitted or to indicate a pause or an unfinished thought.

Chapter 11

CHAPTER 11 REVIEW

L 1.a–d, 2.a–c, 3.a

> **DIRECTIONS**
>
> A. Be sure use conventions you reviewed in this chapter, and what you know about conventions in general, to proofread the essays that you worked on in chapter 10.
>
> B. Read this passage written by a student. Look for any errors that need to be corrected, and answer the questions that follow the passage.

Electoral College

(1) Who chooses the president of the United States? (2) If you said the voter's, you are right, but not completely. (3) When voters cast their ballots on Election Day they are not voting directly for the president. (4) If they did, then some past elections would have turned out differently. (5) They are actually voting for a group of presidential electors.

(6) This system is called the Electoral College, a group of people who meet in their state capitals in December to vote for president. (7) This group has pledged to support the candidate who win the popular vote. (8) The electors cast a total of 538 votes. (9) To be elected president, a candidate must have at leest 270 electoral votes.

(10) Each of the states has a diffrent number of electors. (11) The population of a state determines the number of electors. (12) The electors are equal to the number of senators and representatives in Congress who represent that state. (13) The states with the largest populations have more electoral votes than lesspopulated states. (14) This is why candidates running for president typical spend more time in states like Florida California and New York. (15) They hope to get more electoral votes and win the race!

---

1 How should you edit "If you said the voter's, you are right" in Sentence 2?

    A If you said the voter's you are right

    B If you said, "the voter's," you are right

    C If you said the voters, you are right

    D Correct as is

Conventions

2. What error, if any, needs to be corrected in Sentence 3?

   _____
   _____

3. What is the verb mood in Sentence 4?
   - A Imperative mood
   - B Subjunctive mood
   - C Interrogative mood
   - D Conditional mood

4. What is the correct way to write Sentence 8?
   - A This group have pledged to support the candidate who win the popular vote.
   - B This group has pledged to support the candidate who wins the popular vote.
   - C These group has pledged to support the candidate who win the popular vote.
   - D This group has pledged to support the candidate who winning the popular vote.

5. What error, if any, needs to be corrected in Sentence 9?

   _____
   _____

6. What error, if any, needs to be corrected in Sentence 10?

   _____
   _____

7. In sentence 14, what type of verbal is *running*, and how is it used in this sentence?

   _____
   _____

8. What errors, if any, need to be corrected in Sentence 14?

   _____
   _____

Chapter 11

> **Activity**
>
> **L 1–3**
>
> Have a peer-review session with a group of classmates. Exchange reports or essays that you have been working on for class, and practice finding errors in each other's writing. This will help you to read carefully for errors in the work of another student, as well as point out some of the errors that you may be doing in your own writing. Remember that other students may not always be correct or catch everything. You should still proofread your own work carefully.

Chapter 12
Speaking and Listening

This chapter covers the following eighth grade strand and standards:

<u>Speaking and Listening</u>

Comprehension and Collaboration

1. Engage effectively in a range of collaborative discussions (one-on-one, in groups, and teacher-led) with diverse partners on grade 8 topics, texts, and issues, building on others' ideas and expressing their own clearly.

   a. Come to discussions prepared, having read or researched material under study; explicitly draw on that preparation by referring to evidence on the topic, text, or issue to probe and reflect on ideas under discussion.

   b. Follow rules for collegial discussions and decision-making, track progress toward specific goals and deadlines, and define individual roles as needed.

   c. Pose questions that connect the ideas of several speakers and respond to others' questions and comments with relevant evidence, observations, and ideas.

   d. Acknowledge new information expressed by others, and, when warranted, qualify or justify their own views in light of the evidence presented.

2. Analyze the purpose of information presented in diverse media and formats (e.g., visually, quantitatively, orally) and evaluate the motives (e.g., social, commercial, political) behind its presentation.

3. Delineate a speaker's argument and specific claims, evaluating the soundness of the reasoning and relevance and sufficiency of the evidence and identifying when irrelevant evidence is introduced.

Presentation of Knowledge and Ideas

4. Present claims and findings, emphasizing salient points in a focused, coherent manner with relevant evidence, sound valid reasoning, and well-chosen details; use appropriate eye contact, adequate volume, and clear pronunciation.

5. Integrate multimedia and visual displays into presentations to clarify information, strengthen claims and evidence, and add interest.

6. Adapt speech to a variety of contexts and tasks, demonstrating command of formal English when indicated or appropriate.

In school and elsewhere, you will not only read and write, but you will also listen and speak. When doing so, you can use many of the same skills that you use for effective reading and writing. In addition, there are other skills that can further help you in speaking and listening. This chapter reviews how to analyze and make presentations and some important points about working with others.

Chapter 12

ANALYZING PRESENTATIONS

In chapter 6, you reviewed the various types and purposes of **media**. You know that media can communicate both visually and orally. In this section, you will look specifically at how to evaluate a **speaker's purpose and claims**. You will also read about the **motives** behind a media message. Keep in mind you can use these skills to **analyze presentations** of any kind.

A speech is one type of presentation. It can verbally convey important information. A speech can give a specific view or make a comment on life. A political leader often speaks to the public to let them know about policies or to gain support for a position. An example of this is the State of the Union address made annually by the president of the United States. Important speeches often are made available in printed form. Many historic speeches, like Abraham Lincoln's "Gettysburg Address," are available for you to read. Public speeches may take place as commercials and infomercials, radio broadcasts, and live appearances.

When you listen to a speech, you need to be able to pick out these items:

1   Speaker's argument and specific claim

2   Evidence to support the claim (including which evidence is irrelevant)

3   Reasoning behind the evidence

Analyzing these aspects of a media message or presentation can help you figure out the motive behind it. Motives in media include **social, political, and commercial messages**. Sometimes the way information is presented makes it seem that one idea is presented, when the motive is actually different. Do you recall how you often need to infer the main idea or theme of a text you read? The same is true when you see and hear media messages or speeches. For example, you often see funny and entertaining commercials on television. But the motive behind them is not simply to entertain. They are made by companies who want to sell you their products.

Here is an example from a famous speech by Robert F. Kennedy made just after the assassination of Martin Luther King Jr. Read the speech first. Then look at the explanation after it, which points out some of the ideas discussed so far in this chapter.

> What we need in the United States is not division; what we need in the United States is not hatred; what we need in the United States is not violence and lawlessness, but is love and wisdom, and compassion toward one another, and a feeling of justice toward those who still suffer within our country, whether they be white or whether they be black.

Speaking and Listening

> So I ask you tonight to return home, to say a prayer for the family of Martin Luther King ... but more importantly to say a prayer for our own country, which all of us love— a prayer for understanding and that compassion of which I spoke. We can do well in this country. We will have difficult times. We've had difficult times in the past. And we will have difficult times in the future. It is not the end of violence; it is not the end of lawlessness; and it's not the end of disorder.
>
> But the vast majority of white people and the vast majority of black people in this country want to live together, want to improve the quality of our life, and want justice for all human beings that abide in our land.
>
> Let us dedicate ourselves to what the Greeks wrote so many years ago: to tame the savageness of man and make gentle the life of this world. Let us dedicate ourselves to that, and say a prayer for our country and for our people. Thank you very much.

If you were asked to state the thesis of this speech, what would you say? Consider what the speaker is asking for. He wants Americans to take something positive from a tragic experience. The spring of 1968 was a volatile time when America was tearing itself apart over racial issues. He is asking listeners to feel compassion, rather than hatred, for one another. In this excerpt, the main points that support this thesis are these:

Robert Kennedy

1. "... those who still suffer within our country, whether they be white or whether they be black ..."

Kennedy points out that Americans of all races may suffer, supporting his plea that the races not fight.

2. "... say a prayer for our own country, which all of us love ..."

He suggests that we really are all alike: we are Americans, and we love our country.

3. "... the vast majority of white people and the vast majority of black people in this country want to live together, want to improve the quality of our life, and want justice for all human beings ..."

He speaks to the average American, affirming that everyday people want to get along.

These main points work together to support his thesis. These ideas are about citizens being Americans first and members of a specific race second. In this way, they help make Kennedy's point that this tragedy is a time for people to pull together, not apart. It is also clear that the speaker knows his audience— Americans who are in shock about the assassination and wondering what it will mean for race relations—and directly addresses these thoughts and fears. As you can see, figuring out the thesis helps you to pinpoint the purpose for the speech. In this case, it is to persuade. The motive behind the message is both social and political.

Chapter 12

Although the complete speech is not reprinted here, you can see the structure of the body and conclusion. Notice how the last paragraph closes by rephrasing the thesis.

Finally, what organizational method would you assign to this speech? It reacts to an event, but does not really go through it, so it is not sequential or chronological. It compares black and white people to an extent, but that is not its main point. It looks at the assassination as a possible cause, but the possible effects have not yet happened. In fact, the best answer for how this speech is organized is problem-solution. It examines a terrible event and proposes a solution of people coming together to make the nation stronger, rather than pulling apart and fighting among themselves.

Practice 1: Analyzing Presentations

SL 2, 3

> **DIRECTIONS:** Tommy wrote a report that he then presented in class. Read Tommy's presentation, and answer the questions that follow.

Today's jails and prisons are heavily overpopulated. Most convicts serve only part of their sentences before they are released from prison. Such early release is called parole. A prisoner who is released on parole is called a parolee. Parole may be an efficient way for the state to keep prison populations below the legal limit. But it is also arguably unjust.

Parole is an effective way that prisons can reduce their populations. By law, a prison may not have more than a certain number of convicts. Courts have ruled that a convict's rights include not being forced to be part of an overcrowded prison population. Incarcerated individuals have these rights because of lawsuits their attorneys have won in the courts. If we built more prisons, that would create much-needed jobs as well.

Statistics show that people who have served time behind bars wind up committing crimes again after they are paroled. Assistant District Attorney Amy Wright says, "The courts convict many violent and dangerous criminals, and many of these violent people become convicts who serve only a few years before they are freed on parole. As parolees, they commit more crimes and hurt more people." In short, the evidence suggests that short prison terms combined with parole are ineffective at rehabilitating convicted criminals.

Parole is also a slap in the face to the victims of crimes. People who have suffered from crimes—often violent crimes—are left feeling frustrated and betrayed by the criminal justice system. They watch helplessly as the criminals who victimized them are released on parole after only serving a few years, or sometimes months, of a lengthy sentence. Meanwhile, the only explanation they receive for this injustice is that "criminals have rights." But what about the rights of the victims? Who is worried about their rights?

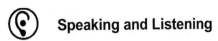 **Speaking and Listening**

Who protects them when they have been victimized? One robbery victim said: "It leaves you furious. How can we feel safe when people can commit violent acts against us, knowing they won't spend much time in jail?"

When all the evidence is considered, it becomes clear that parole is a poor system for dealing with crime. First, it fails to satisfy a basic sense of justice. Victims of crimes are left frustrated, angry, and sometimes living in fear because criminals do not spend the time that they should behind bars. Second, short prison terms and early release fail to rehabilitate criminals, meaning that most will commit more crimes.

Until we are willing to put the rights of victims and everyday citizens above those of convicted criminals, parole will continue to be used. Decisions will continue to be made based on prison population rather than based on what is just and fair. This unfortunate system will not change until citizens desire change, decide to act, and demand more from the government officials who are supposed to be protecting them.

1. This passage could be best described as —
   A persuasive.   B narrative.   C technical.   D entertaining.

2. The speaker presents increased crime as being —
   A a result of criminal convictions.
   B the source of victims' frustrations.
   C an effect of a faulty parole system.
   D a side effect of justice.

3. Give two examples of sound reasoning and strong evidence that the speaker presents.

   _____
   _____
   _____

4. Is there any irrelevant evidence in Tommy's presentation?

   _____
   _____
   _____

Chapter 12

5 Which information, if added to the passage, would best support the author's viewpoint?

    A Testimonials from paroled convicts who were rehabilitated

    B Data showing the average number of people paroled each year

    C A chart of how prison populations have changed over the last twenty years

    D A table showing the number of parolees who commit crimes

6 What could Tommy do to most improve his speech?

_____

_____

_____

_____

MAKING A PRESENTATION

Analyzing the presentations of others can greatly help you do well when you have to present. Just like the speakers you listen to, you must **present your claim** and **provide relevant evidence** to support it. In addition, you must use presentation skills to engage your audience and get your point across.

First, you want to organize your speech for best effect. The choice of organization is similar to when you write. Choose the organizational pattern that best fits the topic. Unlike written text, though, readers can't go back to see what your main points were or flip ahead to see just how many details you will use to make your point. In speeches, you will use more repetition, reminders, and clues about what's coming up than you do in writing. You might have heard the advice, "Tell them what you are going to tell them, then tell them, and then tell them what you told them." It seems simple and repetitive, but it is true for speeches.

STRUCTURE OF A SPEECH

There is no single way to structure a speech. However, here is a general pattern that most good speeches follow:

Introduction

The introduction opens the speech. This is the place to **capture audience attention** with interesting facts, a leading question, or a brief anecdote. Most important is to **state the claim**, usually in a well-organized thesis statement. Also use the introduction to **outline the rest of the speech**, listing the main points you intend to use to support that claim.

Speaking and Listening

Body

The body is the largest portion of the speech. During this portion, you present your main points to **support the thesis**. The great thing about speaking is that you can use your speaking volume, pacing, and gestures to **emphasize the most important points**. Be sure your **evidence and details are relevant** and well chosen. Make your speech **focused and coherent**. Remember to **add multimedia** into your presentation to clarify what you mean and to make your speech more interesting.

Summary

In the summary, briefly **restate the main points and thesis** that you have just presented. This is the time to make sure the audience remembers your main point and how you used evidence to prove it.

Conclusion

Conclude with a final thought or sentence that is memorable and will leave a lasting impression on the audience.

Some presentations, like those you make in class, have one more component. There may be a question-and-answer period that follows the presentation. This allows the audience to ask for clarification on certain points you made or for details that you may not have included. For you, it is a time to shine. This is when you can show that you truly know your subject. Naturally, you can't include everything in your presentation. But if someone asks a question, you can pull out that extra knowledge! Of course, if you don't know the answer to a question, just say so.

DELIVERING A SPEECH

To deliver an effective speech, you should dress and speak in a manner appropriate to the occasion. In addition to the words you use, there are other non-verbal factors to consider when delivering a speech. One factor is appearance. How you look is important. If you are speaking at a formal awards banquet, you will want to dress in a formal manner. If you're giving a pep talk to a football team before it takes the field, you will likely wear the school colors and logo.

So that the audience can understand you, be sure to use **clear pronunciation**. While practicing your speech, give extra attention to any words that you have trouble pronouncing. If there is a particular word you repeatedly trip over, consider replacing it with one you can more easily pronounce. More tips on practicing your speech are included later in this section. You should also be conscious of your **speaking rate** (how quickly or slowly you talk). Unless you are doing so intentionally for effect, you should not talk too slowly or pause too long between sentences or points. At the same time, you should not speak so fast that it is hard for the audience to keep up or mentally process what you say. Try to speak at a normal rate, as though you are talking with friends. A good speech should flow and keep the audience's attention.

Chapter 12

Eye contact is crucial if you are to connect with your audience. If you simply read from a written speech or constantly stare down at notes, then you risk boring your audience and failing to make a positive impression.

When delivering a speech, you could get nervous. When this happens, you might talk too fast or use distracting expressions that take away from the overall message. Distractions can include mumbling, speaking in a monotone voice, and using terms like *um*, *you know*, or *like* repeatedly. It's important to **practice** and weed out these distractions. First, practice on your own. Next, try recording yourself so that you can hear how you sound. Finally, give your speech in front of family members or friends. This will help you relax in front of a friendly audience as well as get some valuable feedback about anything you might need to change.

One more idea to keep in mind is being able to **adapt to a variety of speaking situations**. As you know, this has to do with the speaking task as well as the audience to which you are speaking. You have to be able to demonstrate that you can use formal language when needed in speaking as well as writing. As an example, look at this pep talk a senior cheerleader might give at cheerleading tryouts.

> Gather around here and listen up! If you really want to be cheerleaders, you have to be ready to stretch yourselves to the limit! Be sure you really want to do this, people! You will need to be at practice every day after school. There will be no time for any other extracurricular activities! All of you must be ready to give of yourselves and endure pain as you never have before! You will also need to rely on each other. Some of you will be learning how to trust someone else for the first time in your lives. Above all, cheerleading will bring out your character and show you what you're made of. Now, if you still feel up to the task, I want to see you here tomorrow evening at five o'clock. Be ready to work hard.

Now, say the coach asks this same cheerleader to present this information at a gathering of students, parents, and teachers. The event will be all about the activities available at school, and the coach thinks this will be a great opportunity for everyone to learn about the cheerleading program. How might the language, tone, and message change? Look at this revised example for this new task and audience.

> Students who want to be cheerleaders need to consider what they want to get out of the experience. They also need to be ready to give one hundred percent and stretch themselves to the limit. They must be at practice every day, be physically able to handle routines, and work as part of a team whose members rely on each other. In return for all their hard work, cheerleading builds strong character, self-confidence, and teamwork skills.

Speaking and Listening

Notice how the language changed to address the audience. They are not trying out; rather, they are simply learning about the program. The tone also became more formal since the audience also includes parents and teachers. The message remains similar, however. The presentation still tells what cheerleaders need to give as well as what they gain from their participation.

Practice 2: Making a Presentation

SL 4–6

> **DIRECTIONS**   A. Answer these questions about making a presentation.

1. What is the most effective way to ensure that the audience is listening and sees you are being sincere?

   A   Walk back and forth across the stage.

   B   Speak as loudly as possible.

   C   Maintain eye contact while speaking.

   D   Talk slowly and deliberately.

2. What is the best way to emphasize an important point in your presentation?

   _____

   _____

   _____

> **DIRECTIONS**   B. Use the instructions below to work on a presentation.

Take out your essays that you worked on for chapters 10 and 11. Choose one, and adapt it into a focused, coherent oral presentation or speech. Be sure to include relevant evidence and sound reasoning. Choose a multimedia display to support your speech. Practice your presentation, and then make a recording or give the presentation to a group or in class.

Activity

SL 3

Based on the advice in this section, improve Tommy's speech from Practice 1. Revise the report to include more effective ways to capture audience attention and to make a stronger claim. Develop a speech outline to place in the introduction. Also, think of ways to add emphasis to the most important points, and to build a stronger, more memorable conclusion.

Page 223

Chapter 12

GROUP COMMUNICATION

Whether you belong to a club or youth group, have a lab partner you work with, or discuss various topics in class, you often need to participate in **collaborative discussions**.

When pairs or groups come together, they must communicate effectively. Many times, they do this informally. Their discussions have no formal rules. Some groups, however, such as a student council, community groups, or academic clubs might conduct more formal meetings. They have meeting rules to maintain orderly discussion. No matter how formal or informal, communication needs to be clear and balanced. This section focuses on some ideas to help you excel at such discussions.

Be Prepared

The first step to communicating well is to be ready to do so. This means you need to **come to discussions prepared**. You need to have read the material that you will talk about. If you are working on a project, you need to have done the work requested of you between group meetings.

Express Yourself

As part of the group, you should add value to it. If you're in a class discussion about a story, talk about your impressions of the story and what you took away from it. If you are working on a group presentation, update the group on what you accomplished since the last meeting. **Express your ideas clearly**, listen to others, and **build on others' ideas**. Be sure to **ask and answer questions** that are relevant to the group's task.

Follow the Guidelines

Even groups that do not have formal rules can **follow guidelines**. A group works best when members participate in an orderly and productive way. People can "gain the floor" (get their chance to speak) using methods like raising hands, speaking in a set order, or waiting to be acknowledged by a moderator, the person who makes sure the discussion moves forward and stays focused. It is also important to **assign tasks** so that members know what they are responsible for doing. Finally, be aware of the deadline for the group's work.

Strive for Teamwork

Above all, keep in mind that the group is working together—it is a collaborative process. Each individual has his or her own role in the group and viewpoint and opinions, but the group must agree on important decisions. Sometimes this means the group must **reach a consensus** (an agreement among most members of the group). This can be done by voting. Members who do not agree with the decision still need to follow what the majority of the group decides to do. This is a good way for a group to move forward on a project.

Speaking and Listening

Practice 3: Group Communication

SL 1.a–d

DIRECTIONS Read and answer the questions.

1. The homecoming committee needs to decide on the floats that will ride in this year's parade, but committee members do not agree. To move forward, what does the group need to do?

   A Vote on the top choices.

   B Assign a deadline for the decision.

   C Elect a new committee chair.

   D Decide who can gain the floor.

2. In a photography club meeting, a member wants to discuss a camera lens that you have never heard of. What is the best way to find out more about the lens so the group can discuss it?

   A When it's your turn to talk, ask for details about the lens.

   B After the meeting, research the lens on the Internet.

   C Write to the manufacturer for more information.

   D Interrupt the speaker to point out that no one knows what it is.

3. What is the most important action to take before a meeting?

   _____
   _____
   _____

4. Without an agenda, a deadline, and guidelines for working collaboratively, what might happen in a group meeting?

   A No one would ever take charge of the meeting.

   B The recorder would have nothing to write down.

   C People would not know what they are supposed to do.

   D Everyone would shout, and no one would listen.

5. You are in a meeting and want to add some relevant information while someone else is talking to the group. What should you do?

   _____
   _____

Chapter 12

> **Activity**
>
> SL 1–3
>
> Attend or watch a video of an organized meeting (a city-council meeting, PTA meeting, televised session of Congress, church-group meeting, school-board meeting, student-council meeting, and so on). Note the strategies used to conduct the meeting in an orderly fashion. Then, meet as a class or in small groups to answer the following questions:
>
> - Who appeared to be the leader?
> - What strategies did the group use to ensure orderly communication?
> - How did group members gain the floor?
> - What seemed to be the agenda of the meeting?
> - What consensus, if any, did the group come to?

Speaking and Listening

CHAPTER 12 SUMMARY

Media can communicate visually as well as orally. Oral presentations are one type of media. You must know how to evaluate a **speaker's purpose and claims** and **motives** (**social, political, and commercial messages**) behind a media message in order to **analyze presentations**.

When you speak, you must **present your claim** and **provide relevant evidence** to support it. Your speech should have the following components:

The **introduction** is when you **capture audience attention, state the claim,** and **outline the rest of the speech**.

In the **body** of the presentation, you **support the thesis** you stated in the introduction. Remember to **emphasize the most important points**, provide **relevant evidence and** details, stay **focused and coherent,** and **add multimedia** to clarify what you mean and to make your speech more interesting.

In the **summary**, you can briefly **restate the main points and thesis**.

You can offer a **conclusion** with a final thought that leaves a lasting impression on the audience.

Be sure to use **clear pronunciation** and a well-paced **speaking rate**. Also, make **eye contact** to connect with the audience, and be able to **adapt to a variety of speaking situations**. Remember that the more you **practice** the more polished your speech will be.

Here are some points to keep in mind when you participate in **collaborative discussions**:

- **Come to discussions prepared**.
- **Express your ideas clearly**, listen to others, **build on others' ideas**, and **ask and answer questions** that are relevant to the group's task.
- **Follow guidelines** that help the group work in an orderly and productive way. Be sure to **assign tasks** so that members know what they are responsible for doing.
- If the group does not agree, **reach a consensus** by voting, so the group can move forward.

Chapter 12

CHAPTER 12 REVIEW

SL 1–6

> **DIRECTIONS**   A. Read this speech, and then answer the questions that follow.

    We must remember. We must always remember. "Remember what?" you ask. Well, as you look around this great hall tonight, you can see we are blessed to be seated at fine tables, covered in decorative tablecloths, candles, centerpieces, and such. We have before us plates filled with delicious dinners, and goblets and wineglasses filled with tea and wine. I look around and I see men dressed in tuxedos and women dressed in beautiful evening gowns. In a setting like this … on a night like tonight … surrounded by people like you … it is easy to forget that, out there, beyond this banquet hall—in places we'd never intentionally visit or want our children to grow up in—there are people who live in a much different world. There are people who are starving. There are fathers who cry tears behind closed doors because they don't want their wives or children to see the fear and anxiety in their eyes which says, "I can't pay the rent this month. I can't feed my children tomorrow."

    There are mothers praying that their children will come home alive because so many young people in the neighborhood have died violent deaths at the hands of drug dealers or on the firing lines of a gangland war. There are children whose mothers don't hold them because the mothers are high on crack, and whose fathers aren't around to raise them and teach them how to live.

    You ask, "Remember what?" I would argue the better question is "Remember who?" These are the people we must remember. Why? Because they are our fellow men and women. They are our brothers and sisters.

    Tonight is a call to action. You see, the people I just mentioned are usually not people who are looking for a handout. They are good, decent people who just need help or an advantage. Perhaps you don't think they deserve an advantage. Perhaps you think they should just help themselves. If that is your thought, then I would label you a hypocrite. You place on others a burden you yourself will not shoulder. You have enjoyed advantages. Did you decide the family you would be born into? Did you decide how intelligent you would be? Has no one given you a helping hand along your path to achievement? Of course they have. Tonight represents your opportunity to be that helping hand to another. Tonight you will have the chance to make a commitment. Tonight, you will have the opportunity to impact a life … the life of someone who just wants a fighting chance. Tonight, you have the opportunity to make a statement—to say, "I will remember!"

    May compassion be in your hearts. May kindness rule your minds. May the things you hear, see, and learn tonight forever change you, so that you might forever change those who must never be forgotten. Thank you.

Speaking and Listening

1. What is the main idea of and motive behind this speech?

   _____
   _____
   _____
   _____

2. What is the purpose of this speech?
   A To inform listeners regarding poverty in the inner city
   B To entertain listeners with tales of people who overcame obstacles
   C To persuade listeners to make a difference in the lives of others
   D To explain why it is important to give generously to others

3. Who is most likely the audience for this speech?
   A Wealthy individuals with the resources to devote time and money
   B Low-income individuals who are seeking an opportunity to succeed
   C Students who are looking to launch a community project
   D A civic organization preparing to begin its annual membership drive

4. What is the purpose of the phrase "We must remember" in this speech?

   _____
   _____
   _____
   _____

5. Which of the following is the primary organizational structure used in the speech?
   A Cause and effect   C Compare and contrast
   B Chronological order   D Problem and solution

6. What should the speaker do to keep the interest of the audience during the speech?

   _____
   _____
   _____
   _____

Chapter 12

7   What emotion should the speaker try to communicate through tone while delivering the speech?

   A   Anger
   B   Distress
   C   Humor
   D   Urgency

> **DIRECTIONS** B. Complete the following speaking task.

You have been asked to do a report about innovations in transportation. Do some research, choose a form of transportation you want to present, and prepare a report that you will present in class. Use the information in chapter 11 to help you organize your report. Then use the pointers in this chapter to help make your presentation its best.

> **DIRECTIONS** C. Work in a group to complete the following task.

Your school's annual exhibit of student art work is one month away. The entire community, including parents, has been invited, and prizes will be awarded to the best entries. Your art teacher has assigned a small group of students, including you, to help prepare for the big day. Working in this small group, use the skills of group communication discussed in this chapter to come up with a plan of action. Work together and use your own paper to make notes about what you will do. The committee will be expected to present their plan to the art teacher.

A
active voice 198
affix 121, 133
allusion 128, 133
analogy 129, 133
analysis 46
analyze 79, 90, 91, 92, 100, 106
analyze presentation 216
appositive 207
argument 99, 106, 174, 176, 193
audience attention 220
author purpose 83, 84, 85
author style 86, 90

B
bibliography 143
brainstorming 159

C
cause and effect 96, 106
central idea 15, 16, 18, 79, 90
character 188, 193
characterization 20, 30
chronological order 95, 106
citation 144, 147
claim 99, 193, 220
claim (make a claim) 174
clarity 169
clue 118, 119, 133
clustering 158, 169
coherence 161, 169
comma 206
compare 53, 66, 95, 106
complete sentence 206
compound sentence 206
concluding statement 179, 193
conclusion 93, 106
conclusion (draw conclusion) 48, 66
conclusion (to essay) 188, 193
conflicting information 177, 193
conjunction 206
connotation 128, 133
context clue 118, 119, 133
contrast 53, 66, 95, 106
conventions 197
counterclaim 176, 193

D
dash 207
denotation 128, 133
detail 80, 90, 92, 184, 188, 193, 221
develop idea 157, 169
diagram 159, 169
dictionary 123, 124, 133
direct object 203
drafting 160, 169

E
editing 167, 169
electronic source 138
ellipsis 208
essay
   body 160, 169
   conclusion 160, 169
   informative 174
   introduction 160, 169
   narrative 174
   new approach 164, 169
   organization 160, 169
   persuasive 174
   planning 169
   structure 160
evidence 46, 79, 99, 106, 175, 220, 221
expository writing 184, 193

F
fact 92, 100, 106, 184
fiction 60, 66
figurative language 32, 33, 44
figurative meaning 90, 128, 133
fishbone map 159, 169

G
genre 9, 10, 53
gerund 203
glossary 123, 125, 133
graphic 184, 193

I
idea 15, 16, 18, 79, 90, 106, 157, 169
idiom 129, 133
image 32, 44
inference 46, 92, 93, 106
infinitive 203
information 177, 193
informational text 79, 90, 91, 106, 174
informational writing 184
informative essay 174, 193
informative writing 184
Internet 138, 147
interpret 100, 106
interpretation 92
introduction 184, 188, 193
irony 129, 133

K
key word 139, 149, 197

L
language 184, 188, 193
literal meaning 128, 133
literary devices and elements 11, 31, 44, 188, 193
logical and natural order 188
logical reasoning 175, 193

M
make a claim 99
map 159, 169
mapping 158, 169
meaning nuances 133
media 103, 106, 216, 221
metaphor 129, 133
mood 27, 32, 44, 199, 200

N
narrative essay 174, 193
narrative technique 193
narrative writing 188
nonrestrictive element 207
nuance 119, 133

O

object 203
opinion 92, 106, 176
order 95, 106, 188
organizational features 139, 147, 184
organize speech 218
outline 159, 220

P

pacing 188, 193
paragraph structure 79, 90
paraphrasing 144
participle 203, 204
passive participle 204
passive voice 198
past participle 204
perfect participle 204
persuasive essay 174, 193
plagiarism 143
plot 12, 13, 30, 188, 193
point of view 22, 23, 30, 188, 193
precise language 184, 193
prefix 121, 133
present claim 220
present participle 204
presentation 216
primary source 138
problem 96, 106, 218
pronunciation 221
proofreading 167, 169
publishing 168, 169
pun 129, 133
punctuation 206

Q

quotation 144

R

reasoning 99, 106, 175, 193
relevant evidence 193, 220
research 137, 147, 176
research question 141
restrictive element 207
revising 164, 169
rewriting 165, 169
rhyme 41
rhyme scheme 42, 44
rhythm 42, 44
root 121, 133
rubric 1, 2

S

search engine 139
search term 139, 147
secondary source 138
sensory language 188, 193
sentence 206
sentence structure 79, 90
sequential order 95, 106
setting 27, 30, 188, 193
shifts in mood 200
shifts in voice 200
signal word 119
simile 129, 133
solution 96, 106, 218
sound device 41, 44
source 99, 193
   analyze 142, 147
   cite 143, 147
   electronic 138
   evaluate 141, 142, 147
   finding a source 137, 147
   organizational feature 139, 140
   organize 147
   primary 138, 147
   secondary 138, 147
sources
   electronic 147
speaker claims 216
speaker motives 216
speaker purpose 216
speaking rate 221
speaking situation 222
suffix 121, 133
summary 13, 90, 145, 179, 221
support thesis 221

T

technical meaning 119, 133
text 79, 90, 91, 106, 174
   adaptation 64
   analyze 66
   informational 138, 147
   literary 138, 147
   meaning 53, 66
   style 53, 66
text organization 95, 106
theme 14, 15, 16, 18, 30
thesaurus 123, 124, 133
thesis 217, 221
tone 30
transition 161, 169, 184, 188, 193

V

Venn diagram 159, 169
verb 198
verb mood 198, 199
verb voice 198
verbal 203
vocabulary building 118, 133
voice 198, 200

W

word 119
   meaning 128
   multiple meaning 119
word meaning 32, 44, 118, 133
writing
   audience 169
   clarity 162
   purpose 169
   style 162, 169
   task 169